PEOPLES OF NORTH EAST INDIA
Anthropological Perspectives

PEOPLES OF NORTH EAST INDIA

Anthropological Perspectives

Editor

SARTHAK SENGUPTA

GYAN PUBLISHING HOUSE

New Delhi 110 002

Peoples of North-East India: Anthropological Perspectives

ISBN: 81-212-0519-0

Reprinted in 2011 in India by
Gyan Publishing House
23, Main Ansari Road, Daryaganj,
New Delhi - 110002
Phone : 23282060, 23261060
Fax : (011) 23285914
E-mail : books@gyanbooks.com
website: gyanbooks.com

Printed at: G. Print Process, Delhi

Dedicated to
the sacred memory of my elder brother
Late Samir Sengupta

Preface

North East India, the erstwhile greater Assam, presently the land of seven sister States is very often called an 'anthropological museum' for her providing shelter to numerous populations of various ethnic affiliation, having different social structure and cultural heritages.

North East India's diversified culture and people has attracted the attention of many anthropologists from different parts of the globe. History of anthropological research in North East India started more than one hundred years back from today. During the formative period a number of studies in the sphere of social anthropology in this region was published by a good number of British Administrators and Civil Servants besides reports of travellors and missionaries with main emphasis to know the indigenous people, especially the tribal ones, primarily for administrative purpose. Physical anthropology was also casually dealt with in those monographs in terms of anthropometric characters to understand racial affinity of the constituent population. However, most of these studies suffer from personal bias and other methodological flaws. After India's Independence, a few scholars from India and abroad had taken up ethnographic as well as morphogenetic studies with dedication, and had done commendable works in broadening the horizon of anthropology of the region.

Despite the early start of anthropological research activities in the North East, till today, however, whatever has been done on the life and style of the people of this easternmost remote corner of the country has not been adequate enough compared to its vast and numerous unexplored areas. Further, it has also been realized that, anthropological literature on non-tribal population, which is considered to be a major tool for development of the people and the region, is too scanty, sporadic and sketchy to mention its worthiness as a well-planned research. There has, therefore, been the great need of precise documentation of the reliable information on the people of North East India that needs to be obtained through serious scientific studies by the present day anthropologists. The present volume has been compiled with a view to filling in the lacunae through the writings of a distinguished and dedicated team of anthropologists. The work is expected to provide a glimpse of anthropological perspectives of the People of North East India to all concerned. The scholars who have contributed the articles have longstanding field experience with the people of North East India. The articles dealing with rich empirical data reflect a multidisciplinary approach and have covered a wide range of anthropological panorama. They range from biological issues to social concern.

The volume contains a collection of eighteen articles pertaining to some important facets of anthropology like studies on ethnic elements, inter-group variability, human growth, bio-social and medical anthropological aspects, colourful cultural life, tribal institutions, process of Sanskritization, forms of political system, identity dynamics etc. among the vast and varied types of People of North East India. The volume specially covers the tribal inhabitants, muslim and tea-garden immigrants of the region. The volume, however, in no way can claim to have projected a thorough picture of the multiferious people of the region, but a good cross-section of man, society and culture of North East region is here reflected.

My endeavour will be well rewarded if this treatise proves to be informative, useful and thought provoking to the scholars and researchers as well as administrators, planners and policy makers.

Dibrugarh University
Dibrugarh

Sarthak Sengupta

Acknowledgements

I owe a deep debt of gratitude to all those scholarly contributors for their academic co-operation, patience and forbearence and in making my effort a reality.

My thanks are also due to my friend Mr. Mohendra N. Dutta who helped me in more than one way. I am also thankful to Mrs. Neelanjana Barua for her long hours spent in typing the manuscript meticulously.

It is impossible to forget my sons-Sushruta and Samrat and my wife Kaveeta, as they have suffered the most during my preoccupations. Without their tolerance and encouragement, this book might not have seen the light of the day. I have no words to thank them, but I thrust this small mention atleast records the depth of gratitude.

Last but not the least, my special thanks to M/s Gyan Publishing House, New Delhi for ensuring a prompt and flawless production of this volume.

Sarthak Sengupta

Dibrugarh University

List of Tables, Figures and Charts

TABLES

FIGURES AND CHARTS

CONTRIBUTORS

Dr. Dipak Kumar Adak
Anthropological Survey of India
North Eastern Regional Centre
Shillong, Meghalaya.

Dr. R.P. Athparia
Anthropological Survey of India
North East Regional Centre
Shillong, Meghalaya.

Dr. R.S. Balgir
Division of Community Health and Nutrition
Regional Medical Research Centre
Indian Council of Medical Research
Chandrasekharpur, Bhubaneswar
Orissa.

Dr. P.M. Buzarbarua
Doordarshan Kendra
Guwahati, Assam.

Dr. Dipesh Choudhury
Anthropological Survey of India
27 Jawaharlal Nehru Road
Calcutta, West Bengal.

Dr. A.K. Das
Department of Anthropology
Dibrugarh University
Assam, India.

Smt. Bandana Das
Anthropological Survey of India
North East Regional Centre
Shillong, Meghalaya.

Prof. Dr. B.M. Das
U.G.C. Emeritus Professor
Department of Anthropology
Gauhati University
Guwahati, Assam.

Dr. Bibhash Dhar
Anthropological Survey of India
North East Regional Centre
Shillong, Meghalaya.

Dr. P.C. Dutta
Director of Research (Retd.)
Government of Arunachal Pradesh
Itanagar.

Prof. Dr. Pratap C. Dutta
Department of Anthropology
North Eastern Hill University
Shillong, Meghalaya.

Smt. Mondira Kalita
Department of Anthropology
Dibrugarh University
Assam.

Prof. Dr. R.K. Kar
Department of Anthropology
Dibrugarh University
Dibrugarh, Assam.

Prof. Dr. K.C. Mahanta
Department of Anthropology
Dibrugarh University
Dibrugarh, Assam.

Dr. Birinchi Kumar Medhi
Department of Anthropology
Gauhati University
Guwahati, Assam.

Dr. S.H.M. Rizvi
Anthropological Survey of India
North Western Regional Centre
Dehradun, Uttar Pradesh, India

Dr. Sarthak Sengupta
Department of Anthropology
Dibrugarh University
Dibrugarh, Assam.

Dr. M. Latif Shah
Department of Anthropology
D.M. College of Science
Imphal, Manipur.

Dr. Mutum Bokul Singh
Department of Tribal Studies
Manipur University
Canchipur, Manipur.

Dr. T. Shyamacharan Singh
Department of Anthropology
Manipur University
Canchipur, Manipur.

Dr. Chandra Jyoti Sonowal
Tata Institute of Social Sciences
Sion-Trombay Road
Deonar, Bombay.

Contents

1
Ethnic Elements in North East India

B.M. Das

North East India comprises seven administrative units. These are: Assam, Meghalaya, Manipur, Nagaland, Mizoram, Arunachal Pradesh and Tripura. But considering certain factors like geographical position, historical background, ethnic composition, cultural heritage, this area may be regarded as one geoethnic unit. North East India is surrounded on all sides by foreign countries except one narrow corridor towards west by which it is connected with other parts of India. The northern boundary is formed by Bhutan and China, the eastern by Myanmar, the southern by Myanmar and Bangladesh and the western by Bangladesh. The region is mostly hilly except the Brahmaputra valley. The Brahmaputra flows through the entire region from east to west flooding time to time the fertile plains on the two sides.

This region of India is the homeland of a large number of populations who speak different languages, have diversed socio-cultural traditions and are of different ethnic origins. They came from different directions and at different times by various routes of migration, namely, the northern passes of Bhutan and Tibet, Assam-Myanmar routes on the eastern side and the valleys on the western direction formed by the Ganges and the Brahmaputra.

It is difficult to say anything about the people of North East India of the prehistoric past, as no skeletal remains of man have yet been discovered from this area. However, sporadic occurrences of man-made tools in this region clearly indicate presences of prehistoric cultures.

The Australoids are considered to be the autochthonous people of India. They are very often referred to by different terms like pre-Dravidian, Proto-Australoid, Nishada, Veddid by different authors. They are described as having short stature; dolichocephalic head; platyrrhine nose, which is depressed at the root; dark brown skin colour; wavy or even curly head hair; prominent supraorbital ridges and slightly retreating forehead. Australoid elements are observed sporadically throughout the length and breadth of the country. These elements are present among almost all castes of India, more particularly among the lower castes. There are several Australoid tribes in different parts of middle and south India, but there is no Australoid population as such in any part of North East India. However, a scientific analysis of the available materials on physical anthropology clearly indicates the existence of Australoid traits in several populations of this part of the country. The Khasis of Meghalaya speak Austric language and this language has certain association with the Australoids and in their physical make-up Australoid traits are discernible. A careful observation of the physical features of the Wanchoos, a tribe of Arunachal Pradesh, who use some Austric words in their dialect, also suggests presence of Australoid strains in them. While analysing the anthropometric data of some Bodo group of tribes like Garo, Rabha, Kachari, it appeared probable to the present writer that these tribes contained certain Australoid ethnic stains. In this connection it may be mentioned that long back in 1924 Haddon "tentatively suggested and ancient dolichocephalic-platyrrhine (pre-Dravidian) type which is strong among the Kuki, Khasi, Manipuri, Kachari, etc". Again in 1925 Buxton expressed his opinion that in the eastern frontier of India, "the basal type and probably the aboriginal, is pre-Dravidia, but there is no exact data on this point at present. It is found among many of the more isolated tribes". In 1935 Mills observed "almost entire absence of Mongoloid traits" in the physical features of Mros of Chittagong Hills, which has been called "an old Veddid pocket" by Sarkar and Bhattacharjee (1958). In the same year Guha and Basu identified certain crania found in Nagaland to be of Australoid type. The recent anthropological researches among the Assamese castes by the present writer and his associates support the earlier view that Australoid elements are present in the caste population also. All these informations suggest that the Australoids came North East India before the coming of the Mongoloids.

In this context it should be mentioned that from the second half of the last century with the opening of Tea Gardens in many parts of Assam, peoples of various tribal groups like Munda, Gond, Santhal, Savara, Oraon of some other States of India, e.g., Bihar, Orissa, Madhya Pradesh, etc., migrated to Assam to work in the Tea Gardens. Some of these tribes are of Australoid origin. Hence, in recent years also Australoid elements penetrated to the composition of the people of North East India.

All the tribes of North East India are basically Mongoloid. They came to this part of the country in successive waves at different intervals of time from different directions—north, north-east and south-east. Some groups became confined to certain small geographical areas, while others were distributed over larger regions. Some of them are more or less in complete isolation preserving their ethno-biological traits, while some have got admixtured with non-Mongoloid populations to varying extents. The Mongoloid tribes of India are referred to as the Indo-Mongoloids.

The Indo-Mongoloids on North East India speak different languages of Sino-Tibetan group, which has been divided into two major branches, namely, Tibeto-Burman and Siamese-Chinese. One of the subdivisions of Tibeto-Burman is North-Assam group of languages spoken by most of the tribes of Arunachal Pradesh. Another subdivision is called Assam-Burma group, which has been further divided and subdivided. The Boro group of tribes of Assam, Tripura and Meghalaya, Nagas of Nagaland, Mizo-Kukis of Mizoram, Karbis of Assam, Meitheis of Manipur, etc., speak languages of this group. One of the subdivisions of the Siamese-Chinese is Thai. This language is spoken by Khamti, Khamyang, Phakial, etc., which are distributed in different parts of North East India. The original language of Ahoms, a major Mongoloid population of Assam was Thai. The Khasis of Meghalaya speak an entirely different language called Mon-Khmer, which belongs to Austro-Asiatic linguistic family. The Khasi language has similarities on one hand with certain languages spoken in south East Asia and on the other with Munda language of Central India. It is interesting to find such an isolated pocket of Austro-Asiatic speaker Khasi encircled by populations all belonging to Tibeto-Burman language family.

The Khasis are matriarchal people. In a family, authority is vested on the mother; property is inherited by the daughters; descent is matrilineal and after marriage a girl does not go to live in the house of the husband.

In general it can be said that Khasis have brown skin colour. Their head hair is dark brown with reddish tinge in colour, straight or flat wavy in form and coarse in texture. They have scanty beard and moustache. The colour of eyelid brown to dark brown. The eye slit is mostly oblique and palpebral fissure is medium. Eye fold is present in most of the cases. They are short in stature. Their head is mesocephalic and nose is mesorrhine.

As regards their origin and migration the present writer (Das, 1978) in his monograph on the physical anthropology of the Khasi has suggested two possibilities. One, the Khasis are originally Australoid speaking Austric language. Because of strong intrusive Mongoloid strains at a later time their physical features has undergone remarkable changes, but they have retained their language. The second possibility is that they are basically Mongoloid. They came from northeastern direction perhaps from the same area of dispersion of Tibeto-Burman speakers. On their way to the present habitat they adopted Austric language while they were in northern Burma.

It is said that North East China was the original homeland of Tibeto-Burman speakers, from where at one time they migrated towards south. Somewhere in north Burma they became diversified into three groups. One group entered the Brahmaputra valley by the north-eastern routes, one group moved westward along the sub-Himalayan ranges, while the third group migrated southwards to reach South East Asia. However, at later dates representatives of these three groups entered North East India by various routes mentioned above and became distributed in different parts.

The Garos, who speak Tibeto-Burman language form a major population of Meghalaya State, the other major population being the Khasis. The Garos are also matriarchal people. Both the Khasis and Garos are hill people. However, a section of the Garos has settled in the plains areas of Assam. The present writer found differences in certain physical features between these two sections of the Garos Hill and Plains, suggesting microvariation.

Nagaland is the habitat of various Naga tribes like the Ao, Angami, Sema, Konyak, Lhota, Rengma, Phom, Chang and others. They are Mongoloid. Haddon (1924) suggested an Indonesian ethnic element in them. The Nagas are patriarchal people. The present writer (Das, 1970) analysed the available anthropometric data on the Naga tribes and found that "the medium statured Angamis are the tallest, while the short statured Karbis are the shortest of all. The Aos are also short statured people. The head form varies from dolichocephaly in Ao, Chang and Rengma to mesocephaly in Angami, Sema, Lhota, Konyak and Kabui. The Angami, Ao, Chang, Sema and Rengma are mesorrhine; while Konyak and Lhota are platyrrhine. The Kabuis are leptorrhine. The face is broad in Ao, and medium in Kabui. Thus, the Nagas show a wide range of variation in morphological characters in the sense that the nasal form varies from leptorrhiny in one group to platyrrhiny in the other; head form also varies from dolichocephaly to brachycephaly; stature is also variable, suggesting heterogeneous nature in them. Geographical condition of Nagaland and socio-cultural factors kept the Naga populations is complete isolation from one another for a long time. Various differentiating factors played their respective roles in different manners under different conditions resulting physical variation among them".

The Meitheis are the numerically dominant people of Manipur. Some Kuki-Chin tribes, e.g., Aimol, Hmar, Paite, Thado, Vaipei, etc., and also some Naga tribes like Kabui, Tangkhul in addition to others smaller populations live in Manipur.

The Mizo is the major tribe in Mizoram. However, members of some Kuki-Chin tribes like Hmar, Pawi, Lakher, Paite, Thado are also met with in Mizoram. Each one of those has its own ethnic identity, though they are very much akin to Mizos. Very little information on the physical anthropology of the people of Mizoram is available.

The original inhabitants of Tripura are Tripuri (Tippera) whose language belongs to Tibeto-Burman family. The Riangs who were originally inhabitants of Mizoram now live in Tripura. The Maghs migrated to Tripura from Burma. The Chakmas form another tribe of Tripura. All these tribes are Mongoloid.

A large number of Indo-Mongoloid tribes live in Arunachal Pradesh. Like other Indo-Mongoloids of North East India they are also agriculturist. Some of the major tribes are the Aka, Monpa, Nishi, Sherdukpen, Apatani, Adi, Mishimi, Nocte, Wanchoo, Tangsa, etc. The Arunachal tribes came from the north. The different tribes narrate different stories as regards their movement in that region.

Some of the important Indo-Mongoloid tribes of Assam are the Kachari, Rabha, Karbi, Tiwa, Mishing, Deuri, etc. Most of the Assam tribes live in the plains region. However, a section of Karbi and that of Tiwa and also a section of Kachari, known as Dimasha, live in the hilly regions of Assam. Some of the tribes are included under a bigger group called Boros. Traditional stories prevalent among certain Boro tribes like Garo and Rabha suggest that their ancestral home was Tibet or eastern Sub-Himalayan region from where they migrated to North East India and were distributed in different parts. Another Boro tribes Kachari came from northeastern direction.

In general it may be said that Boro tribes have smooth and flat wavy head hair with coarse texture. Their beard and moustache are scanty in growth. Eyes are oblique having narrow to medium fissure. Mongoloid fold is present in eye. Skin colour is brownish. Zygomatic arches range from medium to marked in prominence. Their stature is below medium in average. Head form varies from dolichocephalic to mesocephaly. Face is medium to broad. Nose is mesorrhine.

The present writer (Das, 1970) compared the tribes of North East India with some of the Asiatic Mongoloids in respect of certain anthropometric traits, more particularly head, face, nose and stature and observed that "the North East Indian tribes show some similarities in one or other character with the other Mongoloid populations of Asia, but they have certain individuality. In general it can be said that they are shorter, they have narrower heads, narrower and lower faces, and broadest noses in comparison to the other Mongoloid people".

It has already been mentioned that Ahoms of Assam were originally Thai or Shan speakers. In the early part of the thirteenth century Ahoms migrated from their original habitat in the upper courses of Irrawaddy in Myanmar and entered Assam crossing the Patkoi ranges. They first established their settlement in the valley of a small river called Namrup. At a later stage they developed it to a kingdom and extended their territory down the Brahmaputra valley covering a large area. The reign of Ahoms came to an end in the year 1926. Coming to Assam Ahoms gradually abandoned their original Thai language and accepted the Assamese language. By the seventeenth century they became Hindu. The Ahoms form a sizable population of Assam being distributed in the districts of eastern Assam valley.

The Ahoms are also Mongoloid in origin. In general they are light brown in skin colour. Their beard and moustache are scanty in growth. Their head hair is black in colour and stretched to flat wavy in form. Their eye colour is mostly black or dark brown. In them eye fold is frequently present. Their head is brachycephalic and nose is mesorrhine. They are below medium in stature.

At later dates Ahoms were followed by some other Shan populations like Tai Phake, Khamyang, Turung, Aiton, etc., to enter Assam. They are distributed in small pockets in the eastern districts of Assam. They are Buddhist people.

Unlike the Mongoloids, the Caucasoids entered North East India from the western direction following the valleys of the Ganges and the Brahmaputra. The Caucasic people are mostly confined in Assam. As a matter of fact the population of Assam may be divided into two broad categories, namely, the "Indid" (the term has been taken from von Eickstedt and the "Mongoloid" Assamese. The Mongoloid Assamese have already been discussed. The people of Assam speak Assamese an Indo-Aryan language.

The "Indid" Assamese are Caucasic in origin. Caucasic, however, is a very broad term and it includes several types and subtypes. The Mediterraneans form a variety of Caucasoid. It is believed that at one time they were distributed from the Mediterranean region to South East Asia forming a some sort of chain, which was broken into pieces because of various reasons at a later date leaving Mediterranean pockets in different areas. This is the "Brown Race" of Elliot Smith. Thus at a very ancient time the Mediterranean variety of the Caucasoid race entered North East India, though it is difficult to ascertain the exact date of their arrival. In this connection it may be pointed out that one type of Mediterranean contributed significantly towards the building of the Indus Valley Civilization. Marked Mediterranean elements are visible in the present-day Assamese population. In general the Mediterraneans are medium statured people with delicately build body and long head. However, it is an established fact that because of several factors, e.g., gene flow, selection environment, isolation, etc., a population can assume different types of physical features in different geographical areas. This is applicable to Mediterraneans of India also and hence in India itself different varieties of this type were evolved. In Assam they might have acquired a distinct physical type.

The Alpino-Armenoid element has also entered into the Assamese population. In contrast to long-headed Mediterranean, they are broad headed. Probably this element also came long back, may be along with Mediterraneans. But they came by a different route via sub-Himalayan region. At present this element is not very frequently found among the Assamese.

Another long-headed element has been contributed by Indo-Aryans who differ from the earlier Mediterraneans in having taller stature, finer nose and lighter complexion. According to some scholars, Indo-Aryans reached northern Bihar at least by 700 B.C. if not earlier, from where they moved eastward in small bands to enter Assam at different times. However, it is difficult to suggest the exact date of their arrival. Indo-Aryan elements are frequently observed in many Assamese populations.

The present writer reported that medium head and medium stature are characteristic features of certain Indid Assamese populations. These perhaps were contributed by Irano-Scythians, who according to some scholars came to India at the same time of the Indo-Aryan migration. Irano-Scythians followed the course of the Indus to arrive at Gujarat-Maharashtra region of Western India from where they migrated eastward following the river valley of the Son and the Narmada and then via Bengal they entered Assam. Thus several varieties of the Caucasoid race have entered into the composition of the Indid Assamese population.

It may be summarised this way that the Australoids first came to North East India. Then came the Mongoloids who partially or fully absorbed the old Australoid strains. The Mongoloids came from different directions and at different times in successive waves. Though the migration of the Mongoloids was a continuous process, yet it can be said that after the Mongoloids came the Caucasoids from the western direction. The Caucasoid migration also occurred in succession. Before the arrival of Indo-Aryans and Irano-Scythians, Mediterraneans and Alpino-Armenoids came to this region.

North East India may be regarded as a meeting place of the Mongoloids and Caucasoids. In many parts of this region people belonging to these two major races are living side by side since long back. As a result admixture to varied degrees has taken place between members of the two groups. In some cases it is not easy to distinguish a man of Mongoloid fold from that of a Caucasic origin by observing the physical features.

Though admixture to certain extent has taken place yet the Mongoloid populations, commonly known as tribes, as a group are distinguishable from the Caucasoid populations, referred to as castes. The populations comprising Mongoloid group are also distinguishable from each other on the basis of physical anthropological and socio-cultural traits. Again, in some cases the constituent sections of a tribe also show microvariation among them. The present writer (Das, 1978) reported such microvariation in the Khasi populations as well as the Chutiya populations. He calls this trend of variation as microevolution (Das, 1981). He observed a distinct microevolutionary trend among certain Boro populations of North East India. One worker (Chakravarty, 1981) observed microevolutionary dynamics in hybrid Mongoloid population called the Man.

The endogamous Hindu castes also exhibit microevolution among them. The present writer (Das, 1979) observed such variations in certain biological traits like ABO blood groups, cerumen type, anthropometry, cross-section of head hair dermatoglyphics, among three Assamese castes, namely, Brahmin, Kalita and Kaibarta, who represent three horizontal strata of the Assamese caste complex. When the castes are arranged in a hierarchical order (i.e., Brahmin at the top, Kalita at the middle and the Kaibarta at the bottom) head hair becomes finer from Kaibarta to Kalita and the Brahmin. Stature shows a gradual increase from the bottom to the top. Similarly head length increasess, while head breadth decreases and as a result head becomes longer and narrower from Kaibarta to Brahmin through Kalita. In the same manner nasal height increases and nasal breadth decreases and consequently nasal index shows a decrease.

In Assam there is a process by which tribal people after conversion to Hinduism can become member of a caste. A caste, called the Rajbanshi (very often referred to as Koch also) has been formed by this process. Like other Assamese Hindu caste this caste also has its defined position in the Assamese caste fold. Rajbanshis are in one sense a heterogeneous population, because members of different tribes after conversion are put into this caste. Thereby their number is also increasing. Through this process Mongoloid elements are entering into the "Indid" Assamese group. Thus tribe caste continuum is observed.

Haemoglobin E (HbβE), a variant of haemoglobin deserves special attention because of its high prevalence in certain populations of North East India. Flatz and his associates (1965) pointed out to an association of high frequencies of HbβE with the Austro-Asiatic language speakers of South East Asia. Accordingly Khasis (Austro-Asiatic language speakers) and Ahoms (whose original language was Thai) were examined and found high prevalence of HbβE in them supporting the hypothesis of Flatz (for detail see Das et al., 1971). But when Kacharis, who speak Tibeto-Burman language were also examined for HbβE, it was found that in them HbβE was so predominant that it was in the process of eliminating HbA even, not to speak of HbβT. Some other populations speaking Tibeto-Burman languages also showed high frequencies of this gene (Das et al., 1980). This gene has penetrated to some Caucasic people also. It may be noted that the frequency of HbβE gene in the Tibeto-Burman is the highest in the world.

The ethnic composition of the population of North East India is such that it provides ample scopes to do different types of anthropological works. Some populations live in complete isolation, others have to some extent mixed up with neighbouring groups. Examples of admixture at a microlevel between two major racial groups—Mongoloid and Caucasoid—are not lacking in this part. Again, some are hill people, some live in the plains. In certain cases section of a hill people has come down to settle in the plains, and thereby two populations from one have emerged. The process of fusion and fission is at work. The Caucasoid people are mostly Hindus. However, a considerable section is formed by the Muslims. Most of the Mongoloid tribes have their own religions, some of them have accepted Christianity; some are Hindus and some are Hinduised; some are Buddhists. All these have made this region colourful and varied. All these populations have contributed their respective shares to the formation of a composite people and composite culture in North East India.

Acknowledgements

This is a part of a lecture delivered in the Institute of Anthropology, University of Rome, in November 1982, under Indo-Italian Cultural Exchange Programme. The author is thankful to Professor Gabriella Spedini and her colleagues for their help and co-operation in undertaking the programme.

REFERENCES

BUXTON, L.H.D., 1925, *The Peoples of Asia*, London.

CHAKRAVARTY, S.K., 1981, *Microevolutionary dynamics in a hybrid population: The Man of Meghalaya*. Unpublished Ph. D Thesis, Gauhati University.

DAS, B.M., 1970, *Anthropometry of the Tribal Groups of Assam, India*. Monograph Field Research Series, Field Research Projects, Miami, Florida, USA.

DAS, B.M., 1971; M.R. CHAKRAVARTHI; H. DELBRUK; G. FLATZ, 1971, High prevalence of Haemoglobin E in two populations of Assam. *Humangenetik*, 12 : 264 - 266.

DAS, B.M., 1978, *Variation in physical characters in the Khasi populations of North East India*. Gauhati, Dutta Barua and Co.

DAS, B.M., 1979, Physical variations in three Assamese castes. *Anthropologischer Anzeiger*, 37, 3 : 204 - 210.

DAS, B.M.; R. DEKA; R. DAS, 1980, Haemoglobin E in six populations of Assam. *Journal of Indian Anthropological Society*, 15 : 153 - 156.

DAS, B.M., 1981, *Microevolution*, New Delhi: Concept Publishing House.

FLATZ, G.; C. PIK; S. SRINGAM, 1965, Haemoglobin E and Beta thalassemia, their distribution in Thailand *Annals of Human Genetics*, 29 : 151 - 170.

GUHA, B.S.; P.C. BASU, 1931, A report on the human relics recovered by the Naga Hills (Burma) expedition for the abolition of human sacrifices during 1926-27. *Anthropological Bulletin*, N.I. Zoological Survey of India.

HADDON, A.C., 1924, *The Races of Man*. Cambridge: Cambridge University Press.

MILLS, J.P., 1935, The Mros of Chittagong Hills. *Census of India*, Volume I, Part III.

SARKAR, S.S.; P. BHATTACHARYA, 1958, The tribal population of West Bengal, *Man in India*, 38, 1 : 60.

2

Intergroup Variability of the Tai People of Assam

T. Shyamacharan Singh

The word Tai denotes a great branch of Mongoloid population of Asia whose habitat extends from Assam in the west to Kwangsi and Hainan in the east, from Yunnan in the north to Thailand in the south (Gogoi, 1968). The Tai people of Assam came originally via mainland of South East Asia, where at present Tai form the most numerous and most widespread of the indigenous population (Terwiel, 1980). The Ahoms were the earliest Tai community who entered in Assam during the beginning of the 13th century. The other Tai communities who came to this region during the period from the middle of the 18th century to the middle of the 19th century were the Khamtis, the Phakes, the Aitons, the Khamiyangs and the Turungs (Grierson, 1967). These peoples, in Assam, are now found in the district of Golaghat, Karbi Anglong (eastern), Jorhat, Sibsagar, Dibrugarh and North Lakhimpur. These areas lie within 26° and 28° north latitude and 93° and 96° east longitude.

Among these Tai communities, the Ahoms, except a few priestly classes, were converted into Hinduism and sacrificed their Tai language (Siamese-Chinese family) in favour of Assamese by the 17th century, before the arrival of the latter immigrants who came as followers of the Hinayana sect of Buddhism. The present-day Khamyangs have also forgotten their Tai language and adopted Assamese. Intermarriage with non-Tai speaking communities is seen to be comparatively higher among them.

This may have led them to sacrifice their own language in favour of Assamese. The Turungs speak a dialect which is a mixture of Tai and Singpho, a Tibeto-Burman speaking tribe. This is due to the fact that they were subdued by the Singphos for a considerable period of time during their migration to Assam (Grierson, 1967). The other communities still retain their Tai language. The Khamtis, however, have been incessantly emigrating to the neighbouring state of Arunachal Pradesh since the last decade. Their number in Assam is now very few and they represent the smallest Tai population in Assam.

So far a few works have been done among these Tai communities of Assam. The Ahoms were studied by Das, et al. (1971, 1975, 1985); Gogoi (1972); Dutta (1978), etc., on various bio-anthropological variables. There are few reports on dermatoglyphics and anthropometry of the Khamyangs made by Das and Bhagabati (1962, 1963, 1964); Das and Das (1972); and Barua (1976). There is a report of fertility and mortality of the Khamyangs and the Turungs made by Das (1985). Another report on some genetical traits of the Turungs has been given by Baruah, et al. (1987). The other sections are still in want of any physical anthropological study. And how far the Tai communities share similarities and differences is yet to be known. In view of such paucity, the present paper attempts to bring out a report on similarities and differences among the Tai populations of Assam in respect of anthropometric measurements, dermatoglyphics, ABO blood groups and taste sensitivity to phenylthiourea.

Materials and Methods

The author has collected data on the aforesaid parameters from the Turungs, the Khamyangs, the Aitons and the Khamtis visiting several villages of the districts of Golaghat Karbi—Anglong, Jorhat, Sibsagar and North Lakhimpur during the period of April to December 1987. Data of the Ahoms have been obtained from Das, et al. (1985). Anthropometric measurements have been taken from the males only, while both the sexes have been included in all the other anthroplogical variables. Proper care has been taken to avoid biologically closely related persons in the samples in all possible ways. Sizes of the samples are shown in the tables. Anthropometric measurements were performed following standard techniques (Singh and Bhasin, 1968), just so dermatoglyphics (Cummins and Midlo, 1961; Holt 1963). ABO blood grouping test was done by direct method using anti-A and anti-B sera. The sorting technique of Harris and Kalmus (1949) was followed to determine the threshold of ability to taste phenylthiourea for comparison, t-test, chi-square test, Nei's G_{ST} X^2 (Roychoudhury, 1978) have been applied. Sanghvi's G (1953) has also been calculated for measuring genetic distance.

Results

Anthropometric study comprises 10 measurements and 6 indices. Mean values and standard errors of these traits are given in table 2.1. It is seen that the Turungs stand for the tallest, being 'medium' in stature (Martin's scale) while the others are all 'below medium'. Cephalic index of the Turungs is also 'mesocephaly' while the others are 'brachycephalic'. In breadth height index, the Ahoms stand apart from the others in the sense that they are 'acrocephalic' while the others are 'metriocephalic'. All of them are, however, 'hypsicephalic' in length height index. Concerning the facial indices the Turungs, the Khamyangs and the Khamtis possess 'euryene' type of upper facial index whereas the Aitons and the Ahoms possess 'mesene' type. But they are all 'euryprosopic' in total facial index and 'mesorrhine' in nasal index.

The values of t-est for comparison among them are given in table 2.2. It should be noted that where the word significant is used it means statistically significant at the 1.0% level. It is apparent from the table that the Turungs agree with the Khamyangs and the Khamtis in all respects. The Aitons and the Khamtis also agree with each other in all the 16 anthropometric traits compared. The Aitons, however, show significant differences from the Turungs and the Khamyangs in 3 traits, viz., head length, circumference of head and cephalic index. The Khamyangs and the Khamtis differ from each other only in 1 measurements, that is nasal height. The Ahoms, in general, show deviation from the others in greater magnitude. They differ from the Turungs and the Aitons in 7 traits and from the Khamyangs and the Khamtis in 6 traits. The anthropometric deviations of the Ahoms from the others, as seen in table 2.2, are as given below :

Deviations from Turungs	: Stature headlength, circumference of head, upper facial height, nasal height, upper facial index and nasal index.
Deviations from Aitons	: Head breadth, bizygomatic breadth, upper facial height, nasal height, upper facial index, total facial index and nasal index.
Deviations from Khamyangs	: Head length, head breadth, bizygomatic breadth, nasal height upper facial height and nasal index.
Deviations from Khamtis	: Head length, head breadth, upper facial height, nasal height, nasal index and upper facial index.

It is, thus, observed that the anthropometric characters of the Tai Buddhists (the Turungs, the Khamyangs, the Aitons and the Khamtis) are more or less uniform and the Ahoms stand somewhat apart from them.

With regard to dermatoglyphics, the present paper covers frequencies of finger patterns and Wilder's main line formulae. The frequencies of finger patterns are given in table 2.3. The trend of whorl, loop and arch distribution among the Turungs, the Khamyangs and the Ahoms is loop > whorl > arch, while it is whorl > loop > arch among the Aitons and the Khamtis. The frequencies of arch is comparatively lower among the Aitons and the Khamtis, whose frequency of whorl is higher than that of the loop. In other words, inverse relation between the frequencies of whorl and arch is seen in the present study also. The ratio of whorl and loop seen in the present populations are 43 : 57 in the Turungs, 45 : 55 in the Khamyangs, 51 : 49 in the Aitons, 56 : 44

in the Khamtis and 41 : 59 in the Ahoms. The Khamtis, thus, stand for the highest frequency of whorl and the lowest frequency of loop while the Ahoms stand for the lowest frequency of whorl and highest frequency of loop. The Tai as a whole display a whorl loop ratio of 47 : 53. The values of chi-square for comparison among them as well as for examination of deviation from the Tai as a whole are given in table 2.4. It is seen that the Turungs and the Ahoms, who have higher frequency of loop than whorl, agree with each other on one side. The Aitons and the Khamtis, who have higher frequency of whorl than loop, agree with each other on the other. Differences between the others are all statistically significant and none of them show agreement with the Tai as a whole.

Distribution of Wilder's main line formulae among these Tai populations are shown in table 2.5. It is at once clear from the table that the frequency of the formula 11.9.7 is the lowest of all other formulae in all the populations. The frequency of 9.7.5 predominates over that of 7.5.5 among the Turungs, the Aitons and the Ahoms thereby showing the trend of distribution as 9.7.5 > 7.5.5 > 11.9.7. The Khamyangs and the Khamtis, however, display higher frequency of 7.5.5. than 9.7.5 thereby showing the trend of distribution as 7.5.5 > 9.7.5 > 11.9.7. The Tai as a whole also shows the latter trend. A keen observation in table 2.5 reveals an interesting feature that the frequency of 11.9.7 seems to have an inverse relation with the frequency of 7.5.5. That is, increase in the frequency 7.5.5 leads to decrease in 11.9.7 and vice versa. Among these Tai populations, the Khamtis whose frequency of 11.9.7 is the lowest of all (8.4%) display the highest frequency of 7.5.5 (44.8%). On the other hand, the Ahoms, whose 11.9.7 frequency is the highest (18.7%) possess the lowest frequency of 7.5.5. (26.7%). Between these two margins frequency of 11.9.7 increases and 7.5.5 decreases successively through the Khamyangs (11.9.7 = 9.8% ; 7.5.5 = 33.8%), the Turungs (11.9.7 = 13.0% ; 7.5.5 = 29.1%) and the Aitons (11.9.7 = 18.1%; 7.5.5 = 27.8%). The values of chi-square for examination of variation among the populations as well as for deviation from the Tai as a whole are given in table 2.6. The Ahoms agree with the Turungs and the Aitons on one side, while the Khamyangs agree with the Khamtis on the other. Differences among the rests are all significant. The Khamtis alone deviate significantly from the Tai as a whole while all the others do not do so, in respect of Wilder's three main line formulae's distribution.

Gene frequencies of two loci, ABO blood group system and taste sensitivity to phenylthiourea among the Tai populations are given in table 2.7. It is interesting that, the Ahoms, who converted themselves into Hinduism before the arrival of other Tai communities, show a trend of allele frequencies which is quite different from those of the others in both the loci. While allele r^O, in the ABO system, is the most frequent one in all of them, allele p^A predominates over allele q^B in the Ahoms and reverse is true in all the remaining populations, who are Buddhist by religion. As such the order of allele frequencies in the Ahoms is $r^O > p^A > q^B$ and that of the others is $r^O > q^B > p^A$. Among the Tai Buddhist the Turungs possess highest frequency of allele r^O and subsequently lowest frequency of alleles q^B and p^A. The Khamtis, on the other hand, display lowest frequency of allele r^O and highest frequencies of alleles q^B and p^A.

With regard to taste sensitivity to phenylthiourea also, the Ahoms stand apart from the others in the sense that the frequency of recessive non taster allele 't' is higher than that of dominant taster allele 'T', while reverse is true among the Tai Buddhist populations. Among the latter populations the Turungs display lowest frequency of allele 't' and the highest by the Khamtis.

The values of Nei's G_{ST}, X^2 for analysis of gene differentiation are given in table 2.8. It is evident that the Tai as a whole is no longer a homogeneous entity in the context of Assam. There is significant difference in all the allele frequencies of the two loci. The biggest difference among them is seen in the alleles of taste sensitivity to phenylthiourea (X^2 = 49.9) followed by alleles r^O (X^2 = 44.516), q^B (X^2 = 37.777) and p^A (X^2 =24.096) of the ABO system. The mean co-efficient of difference between the populations in the ABO system is 1.83%, that of the taste sensitivity to phenylthiourea is 2.49%, and mean value of the two loci is 2.16%.

The values of G, calculated from the abovementioned two loci, for measuring genetic distance among them are shown in table 2.9. The closest affinity is seen between the Aitons and the Khamiyangs while the farthest distance is seen between the Turungs and the Khamtis. The Turungs stand more closer to the Aitons and the Khamyangs than do by the Khamtis. The Ahoms, in general stand apart from all of them.

Discussion

It is learned from the preceding paragraphs that the Tai as a whole is no longer a homogeneous entity in the context of Assam. The Ahoms stand apart from the others in respect of anthropometry, distribution pattern of allele frequencies of both the ABO blood group system and the taste sensitivity to phenylthiourea, whereas such characters are more or less uniform among the Buddhist communities. Preponderance of allele q^B over allele p^A, as seen among the Tai Buddhists, is also found among the Burmese and some Tai populations of South East Asia (Das, 1978 : 21). It may be remembered that the Tai communities came to Assam from these areas. Therefore, higher frequency of allele q^B than p^A may be expected among the Tai communities of Assam. If so, the present-day Ahoms in whom allele p^A is higher than allele q^B, deviate from the general Tai character in respect of allele frequencies of ABO blood group system. Furthermore, the Ahoms have higher frequency of allele 't' than 'T' in respect of taste sensitivity to phenylthiourea, whereas reverse is true among the other Tai populations. Mongoloids generally show a lower incidence of allele 't' with few exceptions as among the Gujaro Indian and Eskimo (c.f. Bhalla, 1972). Even though it may not be the general consensus in the context of North East India, this much is true that the Ahoms, deviate from the general Tai character in this respect too. What causes such deviation of the Ahoms from the general Tai characters? Is it because of their Hinduisation during the 17th century long before the arrival of other Tai communities? Though it is not possible at the present state of knowledge to account definitely for such nature of variability as many factors are likely to be involved, however, the above may be considered as one of the reasons, if not the sole one. By the time the latter Tai immigrants arrived at Assam, the Ahoms had already forgotten their Tai language and adopted Assamese. Conversion into Hinduism may have opened a door for intermarriage with non-Tai communities, the consequence of which may have led them to sacrifice their own language. The present-day Khamyangs have also forgotten their Tai language in favour of Assamese. Intermarriage with non-Tai communities is found very high among them too in comparison to other Tai Buddhist communities. But deviation of the Khamyangs from the general Tai character is not conspicuous like the Ahoms, at the moment.

With regard to dermatoglyphics, the Turungs, the Khamyangs and the Ahoms have higher frequency of loop than whorl and reverse is true among the Aitons and the Khamtis. If 50W : 50L ratio is the character of Mongoloid people (Chakravartti, 1963) only the Aitons (51 : 49) agree with this trend. The Tai as a whole (47 : 53) of course is very near to it. The Khamtis possess a very high frequency of whorl and they also deviate from the Tai as a whole in respect of Wilder's three main formulae. Moreover, they display the lowest frequency of allele r^{O} and highest frequency of p^{A} and q^{B}. Elevation of allele 't' compared to other Tai Buddhists is also seen among them. In this regard, it may be remembered that the Khamtis now stand for the smallest of all the Tai populations in Assam. They have been incessantly emigrating to the neighbouring state of Arunachal Pradesh. During the present author's visit to North Lakhimpur (where the Khamtis are mainly concentrated) for data collection, the biggest Khamti village, Borkhamti, was found to consist of only 25 households while the number of households in the neighbouring 3 villages were 8 to 11 only. It has already been mentioned that the present data have been collected from Assam. Therefore, a possibility of 'genetic drift' in the remaining small Khamti population of Assam cannot be ruled out.

The value of G (table 2.9) demonstrates that the Turungs stand farthest away from the Khamtis. As opposed to the latter, the Turungs possess the highest frequency of allele r^{O}, lowest frequency of allele 't' and a low frequency of whorl. The Turungs agree with the Ahoms in both the dermatoglyphical characters considered in the present study. It is now worthwhile to remember that the Turungs were subdued by the Singphos for a considerable period of time during the time of their migration to Assam. As a result, they now speak a language which is a mixture of Tai and Singpho. Eventually one cannot expect genuine Tai characters from the Turungs.

To conclude it may be recapitulated that the Tai population in Assam do not together constitute a homogeneous Tai entity. Of them, the Aitons seem to be the most conservative one and the Ahoms be the most deviated or evolved one from the general Tai characters. The Tai Buddhists, despite their intergroup variations, still display a more or less common character.

Table 2.1 : Mean value and Standard error of Anthropometric measurements (in cm.) and indices among the Tai populations

Anthropometric trait	Turung n = 98		Khamyang n = 107		Aiton n = 102		Khamti n = 63		Ahom n = 100	
	Mean	± S.E.	Mean	± S.E.	Mean	± S.E.	Mean	± S.E.	Mean	± S.E.
Stature	166.57	0.95	163.73	0.53	163.50	0.54	163.07	0.81	162.83	0.62
Head Length	18.76	0.07	18.79	0.07	18.43	0.07	18.62	0.08	18.24	0.08
Head Breadth	15.12	0.07	15.18	0.06	15.30	0.07	15.27	0.08	14.88	0.07
Head Height	12.71	0.05	12.69	0.06	12.61	0.06	12.81	0.05	12.65	0.14
Head Circumference	56.26	0.18	56.00	0.16	55.24	0.16	55.75	0.19	55.45	0.18
Bizygomatic Breadth	13.89	0.08	14.06	0.06	13.99	0.05	13.48	0.07	13.65	0.05
Upper Facial Height	6.55	0.06	6.77	0.05	6.72	0.05	6.68	0.06	6.98	0.05
Total Facial Height	11.43	0.05	11.62	0.05	11.45	0.07	11.50	0.08	11.46	0.06
Nasal Height	4.98	0.03	5.00	0.03	4.96	0.04	4.85	0.04	5.27	0.04
Nasal Breadth	3.87	0.03	3.82	0.03	3.77	0.02	3.79	0.02	3.78	0.03
Cephalic Index	80.81	0.46	81.06	0.45	82.97	0.42	82.21	0.44	81.71	0.45
Breadth Height Index	84.69	0.52	83.56	0.44	82.76	0.53	83.69	0.51	85.54	0.95
Length Height Index	68.29	0.35	67.58	0.39	68.65	0.39	68.78	0.38	69.05	0.73
Upper Facial Index	47.57	0.44	47.20	0.36	48.29	0.37	47.92	0.50	50.94	0.32
Total Facial Index	82.73	0.60	82.71	0.42	81.65	0.51	83.36	0.62	83.95	0.47
Nasal Index	78.70	0.66	77.35	0.61	76.88	0.68	77.17	0.82	71.67	0.64

Table 2.2 : Values of t-test for comparison in respect of Anthropometric traits among the Tai populations

Anthropometric trait	T × KG	T × A	T × KT	T × AH	KG × A	KG × KT	KG × AH	A × KT	A × AH	KT × AH
Stature	2.611	2.809	2.804	3.297*	0.304	0.682	1.103	0.442	0.815	0.235
Head Length	0.303	3.334*	1.317	4.892*	3.637*	1.599	5.174*	1.787	1.787	3.359*
Head Breadth	0.651	1.818	1.411	2.424	1.302	0.900	3.254*	0.282	4.243*	3.669*
Head Height	1.280	2.305	0.283	0.942	0.943	1.536	0.263	2.561	0.263	1.076
Head Circumference	1.121	4.277*	1.987	3.224*	3.359*	1.006	2.284	2.053	0.872	1.146
Bizygomatic Breadth	1.700	1.060	0.470	2.544	0.896	2.557	5.250*	1.744	4.808*	1.976
Upper Facial Height	2.817	2.177	1.532	5.506*	0.707	1.152	2.970	0.512	3.677*	3.841*
Total Facial Height	2.687	0.232	0.742	0.384	1.976	1.272	2.049	0.470	0.108	0.400
Nasal Height	0.487	0.400	2.600	5.800*	0.800	3.000*	5.400*	1.945	5.480*	7.425*
Nasal Breadth	0.943	2.774	1.886	2.121	1.664	0.943	1.179	0.555	0.277	0.236
Cephalic Index	0.388	3.464*	2.199	1.399	3.103*	1.827	1.021	1.249	2.047	0.794
Breadth Height Index	1.659	2.599	1.373	0.785	1.161	0.193	1.891	1.264	2.556	1.716
Length Height Index	1.355	0.687	0.948	0.939	1.940	2.204	1.776	0.239	0.483	0.328
Upper Facial Index	0.651	1.252	0.525	6.194*	2.111	1.169	7.765*	0.640	5.417*	5.087*
Total Facial Index	0.027	1.371	0.730	1.601	1.604	0.869	1.967	2.130	3.316*	0.758
Nasal Index	1.502	1.921	0.772	7.647*	0.500	0.165	6.413*	0.272	5.579*	5.287*

* Significant at 1.0% level.

T = Turung, KG = Khamyang, A = Aiton, KT = Khamti, AH = Ahom

Table 2.3 : Percentage frequencies of finger patterns among the Tai populations

Population	No.	Whorls	Loops			Arches
			Radial	Ulnar	Total	
Turung	158	41.0	2.6	52.7	55.3	3.7
Khamyang	164	43.2	2.2	49.6	51.8	5.0
Aiton	135	50.5	1.9	46.3	48.2	1.3
Khamti	125	54.7	1.6	42.0	43.6	1.7
Ahom	108	40.0	1.2	55.5	56.7	3.3
Tai	690	45.7	2.0	49.2	51.2	3.1

Table 2.4 : Chi-square values for comparison among the Tai populations in respect of finger pattern types

Population		X^2	Probability lies (d.f. = 2)	Inference
Turung	× Khamyang	6.084	$0.05 > p > 0.02$	Significant
	× Aiton	37.561	$0.001 > p$	Significant
	× Khamti	57.193	$0.001 > p$	Significant
	× Ahom	0.587	$0.80 > 0.70$	Insignificant
Khamyang	× Aiton	40.987	$0.001 > p$	Significant
	× Khamti	51.981	$0.001 > p$	Significant
	× Ahom	8.594	$0.02 > p > 0.01$	Significant
Aiton	× Khamti	5.600	$0.10 > p > 0.05$	Insignificant
	× Ahom	34.463	$0.001 > p$	Significant
Khamti	× Ahom	52.639	$0.001 > p$	Significant
Tai	× Turung	11.842	$0.01 > p > 0.001$	Significant
	× Khamyang	15.825	$0.001 > p$	Significant
	× Aiton	21.261	$0.001 > p$	Significant
	× Khamti	37.783	$0.001 > p$	Significant
	× Ahom	12.341	$0.01 > p > 0.001$	Significant

Table 2.5 : Percentage frequencies of Wilder's three main line formulae among the Tai populations

Population	No.	11.9.7	9.7.5	7.5.5	Others
Turung	158	13.0	38.3	29.1	19.6
Khamyang	164	9.8	30.2	33.8	26.2
Aiton	135	18.1	28.5	27.8	25.6
Khamti	125	8.4	22.8	44.8	24.0
Ahom	88	18.7	34.1	26.7	20.5
Tai	670	13.1	30.9	32.6	23.4

Table 2.6 : Chi-square values for comparison among the Tai populations in respect of Wilder's three main line formulae

Population		X^2	Probability lies (3 d.f.)	Inference
Turung	× Khamyang	8.759	$0.05 > p > 0.02$	Significant
	× Aiton	8.973	$0.05 > p > 0.02$	Significant
	× Khamti	24.079	$0.001 > p$	Significant
	× Ahom	3.279	$0.20 > p > 0.10$	Insignificant
Khamyang	× Aiton	9.041	$0.05 > p > 0.02$	Significant
	× Khamti	7.814	$0.10 > p > 0.05$	Insignificant
	× Ahom	11.185	$0.02 > p > 0.01$	Significant
Aiton	× Khamti	21.814	$0.001 > p$	Significant
	× Ahom	2.250	$0.70 > p > 0.50$	Insignificant
Khamti	× Ahom	23.231	$0.001 > p$	Significant
Tai	× Turung	6.104	$0.20 > p > 0.10$	Insignificant
	× Khamyang	4.739	$0.20 > p > 0.10$	Insignificant
	× Aiton	6.591	$0.10 > p > 0.05$	Insignificant
	× Khamti	17.632	$0.001 > p$	Significant
	× Ahom	6.308	$0.10 > 0.05$	Insignificant

Table 2.7 : Gene frequencies of two loci among the Tai populations

Allele	Turung	Khamyang	Aiton	Khamti	Ahom	Mean
ABO Blood Groups						
p^A	0.100	0.100	0.130	0.197	0.167	0.1342
q^B	0.127	0.227	0.173	0.254	0.118	0.1782
r^O	0.773	0.673	0.697	0.549	0.715	0.6876
Sample size	210	248	204	157	202	1021
P.T.C. Taste Sensitivity						
T	0.6792	0.6135	0.6394	0.5356	0.462	0.5893
t	0.3208	0.3865	0.3606	0.4644	0.538	0.4107
Sample size	204	241	200	153	204	1002

Table 2.8 : Gene differentiation at two loci among the Tai populations

Allele	H_T	H_S	D_{ST}	G_{ST}	Chi-square (D.f. =4)
ABO Blood Groups					
p^A	0.116190	0.114818	0.001372	0.0118	24.096*
q^B	0.146445	0.143740	0.002705	0.0185	37.777*
r^O	0.214806	0.210132	0.004674	0.0218	44.516*
Total	0.477441	0.468690	0.008751	0.0183	
P.T.C Taste Sensitivity					
T	0.242026	0.235997	0.006029	0.0249	49.900*
t	0.242026	0.235997	0.006029	0.0249	49.900*
Total	0.484052	0.471994	0.012058	0.0249	
Grand Total	0.961493	0.940684	0.020809	0.0216	
Average of the two loci	0.480746	0.470342	0.0104045	0.0216	

* Significant at 1% level.

Table 2.9 : Values of genetic distance

	Turung	Khamyang	Aiton	Khamti	Ahom
Turung	—	2.99	1.92	5.57	4.81
Khamyang	5.37	—	1.62	3.41	4.44
Aiton	3.45	2.91	—	3.71	3.85
Khamti	10.00	6.12	6.66	—	4.12
Ahom	8.64	7.97	6.91	7.40	—

Maximum value 5.57 is taken as 10.00 and standardized values are given below the diagonal.

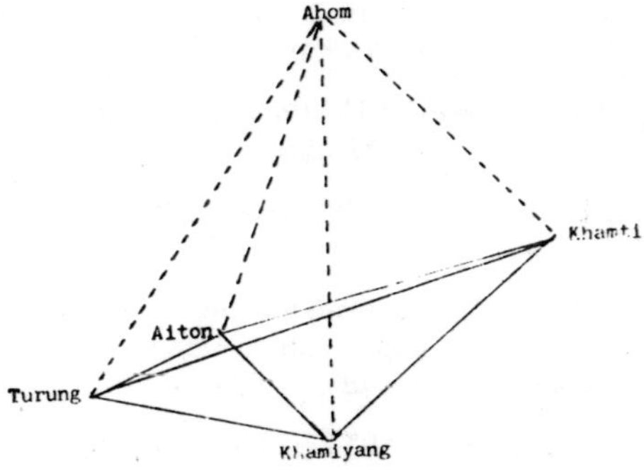

FIGURE 2.1

GENETIC DISTANCE AMONG THE TAI POPULATIONS BASED ON G VALUE OF TWO LOCI (scale unit in cm. with ± 0.5 of the accurate value).

REFERENCES

AHMED HAZARIKA, A.N.Z., 1978, *A Study of growth of head, face, trunk and limbs of the Ahom boys of Assam*. Unpublished Ph. D. Thesis, Dibrugarh University.

BARUAH, G., 1976, A note on palm prints of the Khamyangs: A Mongoloid population of Assam. *Bulletin of the Department of Anthropology, Dibrugarh University*, 5 : 7 - 13.

BARUAH, I.; D.D. DAS; P.M. BUZARBARUAH, 1987, A study of some genetic traits among the Turungs of Assam. *Bulletin of the Department of Anthropology, Dibrugarh University*, 11-12 : 15-20.

BHALLA, V., 1972, Variations in taste threshold for PTC in populations of Tibet and Ladakh, *Human Heredity*, 22.

CHAKRAVARTI, M.R., 1963, Ethnic bearing of the dermatoglyphic studies in India. *Acta Geneticae Medicae et Gemellologiae*, 12, 4 : 374 - 404.

CUMMINS, H.; C. MIDLO, 1961, *Finger prints, palms and Soles: An Introduction to Dermatoglyphics*. New York: Dover Publication Inc.

DAS, B.M., 1978, *Variation in Physical Characteristics in the Khasi populations of North East India*. Gauhati: Dutta Barua and Co.

DAS, B.M.; A.C. BHAGABATI, 1962, Investigations on the finger prints of the Khamyangs. *Journal of Gauhati University*, 13, 1 : 75 - 78.

DAS, B.M.; A.C. BHAGABATI, 1963, Somatometric characters of the Khamyangs. *Journal of Gauhati University*. 14, 2 : 49-54.

DAS, B.M.; A.C. BHAGABATI, 1964, Investigations on the palm prints of the Khamyangs. *Journal of Gauhati University*. 15, 2 : 80-87.

DAS, B.M.; R. DAS, 1972, A note on the ridge counts of finger patterns of the Khamyang : A Mongoloid population of Assam. *Bulletin of the Department of Anthropology, Dibrugarh University*. 1 : 50 - 53.

DAS, B.M.; M.R. CHAKRAVARTTY; H. DELBRUCK; G. GLATZ, 1971, High prevalence of haemoglobin E in two populations of Assam, *Humangenetik*, 12 : 264 - 266.

DAS, B.M.; R. DEKA; G. FLATZ, 1975, Predominence of haemoglobin E gene in a Mongoloid population in Assam (India). *Humangenetik*. 30 : 187 - 191.

DAS, B.M.; P.B. DAS; R. DAS; H. WALTER; H. DANKER HOPFE, 1985, Anthropological studies in Assam, India. 1. Observation on five Mongoloid population. *Anthropologischer Anzeiger*. 43, 3: 193 - 204.

DUTTA, D., 1978, *Intergroup variability in respect of certain dermatoglyphic characters*. Unpublished Ph. D. Thesis, Dibrugarh University.

GAIT, E.A., 1963, *A History of Assam* (3rd Edition). Calcutta : Thacker Spink and Co.

GOGOI, P., 1968, *The Tai and Tai Kingdom.* Gauhati : Department of Publication, Gauhati University.

GOGOI, D., 1972, Menarche and menopause among women of the Ahom village in upper Assam. *Bulletin of the Department of Anthropology, Dibrugarh University,* 1 : 18 - 22.

GRIERSON, G.A., 1967, *Linguistic Survey of India.* Volume II. Delhi : Motilal Banarasidas.

HARRIS, H.; H. KALMUS, 1949, The Measurement of taste sensitivity to phenylthiourea (P.T.C.) *Annals of Eugenics,* 15 : 24 - 31.

HOLT, S.B., 1968, *The Genetics of dermal ridges.* Springfield : Charles Thomas Publisher.

ROYCHOUDHURY, A.K., 1978, Gene differentiation among six tribes in Bihar. *Journal of Indian Anthropological Society.* 13 : 287 -291.

SANGHVI, L.D., 1953, Comparison of genetical and morphological methods for a study of biological differences. *American Journal of Physical Anthropology.* 11 : 385-404.

SENGUPTA. S, 1982, Study of sexual maturation in Ahom girls. *Indian Journal of Physical Anthropology and Human Genetics.* 8, 1 : 63 - 66.

SENGUPTA, S.; M.N. DUTTA; J.L. SHARMAH, 1981, Pattern of C line termination among the Ahoms of Dibrugarh, Assam. *Bulletin of the Department of Anthropology, Dibrugarh University,* 10 : 50-54.

SINGH, I.P.; M.K. BHASIN, 1968, *Anthropometry.* Delhi : Bharati Bhawan.

TERWIEL, B.J., 1980, *The Tai of Assam.* Volume I. Gaya : Centre for South East Asian Studies.

3

A Study on Growth Among the Assamese and Rajasthani Boys

A.K. Das

It has already been shown by many workers that the rate and pattern of growth vary from one population to another. In comparison to other parts of the country, studies on growth are limited in Assam. Mention may be made of the study on Kalita boys and girls (Das, 1966). Das and Das (1969-1971) studied growth of Assamese boys of Guwahati. Das (1974) made a comparative study on the four Hindu castes. Ahmed Hazarika (1974) studied the Ahom boys. Chaudhury (1979) studied the Rabha boys.

In Assam we find various peoples, who speak different language, have different social structure, cultural patterns, religious beliefs and are of different ethnic make-ups. From the ethnic point of view the people of Assam have been divided into two major categories—the 'Indid' and the 'Mongoloid' (Das, 1975). The 'Indid' group exhibits distinct ethnic relation to the Caucasoid population of North India. This group mostly comprises the Assamese Hindu castes and the Assamese Muslims. The Assamese Muslims are biologically similar to the Hindu population of Assam (Ahmed Das, 1977). Thus, the Hindu caste people and Assamese Muslims represent the 'Indid' Assamese group. The Mongoloid group is not included in the present study.

The other group of people considered in the present study is the Rajasthani. Quite a sizable number of them live in Dibrugarh.

They have come to this part of India during the period of 1860 - 1880 (Timberg, 1978). Though they are in Assam for a long time, they are maintaining a separate identity as Rajasthani both culturally and biologically. They marry within their own group. They are strictly vegetarian. The other group, i.e., Assamese people are non-vegetarian.

The data were collected from different educational institutions of Dibrugarh in upper Assam. The data consists of 520 boys of Assamese and 467 of Rajasthani boys. The age of boys ranges from 6 to 17 years. Necessary care was taken to obtain the correct age of the boys. The following somatometric traits are considered in the study; stature, sitting height vertex, lower extremity, biacromial diameter, bicristal diameter, chest girth, waist girth and weight. A distance and a velocity curve on the basis of the data have been drawn. Further, the growth-gradiants of each of the measurements have also been calculated and tabulated.

Stature

From the tables (Table 3.1 and 3.1a) and distance curves (Fig. 3.1), it is found that the mean values for stature increase continuously from 6 years onwards in both Assamese and Rajasthani boys. In the case of Assamese boys, the highest increment in stature is found between 6 and 7 years (10.5 cm) and the next highest in between 8 and 9 years (8.5 cm) and then 11 and 12 years (7.8 cm). But in the case of Rajasthani boys, the highest increment in stature is seen between the 8 and 9 years (9.2 cm). The next highest increment is found between the ages 9 and 10 years (8.6 cm) and then 6 and 7 years (6.7 cm).

The velocity curve (Fig. 3.1a) shows three growth spurts between the ages 8 and 9 years, 11 and 12 years and 14 and 15 years and two growth spurts between the age group 8 and 9 years and 13 and 14 years in Assamese and Rajasthani boys respectively. A small magnitude of growth in stature is visible between the ages 11 and 12 years in Rajasthani boys. The highest peak is observed between the ages of 8 and 9 years in Assamese and Rajasthani boys.

Sitting-height Vertex

It is found from the tables 3.2, 3.2a and figure 3.2 that the sitting height vertex increases continuously from 6 years onwards in both the group. In the case of Assamese boys, the highest increment is found between 6 and 7 years (6.2 cm). The next highest increment is noticed between 11 and 12 years (3.3 cm). But in the case of Rajasthani boys the highest increment in sitting height vertex is almost the same in between 13 and 14 years (3.9 cm) and 6 and 7 years (3.8 cm). The increment between 8 and 9 years is 3.7 cm which comes next.

The velocity curve (Fig. 3.2a) in Assamese boys shows spurts between the ages 11 and 12 years and 13 and 14 years. The highest spurt is seen between the ages of 11 and 12 years. On the other hand, in Rajasthani boys, three sharp peaks are found between 8 and 9 years, 10 and 11 years and 13 and 14 years. The highest peak is found between the ages 8 and 9 years.

Lower Extremity

The mean value of lower extremity (height vertex sitting height vertex) of the two groups, Assamese and Rajasthani increases with age 6 years to 17 years (tables 3.3 and 3.3a). In both the groups the highest mean value is found at 17 years and lowest at 6 years.

The velocity curve (Fig. 3.3a) shows three growth spurts between the ages of 8 and 9 years, 11 and 12 years and 14 and 15 years in Assamese boys. In the case of Rajasthani boys, three peaks are seen in between the ages 8 and 9 years, 10 and 11 years and 12 and 13 years. In both the groups the highest peak is found in between the ages of 8 and 9 years.

Biacromial Diameter

From the table (Tables 3.4 and 3.4a) and distance curves (Fig. 3.4) for biacromial diameter, it is seen that it has a continuous increment from 6 years onwards in both the groups. The total increment observed from 6 to 17 years in 11.8 cm in Assamese group and 12.4 cm in Rajasthani group. The highest increment is found between 11 and 12 years (1.8 cm) in Assamese and between 6 and 7 years (2.2 cm) in Rajasthani boys.

Velocity curve (Fig. 3.4a) shows two spurts between the ages 11 and 12 years and 14 and 15 years in Assamese boys. The highest peak is observed at 11 and 12 years. But in the case of Rajasthani boys, three spurts are seen between the ages of 8 and 9 years, 10 and 11 years and 13 and 14 years. The highest peak is observed between 8 and 9 years.

Bicristal Diameter

The distance curves (Fig. 5.3) show that there is a continuous increase in bicristal diameter from 6 years to 17 years in both Assamese and Rajasthani boys. In case of Assamese boys, the highest peak is found between 6 and 7 years (1.7 cm) while in Rajasthani boys, the highest increment is seen in 9 and 10 years (1.2 cm). The next highest increment is between 14 and 15 years and 16 and 17 years (1.1 cm). The total increment of Assamese and Rajasthani boys between 6 and 17 years are 8.0 cm and 7.5 cm respectively.

The velocity curves (Fig. 3.5a) show three peaks between the age groups of 9 and 10 years, 12 and 13 years and 14 and 15 years in Assamese group and two sharp peaks between 9 and 10 years and 14 and 15 years in Rajasthani boys. A small peak is noticed in 7 and 8 years in Rajasthani boys. The highest peak is found between 12 and 13 years in Assamese boys and between 9 and 10 years in Rajasthani boys.

Chest Circumference

The distance curve (Fig. 3.6) of chest girth shows a continuous increases from 6 to 17 years in both the groups. At 6 years the mean value is slightly higher (53.8 cm) in Assamese group than that of Rajasthani boys (52.2 cm). In Assamese boys, the highest increment is found between the ages of 8 and 9 years (4.3 cm) while it is in between 9 and 10 years (3.6 cm) in Rajasthani boys. The total increment between 6 and 17 years are 22.1 cm and 21.4 cm in Assamese and Rajasthani boys respectively.

The velocity curve (Fig. 3.6a) shows two sharp peaks between the ages of 8 and 9 years and 12 and 13 years with a smaller peak 14 and 15 years in Assamese boys. The highest peak is observed between the ages of 8 and 9 years. In the case of Rajasthani boys, it shows two peaks between the ages 9 and 10 years and 13 and 14 years, the highest being in between 9 and 10 years.

Waist Girth

The mean values of waist girth are 49.0 cm and 50.5 cm at 6 years in Assamese and Rajasthani boys respectively. The tables 3.7 and 3.7a show a total growth of 18.3 cm between the ages of 6 and 17 years in Assamese boys and 17.2 cm in Rajasthani boys. The maximum increment is observed in between the ages of 13 and 14 years (4.0 cm) in Assamese group and between 16 and 17 years in Rajasthani group (3.9 cm). The distance curve (Fig. 3.7) shows a continuous increase in both the groups.

Velocity curve (Fig. 3.7a) shows three distinct spurts between the ages 8 and 9 years, 11 and 12 years and 13 and 14 years in Assamese boys. The spurt between the ages of 13 and 14 years is the highest. In Rajasthani boys two sharp peaks are found between the ages of 9 and 10 years and 13 and 14 years. One more spurt of smaller magnitude is found between the ages of 11 and 12 years. The highest spurt is noticed between the ages of 9 and 10 years.

Weight

It is evident from the tables (3.8 and 3.8a) that there is increases of mean value of the body weight from 6 years to 17 years in both the groups. The total increment between 6 and 17 years is 30.9 cm in the case of Assamese boys and 31.6 cm in the case of Rajasthani boys. In Assamese boys, the highest increment is found between the age of 11 and 12 years while in the Rajasthani boys, the highest increment is found between the ages of 13 and 14 years.

The distance curve (Fig. 3.8) is regular in both the groups and runs almost parallel. The Assamese groups remains at a higher level than the Rajasthani group.

The velocity curve (Fig. 3.8a) shows two spurts between the ages of 11 and 12 years and 13 and 14 years in Assamese boys. In the case of Rajasthani boys, the curves show three prominent peaks between the ages of 8 and 9 years, 10 and 11 years and 13 and 14 years.

The values of growth gradiants of different somatometric traits also suggest that the trend of growth of different traits are similar in both the populations. Of these, more than 60 per cent of the total growth takes place by 6 years of age in both the groups. While more than 70 per cent of growth of its mature size takes place by 6 years in the case of chest girth and waist girth. The body weight grew maximum to reach the mature stage between 6 and 17 years of age, it attains only 35 per cent of its adult stage by 6 years in both the population.

Summary

The present study has been designed to look at the growth patterns of certain metric traits of Assamese and Rajasthani boys of Dibrugarh town in upper Assam. The first group comprises Assamese Hindu caste and the Assamese Muslim while the other group is Rajasthani. They are originally from Rajasthan. A descriptive and a comparative account of each of the character presented in the foregoing pages.

The analysis of the data and the nature of distance curves for all the somatometric characters of Assamese and Rajasthani boys reveal that the mean values of the different measurement increases with the age. The rate of increase is, however, not uniform in all the age groups and all the characters. The Assamese boys show higher values than the Rajasthani boys in all the characters taken into consideration up to 9 years of age indicating a better physique in the early childhood of Assamese boys. But in 11 years of age, the Rajasthani boys are significantly taller and heavier than the Assamese boys. The Rajasthani boys show higher values than the Assamese groups in biacromial diameter, bicristal diameter at 11 years. The differences are found to be statistically significant. At 11 years the differences between Assamese and Rajasthani boys in stature are not statistically significant.

From the analysis of the velocity curve, it is observed that there are three distinct spurts in most of the characters in both the populations. Among the Assamese boys an early spurt is seen between the age group 7 and 8 years, 8 and 9 years and 9 and 10 years. In most of the characters this spurt occurred in between 8 and 9 years. A similar picture is observed in Rajasthani boys also. This spurt which occurs before adolescence may be termed as pre-adolescent growth spurt. Pre-adolescent growth spurt occurred mostly in between 8 and 9 years and it is followed by 9 and 10 years. From the present investigation of the Assamese boys, it is observed that the adolescent spurt occurs between 14 and 15 years, namely, in stature, sitting height vertex, biacromial diameter, bicristal diameter and chest girth. This spurt occurs in between 13 and 14 years in waist girth and weight.

The Rajasthani sample shows three distinct growth spurt. The first spurt is seen between 7 and 10 years. Out of 8 characters, this early spurt occurs at the age group 8 and 9 years in four character, namely, stature, sitting height vertex, biacromial diameter and weight. In the case of waist girth and chest circumference, this spurt occurs between 9 and 10 years.

Thus, from the above findings it is evident that there are three growth spurts in both the populations. The period of extension for the three spurts in both the groups is comparable. It also indicates that the trend of growth is similar in both the groups.

Acknowledgement

The author is grateful to Professor Dr. B.M. Das of Gauhati University under whose guidance and supervision the work was done.

Table 3.1 : Statistical Constants of Height Vertex (Cm.) of Assamese Boys

Age groups (in years)	No.	Mean ±	S.E.	S.D. ±	S.E.	Difference between Mean age groups (Cm.)	Rate of growth (%)	Growth Gradiants
6	30	109.6	1.1	6.0	0.77	-	-	67.32
7	30	120.1	1.1	6.0	0.77	10.5	9.6	73.77
8	30	125.4	1.8	9.6	1.20	5.3	4.4	77.03
9	30	133.9	1.5	8.0	1.00	8.5	6.8	82.25
10	50	134.9	1.1	7.6	0.76	1.0	0.7	82.86
11	50	136.7	1.1	7.7	0.77	1.8	1.3	83.97
12	50	144.5	1.2	8.7	0.87	7.8	5.7	88.76
13	50	149.8	1.3	9.2	0.92	5.3	3.7	92.01
14	50	153.6	1.6	11.4	1.10	3.8	2.5	94.35
15	50	159.1	1.1	7.8	0.78	5.5	3.6	97.73
16	50	160.7	1.0	7.3	0.73	1.6	1.0	98.71
17	50	162.8	0.8	6.1	0.61	2.1	1.3	100.00

Table 3.1a : Statistical Constants of Height Vertex (Cm.) of Assamese Boys

Age groups (in years)	No.	Mean ±	S.E.	S.D. ±	S.E.	Difference between Mean age groups (Cm.)	Rate of growth (%)	Growth Gradiants
6	30	109.3	0.80	4.6	0.60	-	-	66.16
7	30	116.0	0.58	3.2	0.41	6.7	6.1	70.22
8	35	119.6	1.30	7.5	0.90	3.6	3.1	72.40
9	30	128.8	1.40	7.5	0.97	9.2	7.7	77.97
10	40	137.4	1.30	7.9	0.88	8.6	6.7	83.17
11	45	140.8	1.40	9.0	0.95	3.4	2.5	85.23
12	50	144.7	1.30	9.3	0.93	3.9	2.8	87.59
13	50	148.4	1.20	8.3	0.83	3.7	2.6	89.83
14	40	153.8	1.31	8.5	0.95	5.4	3.6	93.10
15	32	158.1	1.30	7.0	0.90	4.3	2.8	95.70
16	50	158.6	1.10	7.9	0.79	0.5	0.3	96.00
17	35	165.2	0.90	5.3	0.64	7.6	4.8	100.00

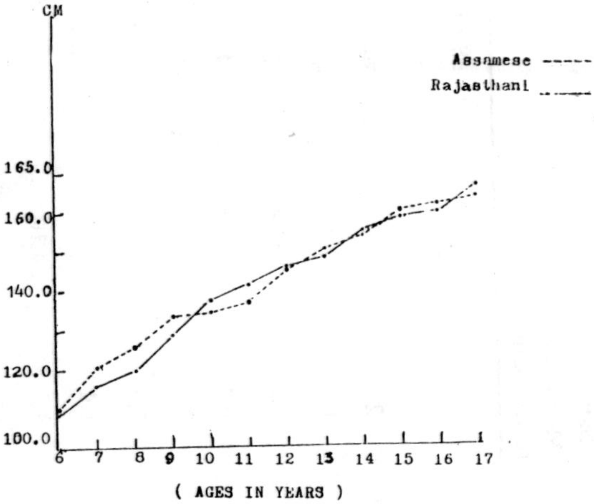

FIGURE 3.1
Distance Curve : Height Vertex

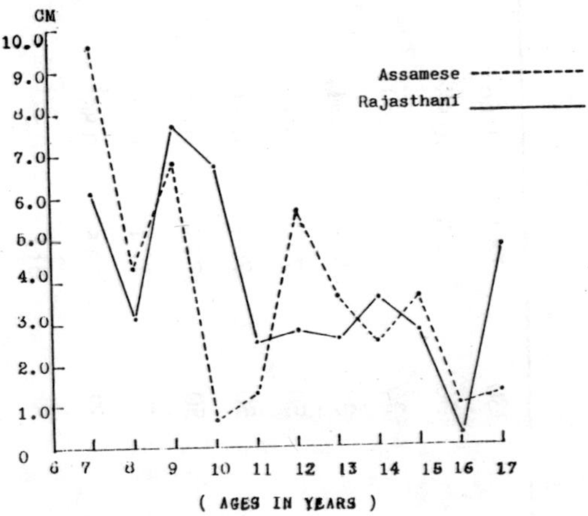

FIGURE 3.1a
Velocity Curve : Height Vertex

Table 3.2 : Statistical Constants of Sitting Height Vertex (Cm.) of Assamese Boys

Age groups (in years)	No.	Mean ±	S.E.	S.D. ±	S.E.	Difference between Mean age groups (Cm.)	Rate of growth (%)	Growth Gradiants
6	30	58.1	0.66	3.6	0.46	-	-	68.84
7	30	64.3	0.55	3.0	0.39	6.2	10.70	76.18
8	30	67.1	0.80	4.4	0.57	2.8	4.30	79.30
9	30	69.8	0.64	3.6	0.32	0.2	0.29	82.70
10	50	70.0	0.45	3.2	0.32	0.2	0.29	82.93
11	50	70.9	0.59	4.2	0.42	0.9	1.30	84.00
12	50	74.2	0.64	4.5	0.45	3.3	4.70	87.91
13	50	77.1	0.69	4.9	0.49	2.9	3.90	91.33
14	50	78.5	0.86	6.1	0.61	1.4	1.80	93.01
15	50	81.7	0.57	4.0	0.40	3.2	4.10	96.80
16	50	82.9	0.54	3.8	0.38	1.2	1.50	98.22
17	50	84.4	0.51	3.6	0.36	1.5	4.30	100.00

Table 3.2a : Statistical Constants of Sitting Height Vertex (Cm.) of Rajasthani Boys

Age groups (in years)	No.	Mean ±	S.E.	S.D. ±	S.E.	Difference between Mean age groups (Cm.)	Rate of growth (%)	Growth Gradiants
6	30	58.7	0.57	3.1	0.40	-	-	69.14
7	30	62.5	0.82	4.5	0.58	3.8	6.5	73.62
8	31	63.0	0.76	4.2	0.53	0.5	0.8	74.20
9	30	66.7	0.69	3.8	0.49	3.7	5.9	78.56
10	40	68.3	0.60	3.8	0.43	1.6	2.4	80.45
11	45	71.7	0.72	4.8	0.51	3.4	5.0	84.45
12	50	74.0	0.71	5.0	0.50	2.3	3.2	87.16
13	50	74.6	0.55	3.9	0.39	0.6	0.8	87.87
14	40	78.5	0.74	4.7	0.53	3.9	5.2	92.46
15	32	80.6	0.87	4.9	0.61	2.1	2.7	94.94
16	50	81.1	0.65	4.6	0.46	0.5	0.6	95.52
17	35	84.9	0.59	3.5	0.35	3.8	4.7	100.00

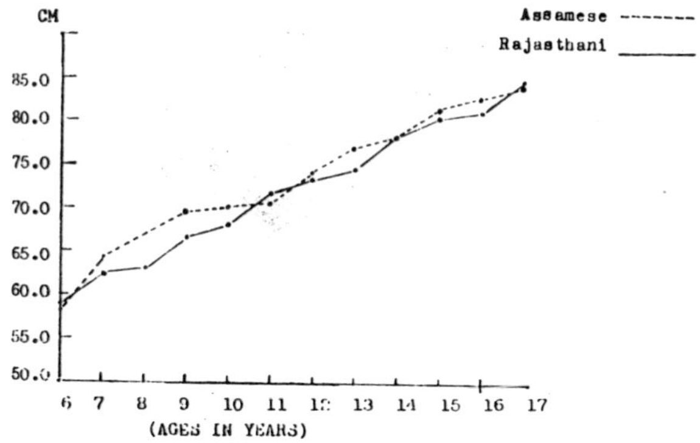

FIGURE 3.2
Distance Curve : Sitting Height Vertex

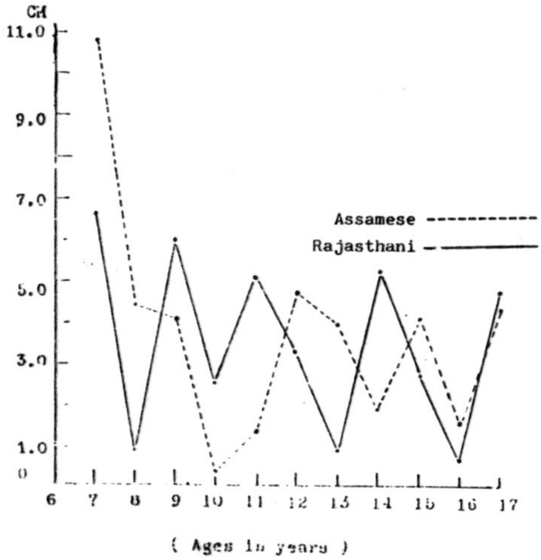

FIGURE 3.2a
Velocity Curve : Sitting Height Vertex

Table 3.3 : Statistical Constants of Lower Extremity (Cm.) of Assamese Boys

Age groups (in years)	No.	Mean ±	S.E.	S.D. ±	S.E.	Difference between Mean age groups (Cm.)	Rate of growth (%)	Growth Gradiants
6	30	52.1	0.86	4.8	0.62	-	-	66.71
7	30	56.3	0.78	4.3	0.55	4.2	8.1	72.09
8	30	59.1	1.0	5.7	0.74	2.8	4.9	75.69
9	30	64.4	0.82	4.5	0.58	5.3	8.9	82.46
10	50	64.8	0.75	5.3	0.53	0.4	0.6	82.97
11	50	65.0	0.75	5.3	0.53	0.2	0.3	83.23
12	50	70.3	0.72	5.1	0.51	5.3	8.2	90.01
13	50	73.1	0.75	5.3	0.53	2.8	4.0	93.60
14	50	74.7	0.85	6.0	0.60	1.6	2.2	95.65
15	50	77.4	0.61	4.3	0.43	2.7	3.6	99.10
16	50	77.8	0.66	4.7	0.47	0.4	0.5	99.62
17	50	78.1	0.55	3.9	0.39	0.3	0.4	100.00

Table 3.3a : Statistical Constants of Lower Extremity (Cm.) of Rajasthani Boys

Age groups (in years)	No.	Mean ±	S.E.	S.D. ±	S.E.	Difference between Mean age groups (Cm.)	Rate of growth (%)	Growth Gradiants
6	30	50.9	0.66	3.6	4.60	-	-	63.15
7	30	54.8	0.78	4.3	0.55	3.9	7.7	67.99
8	35	57.5	0.71	4.2	0.50	2.7	4.9	71.34
9	30	62.4	0.86	4.7	0.61	4.9	8.5	77.42
10	40	64.4	0.74	4.7	0.53	2.0	3.2	79.90
11	45	69.3	0.75	5.0	0.53	4.9	7.6	85.98
12	50	70.8	0.74	5.2	0.52	1.5	2.2	87.84
13	50	73.5	0.79	5.6	0.56	2.7	3.8	91.19
14	40	75.5	0.82	5.2	0.58	2.0	2.7	93.67
15	32	76.8	0.94	5.3	0.66	1.3	1.7	95.29
16	50	78.7	0.86	6.1	0.61	1.9	2.5	97.64
17	35	80.6	0.74	4.4	0.53	1.9	2.4	100.00

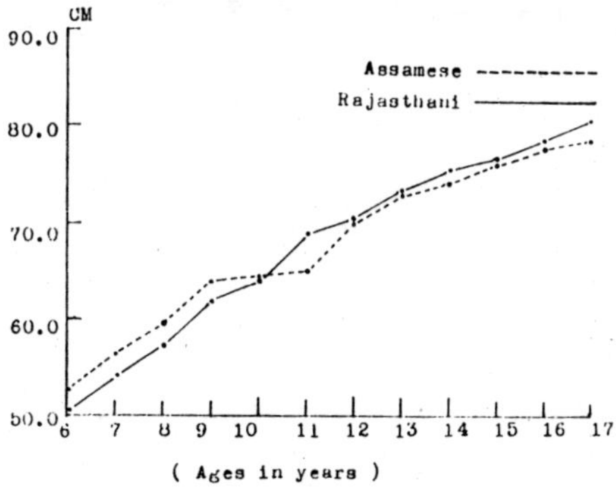

FIGURE 3.3
Distance Curve : Lower Extremity

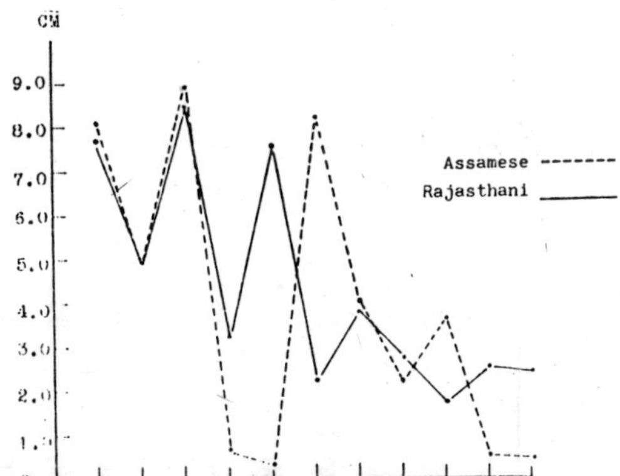

FIGURE 3.3a
Velocity Curve : Lower Extremity

Table 3.4 : Statistical Constants of Biacromial Diameter (Cm.) of Assamese Boys

Age groups (in years)	No.	Mean	± S.E.	S.D.	± S.E.	Difference between Mean age groups (Cm.)	Rate of growth (%)	Growth Gradiants
6	30	23.5	0.33	1.8	0.23	-	-	66.75
7	30	25.0	0.35	1.9	0.24	1.5	6.4	70.82
8	30	26.3	0.53	2.9	0.37	1.3	5.2	74.50
9	30	27.3	0.31	1.7	0.22	1.0	3.8	77.34
10	50	28.1	0.30	2.1	0.21	0.3	1.1	79.60
11	50	28.2	0.31	2.2	0.22	0.1	0.3	79.89
12	50	30.0	0.45	3.2	0.32	1.8	6.4	84.99
13	50	30.9	0.30	2.1	0.21	0.9	3.0	87.54
14	50	32.0	0.45	3.2	0.32	1.1	3.6	90.65
15	50	33.6	0.38	2.7	0.27	1.6	5.0	95.18
16	50	34.8	0.38	2.7	0.27	1.2	3.6	98.58
17	50	35.3	0.38	2.7	0.27	0.5	1.4	100.00

Table 3.4a : Statistical Constants of Biacromial Diameter (Cm.) of Rajasthani Boys

Age groups (in years)	No.	Mean ±	S.E.	S.D. ±	S.E.	Difference between Mean age groups (Cm.)	Rate of growth (%)	Growth Gradiants
6	30	22.6	0.26	1.4	0.26	-	-	64.57
7	30	24.8	0.38	2.1	0.27	2.2	9.7	70.86
8	35	25.3	0.32	1.9	0.23	0.5	2.0	72.29
9	30	26.9	0.36	2.0	0.26	1.6	6.3	76.86
10	40	27.8	0.33	2.1	0.23	0.9	3.3	79.43
11	45	29.4	0.36	2.4	0.23	1.6	5.8	84.00
12	50	29.9	0.38	2.7	0.27	0.5	1.7	85.43
13	50	30.7	0.30	2.1	0.21	0.8	2.7	87.71
14	40	32.2	0.33	2.1	0.23	1.5	4.9	92.00
15	32	33.1	0.53	3.0	0.38	0.9	2.8	94.57
16	50	33.7	0.45	3.2	0.32	0.6	1.8	96.29
17	35	35.0	0.37	2.2	0.26	1.9	5.7	100.00

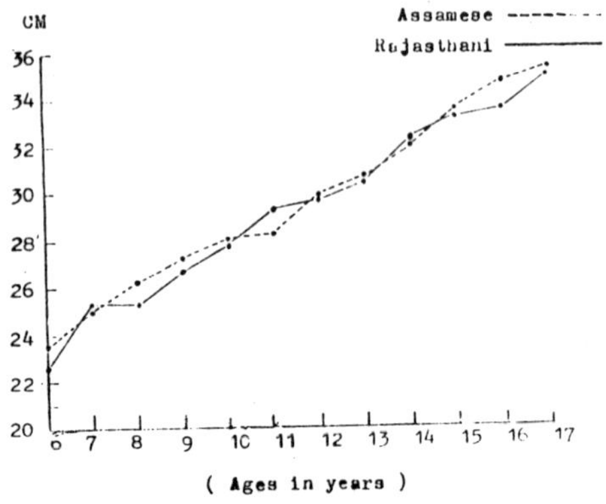

FIGURE 3.4
Distance Curve : Biacromial Diameter

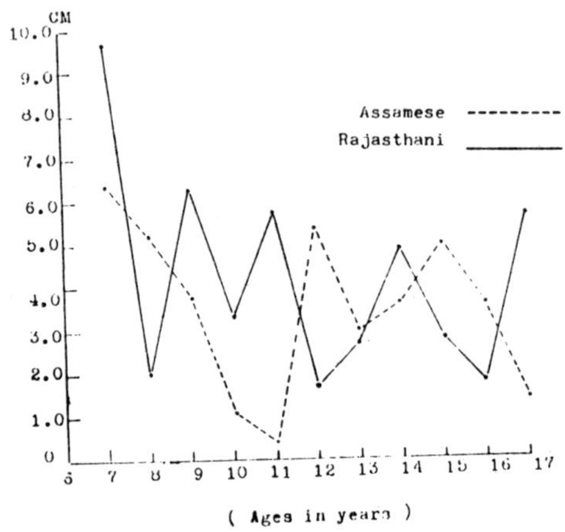

FIGURE 3.4a
Velocity Curve : Biacromial Diameter

Table 3.5 : Statistical Constants of Bicristal Diameter (Cm.) of Assamese Boys

Age groups (in years)	No.	Mean	± S.E.	S.D.	± S.E.	Difference between Mean age groups (Cm.)	Rate of growth (%)	Growth Gradiants
6	30	17.0	0.18	1.0	0.13	-	-	68.0
7	30	18.7	0.29	1.6	0.21	1.7	10.0	74.8
8	30	18.9	0.36	2.0	0.26	0.2	1.1	75.6
9	30	19.0	0.26	1.4	0.18	0.1	0.5	76.0
10	50	19.9	0.27	1.9	0.19	0.9	4.7	79.6
11	50	20.1	0.27	1.9	0.19	0.2	1.0	80.4
12	50	20.5	0.23	1.6	0.16	0.4	2.0	82.0
13	50	22.0	0.23	1.6	0.16	1.5	7.3	88.0
14	50	22.3	0.37	2.6	0.26	0.3	1.4	89.2
15	50	23.6	0.35	2.5	0.25	1.3	5.8	94.4
16	50	24.3	0.20	1.4	0.14	0.7	3.0	97.2
17	50	25.0	0.27	1.9	0.19	0.7	2.9	100.00

Table 3.5a : Statistical Constants of Bicristal Diameter (Cm.) of Rajasthani Boys

Age groups (in years)	No.	Mean ±	S.E.	S.D. ±	S.E.	Difference between Mean age groups (Cm.)	Rate of growth (%)	Growth Gradiants
6	30	16.8	0.14	0.8	0.10	-	-	69.14
7	30	17.4	0.29	1.6	0.21	0.6	3.5	71.60
8	35	18.3	0.24	1.4	0.17	0.7	4.0	75.31
9	30	18.7	0.27	1.5	0.19	0.4	2.2	76.95
10	40	19.9	0.24	1.5	0.17	1.2	6.4	81.89
11	45	20.8	0.30	2.0	0.21	0.9	4.5	85.60
12	50	21.0	0.23	1.6	0.16	0.2	0.9	86.42
13	50	21.3	0.24	1.7	0.17	0.3	1.4	87.65
14	40	22.0	0.33	2.1	0.23	0.7	3.3	90.53
15	40	23.1	0.30	1.9	0.21	1.1	5.0	95.06
16	50	23.2	0.25	1.8	0.18	0.1	0.4	95.47
17	35	24.3	0.29	1.7	0.20	1.1	4.7	100.00

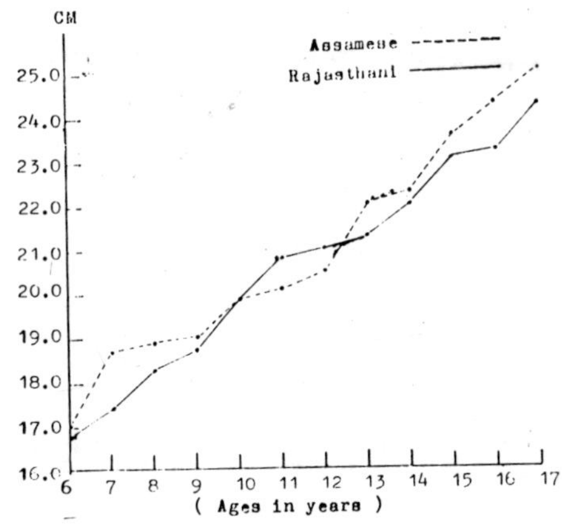

FIGURE 3.5
Distance Curve : Bicristal Diameter

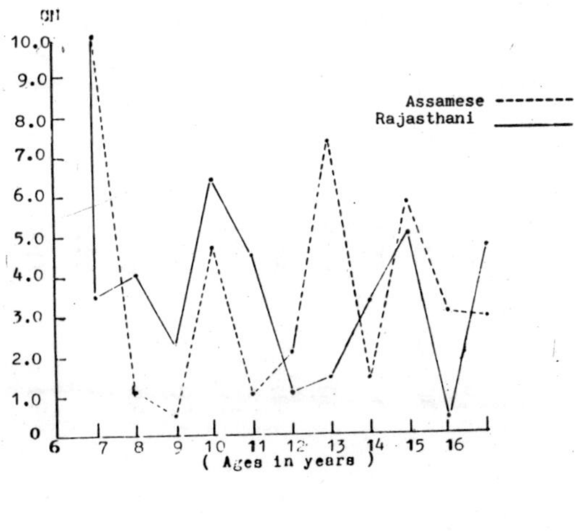

FIGURE 3.5a
Velocity Curve : Bicristal Diameter

Table 3.6 : Statistical Constants of Chest Circumference (Cm.) of Assamese Boys

Age groups (in years)	No.	Mean ±	S.E.	S.D. ±	S.E.	Difference between Mean age groups (Cm.)	Rate of growth (%)	Growth Gradiants
6	30	53.8	0.75	4.1	0.53	-	-	70.8
7	30	54.7	0.58	3.2	0.41	0.9	1.7	72.0
8	30	55.3	0.60	3.3	0.43	0.6	1.1	72.8
9	30	59.6	0.56	3.1	0.40	4.3	7.8	78.5
10	50	60.4	0.52	3.7	0.37	0.8	1.3	79.5
11	50	61.4	0.51	3.6	0.36	1.0	1.7	80.9
12	50	62.3	0.52	3.7	0.37	0.9	1.5	82.0
13	50	66.2	0.75	5.3	0.53	3.9	6.3	87.2
14	50	68.6	0.95	6.7	0.67	2.4	3.6	90.3
15	50	71.8	0.54	3.8	0.38	3.2	4.7	94.6
16	50	75.0	0.66	4.7	0.47	3.2	4.5	98.8
17	50	75.9	0.74	5.2	0.52	0.9	1.2	100.00

Table 3.6a : Statistical Constants of Chest Circumference (Cm.) of Rajasthani Boys

Age groups (in years)	No.	Mean ±	S.E.	S.D. ±	S.E.	Difference between Mean age groups (Cm.)	Rate of growth (%)	Growth Gradiants
6	30	52.2	0.36	2.0	0.26	-	-	70.92
7	30	53.4	0.49	2.7	0.31	1.2	2.3	72.55
8	35	53.7	0.63	3.7	0.44	0.3	0.5	72.96
9	30	56.9	0.51	2.8	0.36	3.2	6.0	77.31
10	40	60.5	0.66	4.2	0.47	3.6	6.3	82.20
11	45	62.7	0.63	4.2	0.44	2.2	3.6	85.19
12	50	63.6	0.66	4.7	0.47	0.9	1.4	86.41
13	50	64.9	0.58	4.1	0.41	1.3	2.0	88.18
14	40	68.1	0.71	4.5	0.50	3.2	4.9	92.53
15	32	70.9	0.92	5.2	0.65	2.8	4.1	96.33
16	50	71.4	1.00	7.2	0.72	0.5	0.7	97.01
17	35	73.6	0.81	4.8	0.57	2.2	3.1	100.00

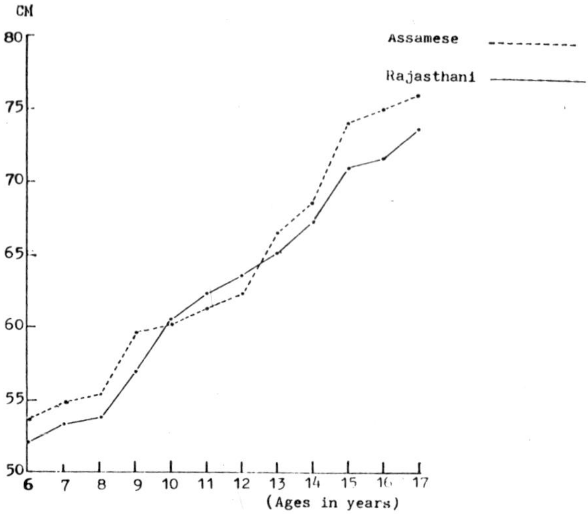

FIGURE 3.6
Distance Curve : Chest Circumference

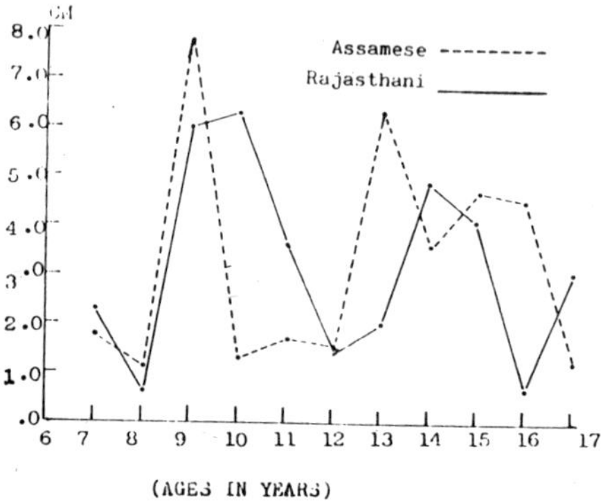

FIGURE 3.6a
Velocity Curve : Chest Circumference

Table 3.7 : Statistical Constants of Waist Girth (Cm.) of Assamese Boys

Age groups (in years)	No.	Mean ± S.E.		S.D. ± S.E.		Difference between Mean age groups (Cm.)	Rate of growth (%)	Growth Gradiants
6	30	49.0	0.55	3.0	0.39	-	-	72.81
7	30	52.1	0.57	3.1	0.40	3.1	6.3	77.41
8	30	53.4	0.78	4.3	0.55	1.3	2.5	79.35
9	30	55.2	0.38	2.1	0.27	1.8	3.4	82.02
10	50	55.3	0.61	4.3	0.43	0.1	0.1	82.17
11	50	55.9	0.52	3.7	0.37	0.6	1.1	83.06
12	50	57.8	0.55	3.9	0.39	1.9	3.4	85.88
13	50	58.1	0.59	4.2	0.42	0.3	0.5	86.33
14	50	62.1	0.76	5.4	0.54	4.0	6.9	92.27
15	50	63.7	0.71	5.0	0.50	1.6	2.6	94.65
16	50	65.5	0.75	1.8	0.53	1.8	2.8	97.34
17	50	67.3	0.82	5.8	0.58	1.8	2.7	100.00

Table 3.7a : Statistical Constants of Waist Girth (Cm.) of Rajasthani Boys

Age groups (in years)	No.	Mean ±	S.E.	S.D. ±	S.E.	Difference between Mean age groups (Cm.)	Rate of growth (%)	Growth Gradiants
6	30	50.5	0.44	2.4	0.31	-	-	74.59
7	30	51.1	0.60	3.3	0.43	0.6	1.2	75.48
8	35	51.9	0.44	2.6	0.31	0.8	1.6	76.66
9	30	53.6	0.55	3.0	0.39	1.7	3.3	79.17
10	40	56.2	0.82	5.2	0.58	2.6	4.9	83.01
11	45	57.1	0.75	5.0	0.53	0.9	1.6	84.34
12	50	58.3	0.76	5.4	0.54	1.2	2.1	86.12
13	50	59.4	0.61	4.3	0.43	1.1	1.9	87.74
14	40	61.7	0.74	4.7	0.53	2.3	3.9	91.13
15	32	62.1	1.00	5.9	0.74	0.4	0.6	91.73
16	50	62.8	0.82	5.8	0.58	0.7	1.1	92.76
17	35	67.7	1.2	7.1	0.85	4.9	7.8	100.00

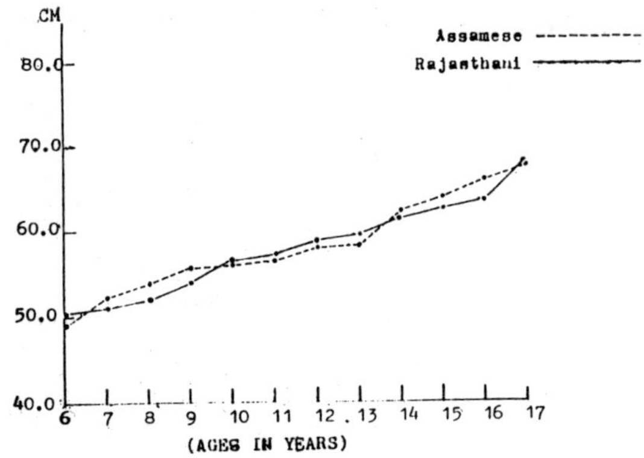

FIGURE 3.7
Distance Curve : Waist Girth

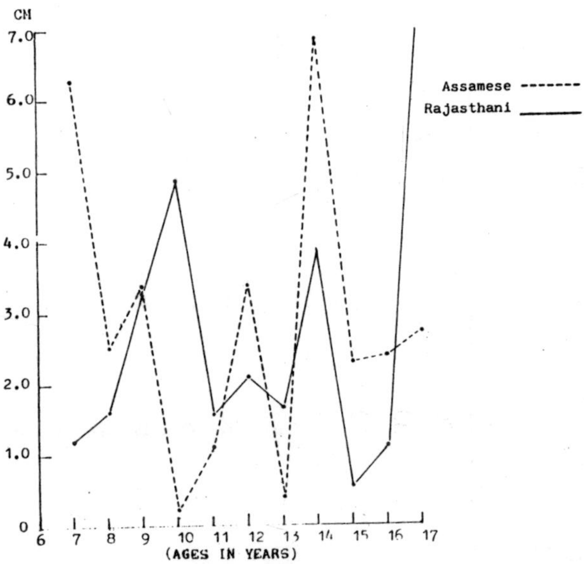

FIGURE 3.7a
Velocity Curve : Waist Girth

Table 3.8 : Statistical Constants of Weight (Kg.) of Assamese Boys

Age groups (in years)	No.	Mean ±	S.E.	S.D. ±	S.E.	Difference between Mean age groups (Kg.)	Rate of growth (%)	Growth Gradiants
6	30	16.6	0.66	3.6	0.46	-	-	34.95
7	30	19.9	0.53	2.9	0.37	3.3	19.9	41.89
8	30	23.1	0.93	5.1	0.66	3.2	16.1	48.63
9	30	25.4	0.71	3.9	0.50	2.3	10.0	53.47
10	50	25.7	0.52	3.7	0.37	0.3	1.2	54.11
11	50	26.1	0.68	4.8	0.48	0.4	1.6	54.93
12	50	31.2	0.89	6.3	0.63	5.1	19.5	65.68
13	50	34.3	0.93	6.6	0.66	3.1	9.9	72.21
14	50	38.6	1.20	8.3	0.83	4.3	12.5	81.26
15	50	43.2	0.89	6.3	0.63	4.6	11.9	90.95
16	50	44.5	0.91	6.4	0.64	1.3	3.0	93.68
17	50	47.5	0.99	7.1	0.71	3.0	6.7	100.00

Table 3.8a : Statistical Constants of Weight (Kg.) of Rajasthani Boys

Age groups (in years)	No.	Mean ±	S.E.	S.D. ±	S.E.	Difference between Mean age groups (Kg.)	Rate of growth (%)	Growth Gradiants
6	30	16.9	0.40	2.2	0.28	-	-	34.85
7	30	18.1	0.40	2.2	0.28	1.2	7.1	37.32
8	35	19.9	0.69	4.1	0.49	1.8	9.9	41.03
9	30	23.3	0.62	3.4	0.44	3.4	17.1	48.04
10	40	25.4	0.74	4.7	0.53	2.1	9.0	52.37
11	45	29.4	0.89	6.0	0.63	4.0	15.7	60.62
12	50	31.5	0.88	6.2	0.62	2.1	7.1	64.95
13	50	32.7	0.65	4.6	0.46	1.2	3.8	67.42
14	40	37.6	0.85	5.4	0.60	4.9	14.9	77.53
15	32	41.0	1.50	8.6	1.20	3.4	9.0	84.54
16	50	41.2	1.20	8.3	0.83	0.2	0.4	84.95
17	35	48.5	1.20	6.9	0.82	7.3	17.1	100.00

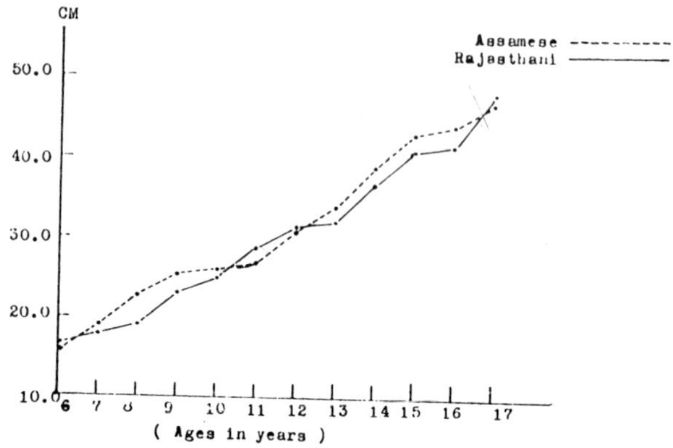

FIGURE 3.8
Distance Curve : Weight

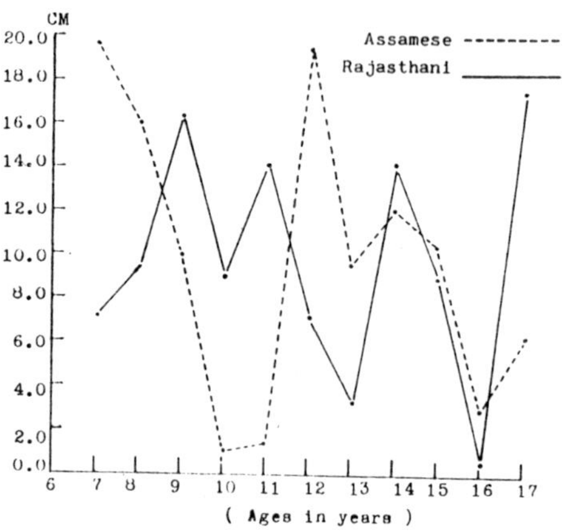

FIGURE 3.8a
Velocity Curve : Weight

REFERENCES

AHMED DAS, F., 1977, *A Study on the genetic composition of Assamese Muslim of Dibrugarh, Assam.* Unpublished Ph. D Thesis, Dibrugarh University, Assam.

AHMED HAZARIKA, A.N.Z., 1974, A comparative study of growth of stature, girth of thorax and weight of Ahom and Kalita boys of Assam. *Contemporary Anthropological Research in North East India.* Edited by B.M. Das, Dibrugarh University, pp 73 - 77.

DAS, B.M., 1969-1971, A study on some aspect of growth of the Assamese boys. *Journal of Gauhati University* (Science), 20 - 22 : 51 - 65.

DAS, P.B., 1966, *A Study of growth of somatometric characteristics of a selected caste of Assam.* Unpublished Ph. D Thesis, Gauhati University, Assam.

DAS, P.B., 1974, A comparative study of growth in respect of height, weight and chest circumference of rural Assamese boys. In *Contemporary Anthropological Research in North East India.* Edited by B.M. Das Anthropology Department Dibrugarh University 3 : 43 - 55.

CHOWDHURY, B., 1979, *A cross-sectional study of growth of some somatometric characters of Rabha boys of Kamrup District, Assam.* Unpublished Ph. D Thesis, Gauhati University, Assam.

TIMBERG, T.A., 1978, *The Marwaris: From Traders to Industrialist.* New Delhi : Vikas Publishing House.

4
The Garias of Assam : A Biodemographic Study

P.M. Buzarbarua, S.H.M. Rizvi

In recent time growing interest in the study of bio-demography has been observed among the human biologists. Spuhler (1959) pointed out that physical anthropology, demography and population genetics are closely interrelated and clearly presented an overlapping area of these three major disciplines. Fertility and mortality are important demographic variables which are the major measures of micro-evolutionary dynamics. Differential fertility and differential mortality acting individually or jointly are the most fundamental events of natural selection which is one of the major evolutionary factors that brings about change in the gene frequencies in a population.

In the present study an attempt has been made to study the demographic structure of the Garia-Muslims of Assam. In Assam according to 1971 Census, Muslims constitute 24.03 per cent total population of the state and is the single largest religious minority. On the basis of economy, socio-cultural traits including linguistic affinities, Muslim community of Assam may be subdivided into various categories. Since, like Muslims of other regions, in Assam, too, they are not a single homogeneous community but a conglomeration of several socio-culturally distinctive identifiable historical communities evolved at different stages of historical development of the state. The Garia Muslims are also known as *'Asomiya'* (Assamese) or *'Thalua'* (local) Musalman. They claim their migration from Gaur Desh (medieval capital of

Bengal). It is claimed that the first settlement of Muslim in Assam in the form of stay of Muslim soldiers took place during thirteenth century when in 1203 A.D. Mahammad Bin Bakhtiar Khilizi, a general of Kutubuddin invaded Assam and was defeated. Thus, the settlement of soldiers has been regarded as the first batch of Muslim immigrants even before the arrival of Ahom who ruled for about 600 years. The Garia Muslims are an endogamous group and basically an agriculturist community.

Material and Method

Data were collected by interviewing 1930 ever-married Garia Muslim women who have completed her fertility period by random sampling from the Lachima, Belbari, Sala, Barmara and Lauli villages of the Sarthebari police station of Barpeta district of Assam during the month of January 1990 to August 1990. Geneologies were collected from all the ever-married women by prolonged and in-depth interview. Here emphasis was given on (i) the Phratry, to which each male belong and their natal clan, (ii) number of total pregnancies, (iii) embryonic death, and (iv) age at the time of death of children.

Results and Discussion

Fertility is one of the important demographic variables that provide the measures and indices for estimating the rate of contribution of certain genes or genotypes to the next generation. Fertility record of ever-married Garia women are given in table 4.1. From the table it has been observed that 1930 ever-married women (who have completed their reproductive span) had a average 5.36 pregnancies with a 5.18 live births. The mean number of live births per mother (5.18) was found to be lower than Bengali Kayastha (8.70; Sen 1953), Bengali Vaidya (7.98; Sen, 1953), Maharashtra Brahman (7.14; Rakshit, 1962), Mundas of Assam (6.82; Buzarbarua, 1990), Bengali Brahman (6.71; Sen, 1953), Irula (6.55; Basu, 1968), Turung (6.33; Das, 1985), Santals of Assam (6.20; Buzarbarua, 1982), Santal of Bihar (6.10; Sarkar, 1944), Hajong of Meghalaya (6.04; Barua, 1983), Pahira (6.00; Basu, 1969), Mishing (5.81; Buzarbarua and Phookan, 1985), Maler (5.80; Sarkar, 1944), Non Christian Khasi (5.70; Nag, 1965), Chutia

(5.54; Das, 1980), Moran (5.52; Das, 1980), Khamiyang (5.45; Das, 1985), Kota of Nilgiri (5.37; Basu, 1972), Wancho (5.35; Kar and Sharma, 1982-1983), Mishing (5.34; Das, 1980). But it is higher than the Puttusali (4.04; Mukherjee, 1974), Gond (4.61; Devi, 1975), Mokashi Gond (4.71; Sharma et. al., 1988), Kanikkar (4.74; Nag, 1954), Dorla (4.86; Rakshit, 1959), Raj Gond (4.88; Sharma et. al., 1988), Dhurwa (5.17; Rakshit, 1959).

All ever-married living women with at least one pregnancy are considered as mother. It is observed from the table 4.2 that 1921 mothers had a total of 10349 pregnancies including still-births and abortions. The respective percentages of live-births and abortions of the total number of 10349 pregnancies are 96.52 and 0.96 only. Table 4.2 also shows the average number of miscarriage/abortion and still-birth per ever-married woman. The average number of miscarriage/abortion per married woman (0.5) is much lower than that of Dule Bagdi (Poddar, 1975; Talukdar, 1979), Kota (Basu, 1972), Muslims of 24 Parganas (Barua, 1981), Mishing (Buzarbarua and Phookan, 1984), Santals and Mundas of Assam (Buzarbarua, 1982, 1990). But it is higher than the Hajongs (Barua, 1983) of Meghalaya. The average number of still-birth per mother (0.14) is also much higher than the aforesaid populations.

The best index of early postnatal mortality is the infant mortality, which is related to the number of live-born children and it is expressed in percentage. The juvenile mortality rate related to the number of deaths from one year to fourteen years of life to the number of live-born children and it is also expressed in terms of percentage. In the present study, postnatal mortality measured in terms of infant death rate and juvenile death rate. Average number of infant death and juvenile death per mother have been shown in table 4.3. From the table it has been found that infant mortality rate 1.37 per cent and the juvenile mortality rate is 1.23 per cent. Therefore, as a whole 2.60 per cent of the offspring failed to reach the reproductive age.

Sex Ratio

Sex ratio is an indicator of relative number of males and females in a population. For the purpose of present study, it has been considered as male/female × 1000. Generally sex ratio is classified into the following categories:

(i) Primary sex ratio or sex ratio of the zygotes.

(ii) Secondary sex ratio or sex ratio of the live-birth.

(iii) Tertiary sex ratio or sex ratio of different ages of a particular population.

For the present study following sex ratio has been estimated:

Crude primary sex ratio: It is the number of male still-birth plus live-births per 100 female still-birth plus live births.

$$\text{Crude primary sex ratio} = \frac{\text{Male still-births + live - births}}{\text{Female still-births + live - births}} \times 100$$

The crude primary sex ratio is an underestimate of the true primary sex ratio as in the miscarriage/abortion, the sex cannot be determined.

Secondary sex ratio: It is the sex ratio of the live-births, i.e., the number of live-birth of male offspring per 100 live-births of female offspring.

$$\text{Secondary sex ratio} = \frac{\text{Male live-births}}{\text{Female live-births}} \times 100$$

Table 4.4 shows the sex ratio of the still-births plus live-births as well as the sex ratio of the live-births offspring among the Garia Muslim population of Assam. The crude primary sex ratio do not deviate much from the approximate 1 : 1 ratio. That means, the sexual selection within the populations is very negligible.

The Genetical Implication of Demographic Variables

The parameters used in calculating the index of opportunity of selection is shown in table 4.5. From the table it is observed that 96.52 per cent zygote survive to birth, but only 93.92 per cent survives to reproductive age. 2.6 per cent zygote died before they reach 15 years of age and 3.6 per cent died within embryonic stage.

In the present study it has been found that 6.8 per cent zygote in the present population do not contribute their gene pool to the next generation. In other words, 93.92 per cent of the total population actually contributes their gene pool to the next generation.

Selection Intensity

Selection is one of the process that brings in changes in the evolution of a population be that micro and macro levels. It is the measure of fitness of a population in a particular environment as revealed by the ongoing patterns of fertility and mortality. Selection intensity has been calculated after Crow (1958) and also from early embryonic stage (Jhonston and Kensinger, 1971) which separates the index due to mortality into prenatal and postnatal components.

The statistical formula proposed by Crow (1958) is as follows:

$$I = I_m + \frac{I_f}{P_S}$$

$$I_m = \frac{P_d}{P_s}$$

$$I_f = \frac{V_f}{(x)^2}$$

where:

I = index of total selection intensity.

I_m = index of selection due to infant mortality.

I_f = index of selection due to fertility.

X = average number of live-births per woman aged 45 years and above.

V_f = variance in the number of live-births due to fertility.

P_d = Proportion of premature deaths (died before 15th year of life), i.e., proportion of pre reproductive death of children.

P_s = $1 - P_d$, or proportion of survivors up to 15th year and above.

Modification of Crow's formulae (1958) by Johnston and Kensinger (1971), which stands as:

$$I = I_{me} + \frac{I_{mc}}{P_b} + \frac{I_f}{P_b P_s}$$

$$I_{me} = \frac{P_{ed}}{P_b}$$

$$I_{mc} = \frac{P_d}{P_s}$$

$$I_f = \frac{V_f}{(x)^2}$$

where:

I = index of total selection intensity.

I_{me} = index of selection due to embryonic mortality (i.e., prenatal mortality).

I_{mc} = index of selection due to child mortality (before 15 years).

I_f = index of selection due to fertility.

X = number of live births per woman of completed fertility (i.e., 45 years and above).

P_{ed} = proportion of embryonic death (i.e., prenatal deaths).

P_b = proportion of survivors to birth or $(1 - P_{ed})$.

P_d = proportion of child death (i.e., died before 15 years of age).

P_s = $1 - P_d$ or proportion of survivors, birth to reproductive age.

$P_b P_s$ = proportion of survivors, early embryo to reproductive age.

V_f = variance in the number of live-births due to fertility.

Table 4.7 shows the values of selection intensity index for Garia Muslims of Assam. The values of Selection intensity calculated following Crow's (1958) method is lower than the values obtained by Johnston and Kensinger's (1971) method. This indicates that the component of prenatal death is contributing more to the selection intensity index (I) in the said population. The values of 'I' as observed in the Kota (2.52; Basu, 1972) is the highest and Punjabi Sonar of Shillong (0.107; Jawal, 1977) is lowest for any Indian population so far studied.

Table 4.1 : Fertility record of the ever-married Garia Muslim women

	Pregnancy $\overline{X}$	Live-birth $\overline{X}$
Ever-married women who have cross their fertility period (N = 1930)	5.36	5.18
Ever-Pregnant women who have cross their fertility period (N = 1921)	5.39	5.20

Table 4.2 : Number of children ever born to mothers of all ages

Total number of mothers	1921	
Total number of pregnancies	10349	
Total number of live-born male children	5026	(48.56%)
Total number of live-born female children	4963	(47.96%)
Total number of live-born children	9989	(96.52%)
Total number of dead male children	64	(0.62%)
Total number of dead female children	59	(0.57%)
Total number of dead children	123	(1.19%)
Total number of male still-birth	154	(1.49%)
Total number of female still-birth	107	(1.03%)
Total number of still-birth	261	(2.52%)
Total number of miscarriage/abortion	99	(0.96%)
Total number of reproductive wastage	360	(3.48%)
Average number of still-birth per mother	0.14	
Average number of miscarriage/abortion per mother	0.05	
Average number of reproductive wastage per mother	0.19	

Table 4.3 : Postnatal deaths among the offspring

Total number of mothers	1921
Total number of live births	9989
Total number of infant deaths	137
Total number of juvenile deaths	123
Infant death rate	1.37%
Juvenile death rate	1.23%
Average number of infant death per mother	0.07
Average number of juvenile death per mother	0.06

Table 4.4 : Sex ratio of the offspring

	Male	Female	Sex ratio
1. Still-birth + live-birth	5180	5070	102.17 (Crude primary sex ratio)
2. Live-birth	5026	4963	101.27 (Secondary sex ratio)

Table 4.5 : Parameter used in calculating the index of opportunity for selection

Total number of mothers who have cross their fertility period	1921
Number of pregnancy reported	10349
Number of live-birth	9989
Number of survivor to marriageable age	9729
Proportion of survivors to birth	0.9652
Proportion of embryonic death	0.0360
Proportion of survivors, birth to reproductive age	0.9392
Proportion of premature death (died before 15 years)	0.0260
Proportion of early embryo to reproductive age	0.9401
Mean number of live-birth	5.20
Variance in the number of live-birth due to fertility	11.90

Table 4.6 : Parameters used in calculating the rate of contribution to the next generation gene pool

Proportion of individuals not contributing their gene pool to the next generation (women those were completed their fertility period included only)	9
Proportion of prenatal death (embryonic and foetal deaths)	0.013
Proportion of offspring dying before 15 years of age	0.012
Proportion of unmarried individuals (who have attained their menoposal age)	Nil

Table 4.7 : Indices of selection potential

Calculated from birth (Crow, 1958)			Calculated from early embryonic stage (Jhonston & Kensinger, 1971)			
I_m	I_f	I	I_{me}	I_{mc}	I_f	I
0.0267	0.4401	0.4785	0.9731	0.0267	0.4401	0.5227

REFERENCES

BARUA, S., 1981, *A Demogenetic Study among the Muslims of West Bengal.* (Unpublished Ph. D Thesis), Calcutta University.

BARUA, S., 1983, The Hajongs of Meghalaya: A Bio-demographic study. *Human Science*. 32 : 190 - 200.

BASU, A, 1969, The Pahira: A Population Genetical Survey. *American Journal of Physical Anthropology*. 31 : 399 - 416.

BASU, A, 1972, A Demographic Study of the Kota of Nilgiri Hills. *Journal of Indian Anthropological Society*. 7 : 29 - 55.

BASU, M.P., 1968, A Demographic Profile of the Irula. *Bulletin of the Anthropological Survey of India*. 16 : 267 - 289.

BUZARBARUA, P.M., 1982, A Short Note on Fertility among the Santal Women of Nagrijuli area, Kamrup District, Assam. *North East Quarterly*. 1.

BUZARBARUA, P.M., 1990, A Bio-Demographic Study of the Munda Population of Assam. *Social Sciences*. 3 : 171 - 178.

BUZARBARUA, P.M.; M.N. PHOOKAN, 1985, Effect of birth orders and mother age on reproductive wastage of the Mishing of Disangmukh of Sibsagar, Assam. *Indian Journal of Physical Anthropology and Human Genetics*. 10 : 155 - 158.

CROW, J.F., 1958, Some Possibilities for measuring Selection Intensities in Man. *Human Biology*. 30 : 1 - 13.

DAS, B., 1985, Fertility and Mortality Differentials among the Khamyang and Turung Population of Jorhat District Assam. *Journal of Assam Science Society*. 28 : 14 - 19.

DEVI, B., 1975, A Note on the Reproductive Life of Kond Women. In *Bioanthropological Research in India*. Edited by H.K. Rakshit. Calcutta : Anthropological Survey of India.

GHOSH, A.K., 1970, Selection Intensity in the Kota of Nilgiri Hills, Madras. *Social Biology*. 17 : 224 - 225.

JHONSTON, F.F.; K.M. KENSINGER, 1971, Fertility and Mortality Differentials and their Implication for Micro-evolutionary change among the Cachinahua. *Human Biology*. 43 : 356 - 364.

KAR, R.K.; J.L. SHARMAH, 1982-1983, A Study of Fertility among the Wanchos: A Tribe in Arunachal Pradesh. *Bulletin of the Department of Anthropology. Dibrugarh University*. 11 - 12 : 67 - 80.

NAG, M.K., 1954, A Demographic Study of the Kanikkar of Travancore. *Bulletin of the Anthropological Survey, Government of India*. 3 : 95 - 116.

NAG, M.K., 1965, Effects of Christianity on a few aspects of Khasi Culture. *Bulletin of the Anthropological Survey, Government of India*. 14 : 1 - 34.

PODDAR, S., 1975, 'Effects of birth orders and mother's age on reproductive wastage'. In *Bio-Anthropological Research in India*. Edited by H.K. Rakshit. Calcutta: Anthropological Survey of India.

RAKSHIT, S., 1962, Reproductive life of some Maharashtrian Brahman women. *Man In India*. 42 : 139 - 159.

SARKAR, S.S., 1944, The Reproductive life of the Maler Women. *Man In India*. 24 : 29.

SEN, T., 1953, Reproductive life of some Indian women. *Man in India*. 33 : 31 - 54.

SHARMA, M., 1988, Preferential mating patterns and selection intensity among the Gond. In *Marriage in India*. Edited by B.B. Goswami, D. Danda, and J. Sarkar. Calcutta : Anthropological Survey of India.

SPUHLER, J.N., 1959, 'Physical Anthropology and Demorgaphy. In *'The Study of Population: An Inventory and Apprisal'*. Edited by P.M. Hauser and O.D. Duncun. pp 729 - 758.

TALUKDAR, S., 1979, Genetical demography of two Dule Bagdi demes. *Man in India*. 50 : 43 - 70.

5

Selection Intensity Among the Sonowals of Assam

Sarthak Sengupta, Mondira Kalita

Introduction

Natural selection is one of the major evolutionary forces that acts on population causing gradual modification by bringing about changes in the genetic makeup. Crow (1958) suggested an index of opportunity for selection in a population. It comprises two components, differential mortality and differential fertility. The index of total selection intensity indicates the maximum potential rate of change through selection assuming that variations in mortality and fertility are genetically determined and fitness is completely heritable. Livingstone and Spuhler (1965) suggests that there would be no change in the genetic make up of a population through selection, if the computed value of the index comes to zero. Johnston and Kensinger (1971) subsequently extended Crow's original approach and separated the mortality component 'into a component due to variance in prenatal loss and another due to postnatal mortality'.

In the present paper an attempt has been made to examine the intensity of natural selection in the Sonowal population of Dibrugarh, Assam as well as to compare the present findings with those from other populations of North East India, obtained by others. The Sonowal is an endogamous branch of Kachari tribe and a populous plain scheduled tribal population of Assam. At present, they are mainly concentrated in Dibrugarh district.

Material and Method

The sample consists of 72 Sonowal mothers age of 45 years and above. In order to estimate the total selection intensity, we have followed the method proposed by Crow (1958). We have also used the modified formula of Johnston and Kensinger (1971) which takes care of embryonic deaths. This has been done with a view to identifying how these two estimates of the total selection intensity in the Sonowal population, differ from each other.

Results

Pre-reproductive mortality, which is one of the important demographic variables, indicate the loss of certain genotypes in the population. Table 5.1 shows that there are 72 Sonowal mothers, who are aged 45 years and above. They had altogether 433 pregnancies, out of which 411 terminated into live-births and the number of premature death is 59. Thus, in the present sample, proportion of offspring mortality before 15 years of age is 0.1436 or 14.36%. The average number ($\bar{X}$) of live-births per woman aged 45 years or more is 5.71 with a variance (V_f) of 5.34.

The mortality (I_m) and fertility (I_f) components and the index of total selection intensity (I) computed for the present Sonowal sample (Table 5.2) according to Crow's (1958) formula is 0.1676, 0.1638, and 0.3589 respectively. The indices for the Sonowal relating to prenatal mortality (I_{me}), postnatal mortality up to reproductive age, i.e., 15 years (I_{mc}), fertility (I_f) and the total selection intensity (I) also estimated according to Johnston and Kensinger's (1971) method and are set out in table 5.2. The I_{me}, I_{mc}, I_f and I in the Sonowal population under study are 0.0535, 0.1677, 0.1638 and 0.4321 respectively.

Recently, studies of Reddy and Lakshmanudu (1979), Rao and Choudhury (1986), Reddy and Chopra (1990) reported that 'I' in Indian population varies between 0.24 and 2.25, I_m between 0.01 and 0.81 and I_f between 0.17 and 0.83. The present data indicate that the 'I' among the Sonowal is more towards the lower limit of the range and so is the case with I_m. However, the index of selection due to fertility, i.e., I_f in the Sonowal is slightly lower than the minimal Indian level.

Another points merit noting here that the index of total selection intensity according to Johnston and Kensinger's method shows considerably higher value that of the value calculated according to Crow's formula. It is also noteworthy that opportunity for selection (estimated by both methods) operates mainly through differential mortality. In this regard the contribution of postnatal mortality is more than prenatal mortality.

A comparison of the present data with that of the other North East Indian population reported so far is also attempted. No test of significance of the difference between the population with respect to 'I' was possible, however.

The present Sonowal samples are very different from the results that obtained on the same population by Deka (1980). The I_m, I_f, and I among the Sonowal reported by Deka (1980) are 0.185, 0.179 and 0.364 respectively. The study reveals that the value of index of opportunity for selection (I), as well as its fertility (I_f) and mortality (I_m) components are comparatively greater than those obtained for the Sonowal of the present study. As in the present series, in his sample too, greater contribution of mortality components than the fertility components was observed. Prenatal mortality (I_{me}) postnatal mortality up to reproductive age, i.e., 15 years (I_{mc}), fertility (I_f) and the total selection intensity (I) also estimated which are 0.103, 0.185, 0.179 and 0.541 respectively. It is noteworthy that the index of selection due to embryonic mortality, i.e., prenatal mortality is much higher in the former sample (Deka, 1980) and it is almost double to that of the present one. The index of total opportunity for selection is also much higher among the Sonowal reported earlier to that of the present study.

Guha and Mukherjee (1990) reports that the I_m, I_f, and I among the Boro Kachari of Lower Assam as 0.110, 0.130 and 0.250 respectively. The values of all these indices are much lower than the Sonowal population. In this connection, it is worth mentioning that among the Boro Kachari, mortality component of selection is lower than its fertility component, which is just reverse of the situation in other population groups where I_m is higher than I_f. The data summarised in the table also shows that the index of total selection (I) in the Punjabi Sonar of Shillong (Jaswal, 1977) is the lowest in which both I_m and I_f are the lowest, while it is highest in the Singpho of Arunachal Pradesh (Padmanabham and Jaswal, 1982) in which I_f is the highest and I_m is also high. There are also wide variations between the two Jaintia sample (Deka, 1978; Khongsdier, 1990). The index of total opportunity for selection in the Hajong (Barua, 1983) is almost the same as found among the Pnar of Meghalaya.

Spuhler (1962, 1963) has suggested that socio-economic factors, particularly, the economic conditions effect the index of total selection intensity. A few recent studies on tribal populations of India demonstrate the effect of, particularly, two major socio-cultural factors, viz., rural urban residence and religion on the index.

In view of the above findings, it is worth mentioning that Deka (1980) collected data from some interior villages located within a radius of 50 kms of Dibrugarh town and as such his data represent a rural population. On the other hand the present sample collected from villages which are very close (located within a radius of 0 to 2 kms) to Dibrugarh township and thus represent an urban population on the presumption that these villages were exposed to and benefited by the urban facilities maximally. It is apparent from the present study that the value of mortality and fertility components and index of opportunity for selection in rural Sonowals have higher values than that of their urban counterparts.

From the above findings, thus, it may be suggested that among the Sonowal tribe of Dibrugarh, the variation which occurs in two samples with respect to the index of selection intensity is mainly due to micro socio-cultural variation, i.e., due to rural-urban residence, as there are no physical environmental variations among the samples studied. The above findings is in conformity with the observation made by earlier researcher (Mukherjee, 1989; Bharati, 1981, etc.), who observed that I_m, I_f and I usuallly differ in relation to rural-urban residence of population.

Table 5.1 : Parameters used in calculating the total selection intensity in Sonowal

i.	Number of mothers aged 45*	=	72
ii.	Number of pregnancy/conception	=	433
iii.	Number of live-births	=	411
iv.	Number of embryonic death (miscarriage, abortion and still birth)	=	22
v.	Number of dead child up to 15 years of age	=	59
vi.	Survivors up to 15 years of age and above	=	352
vii.	Number of live-births per woman of completed fertility (i.e., 45* years)	=	5.71
viii.	Variance of mean live-birth	=	5.34

Table 5.2 : Indices of Selection Intensity : The Sonowal and other population groups of North East India

Population	Crow's (1958) Formula			Johnston and Kensinger's (1971) method				Source
	I_m	I_f	I	I_{me}	I_{mc}	I_f	I	
ASSAM								
Sonowal	0.1676	0.1638	0.3589	0.0535	0.1777	0.1638	0.4321	Present Study
Sonowal	0.185	0.179	0.364	0.103	0.185	0.179	0.541	Deka, 1980
Boro Kachari	0.110	0.130	0.250					Guha & Mukherjee, 1990
Bengali Muslim of Cachar	0.43	0.31	0.87					Chakravarty, 1976
ARUNACHAL PRADESH								
Apatani (Guchi)	0.435	0.195	0.710					Padmanabham & Jaswal, 1982
Apatani (Guth)	0.440	0.312	0.889					—do—
Singpho	0.437	0.406	1.020					—do—
MEGHALAYA								
Pnar	0.2362	0.1335	0.4012	0.2016	0.2362	0.1335	0.6807	Khongsdier, 1990
Jaintia	0.456	0.125	0.638					Deka, 1977
Hajong				0.0320	0.4430	0.1310	0.6840	Barua, 1983
Punjabi Sonar (Shillong)	0.050	0.054	0.107					Jaswal, 1977

REFERENCES

BARUA, S., 1983, The Hajong of Meghalaya: A Biodemographic study. *Human Science*. 32 : 190 - 200.

BHARATI, P., 1981, Economic condition and demography among the Mahishyas of Chakpota village, Howrah district, West Bengal. *Journal of Biosocial Science*. 13 : 345 - 356.

CHAKRAVARTY, S.K., 1976, Selection potential among the Bengali Muslim of Cachar. *Proceedings of Third Annual Conference of Indian Anthropological Society*, Santiniketan.

CROW, J.F., 1958, Some possibilities for measuring selection intensities in man. *Human Biology*. 30 : 1 - 13.

DEKA, A., 1978, Reproductive performance and selection among the Jaintias of village, Sa-phai. In *Genetical Demography of Indian Population*. pp 6 -11, Calcutta : Anthropological Survey of India.

DEKA, R., 1980, Selection potential among the Sonowal Kachari of upper Assam. *Bulletin of the Department of Anthropology, Dibrugarh University*. 9 : 136 - 140

GUHA, A.; D.P. MUKHERJEE, 1990, Influence of cultural traditions and social movements on the genetic structure of the Boro Kachari population. *Journal of Indian Anthropological Society*. 25 : 73 - 81.

JOHNSTON, F.F.; K.M. KENSINGER, 1971, Fertility and mortality differentials and their implications for micro-evolutionary change among the Cashinahua. *Human Biology*. 43 : 356 - 364.

KHONGSDIER, R., 1990, The Pnar of Sutnga and Moopala villages: A study in selection intensity. *Journal of Indian Anthropological Society*. 25 : 182 - 184.

LIVINGSTONE, F.B.; J.N. SPUHLER, 1965, Cultural determinants of natural selection. *International Social Science Journal*. 17 : 118 - 120.

MUKHOPADHYAY, B., 1989, Socio-cultural variation and selection intensity among the Lepcha of Kalimpong subdivision, Darjeeling district, West Bengal. *Journal of Indian Anthropological Society*. 24 : 197 - 200.

PADMANABHAM, P.B.S.V.; I.J.S. JASWAL, 1982, A demographic study of Apatanis. *Proceedings of the Seminar on Biological and Cultural Variation of the People of North East India*. Guwahati : Anthropology Department, Gauhati University.

RAO, K.R.; D. CHOUDHURY, 1986, Indices of selection intensity among four sub-groups of Telis in Vidarbha region, Maharastra. *Human Science*. 35 : 328 - 333.

REDDY, B.M.; V.P. CHOPRA, 1990, Opportunity for natural selection among the Indian population. *American Journal of Physical Anthropology*. 83 : 281 - 296.

REDDY, P.C.; M. LAKSHMANUDU, 1979, Indices of opportunity of selection in Mala, Madiga and other Indian population. *Journal of Indian Anthropological Society*. 14 : 245 - 252.

SPUHLER, J.N., 1962, Empirical studies on quantitative human genetics. In: *United Nations Seminar on the Use of Vital and Health Statistics for Genetics and Radiation Studies*. pp 241 - 252; Geneva: World Health Organization.

SPUHLER, J.N., 1963, The scope of natural selection in man. In *Genetic Selection in Man*. Edited by W.I. Schull, pp 1 - 111. Ann Arbor: University of Michigan Press.

6
Body Build and Menarcheal Age in Rural Assamese Women

Bandana Das

The physiological processes controlling the reproductive function differ in both the sexes of Homo sapians. The onset of menstrual cycle in female which is termed as menarche indicates the sexual maturity and marks a definite stage of uterine development in association with development of other related secondary sex organs for attainment of reproductive function. Thus, it is an important factor in considering the reproductive life of a woman, a valuable demographic variable, often considered in physical anthropological studies. Several investigations have revealed the influence of various factors, e.g., body build, nutrition, heredity and environment towards the observed variation in the onset of menarche among different populations (see Valsik, et al., 1973 for detail).

In the study of the mechanism of evolutionary change, and the study of individual differences in structure and function; growth and development occupies a central place which is influenced by a mixture of heredity and environmental effects. The genetical control of growth rate is manifested most simply in the inheritance of age at menarche, the same pattern of inheritance as that shown by height and other body measurements. The height, weight or body build of an adult as well as the menarcheal age always represent the resultants of both the genetical and external environmental forces such as dietary restriction or socio-economic condition, manual labour or exercise, etc.

As both the processes, the body build and menarche are influenced by similar kind of factors they are interrelated to a great extent. In the present study an attempt has been made to find out the interrelationship between the menarcheal age and body size.

Many investigations have been carried out on this problem by various workers in India and abroad and considerable literature exists on the general relationship at adolescence between body size and sexual maturation. Palmar and Read (1935) using longitudinal growth data of school children, related stature with sexual maturity of girls and found a positive relationship. Jacobson (1954) also studied menarcheal age in relation to adult body structure. Tanner (1962) related body size with puberty. Livson and Neill (1962) found a strong association between ponderal index and sexual maturity. Joseph (1971) studied physical growth and menarche, showed a close relationship between body build and age at menarche. Eggers, et al. (1967) and Firsch and Roger (1969, 1970, 1971) studied menarche in relation to height and weight. In India, Bardhan (1962) studied anthropometric measurements in relation to menarcheal age. Bali and Randhawa (1979) studied the relationship of variation in sexual maturation to various body girths.

With special reference to Assam, only a few studies have so far been carried out by different researchers and mostly these are concentrated upon reporting mean menarcheal age only. Studies conducted by Rakshit (1960), Das and Das (1967), Srivastava and Goswami (1968) and Das and Sengupta (1984) on the caste populations of Assam may be mentioned in this connection. Besides these, there are few other studies made within this region, like the menarche of the Ahom female reported by Gogoi (1972), Singpho by Kar and Mahanta (1975) and so on. The relationship of menarcheal age with haemoglobin variants has been examined by Deka (1976b) and reports late onset of menarche in women homozygous for haemoglobin E as compared to normal heterozygotes and homozygotes.

Material and Method

The present study is based on two caste populations, i.e.,

the Brahmin and the Kaibarta and the Assamese Mulim community. The data were collected during the period extending from March to June 1981 from the village area under the police station of Hajo, Nalbari and Patacharkuchi of erstwhile Kamrup district, Assam. From each group 200 individuals were taken, the total sample size thus, includes 600 individuals in the age group between 9 and 16 years. The girls originated from all the population groups were apparently healthy.

Information on age at menarche was obtained from the subjects by retrospective method depending on recall. To get the accuracy, cross examination was done comparing the age with the horoscope records.The body height and weight were the measurements recorded as the parameters of general body build following Martinand Saller (1957).

Results and Discussion

The girls have for the purpose of the study been classified under eight age classes, each age-class being for 12 months. Accordingly, age group framed from 9.00 to 9.99 included the individuals from 9 years to 9 years 11 months of age. Each age group includes 25 individuals. Enquiry been made to each individuals about the áttainment of puberty and the measurements were taken from each individuals from the menstruating as well as non-menstruating girls. The body measurements of the menstruating girls is compared with the non-menstruating girls in each group.

The percentage of menstruating girls and the mean age at menarche has been calculated separately for each caste group and are presented in table 6.1. It shows that out of 600 individuals, 263 girls (43.83%) experienced puberty while 337 (56.17%) were not. Except Muslim, the other two Hindu caste groups show almost similar percentage. The mean menarcheal age of all three population groups also do not deviate much from the mean age at menarche of the pooled sample.

To find out the relationship of the body build and menarcheal age, the data has been pooled together and the mean of the height and weight of menstruating girls has been compared with the mon menstruating girls of the same age group separately. The mean difference were measured by applying the t-test of significance.

Table 6.2 shows the difference of mean height of menstruating and non-menstruating girls from 11.00 years to 15.99 years of age group. The table reveals that in each group, the menstruating girls are significantly taller than non-menstruating girls. In the same way calculation has been made to find out relations between weight and menstruation and it also shows similar result as in the case of height (Table 6.3).

Height-weight ratio is one of the simplest index, used to measure body-build. Higher height-weight ratio shows the superior body build and it is calculated following Martin and Saller (1957 : 354)

$$\text{Height-weight index (Quetelet Bouchard)} = \frac{\text{Weight (Kgs)}}{\text{Height (mm)}} \times 100$$

The value of height weight index of menstruating girls has been compared with the non-menstruating girls (Table 6.4). It shows higher value in case of menstruating girls compared to non-menstruating girls in the same age group. It thus appears that the menstruating girls are robust in build than the non-menstruating girls, or in other words the girls with big build menstruate earlier than the others.

The findings of the present study agree well with the observation of Tanner (1966), 'that portion of greater size in children which reflects earlier menstruation'.

Table 6.1 : Number of menstruating girls at different age groups

Age-group	Brahmin	Kaibarta	Muslim	Pooled sample
9.00 - 9.99	-	-	-	-
10.00 - 10.99	-	-	-	-
11.00 - 11.99	-	1 (4.00)	2 (8.00)	3 (4.00)
12.00 - 12.99	4 (16.00)	7 (28.00)	6 (24.00)	17 (22.66)
13.00 - 13.99	13 (52.00)	10 (40.00)	14 (14.00)	37 (49.33)
14.00 - 14.99	19 (76.00)	22 (88.00)	23 (92.00)	64 (85.33)
15.00 - 15.99	24 (96.00)	19 (76.00)	24 (96.00)	67 (89.33)
16.00 - 16.99	25 (100.00)	25 (100.00)	25 (100.00)	75 (100.00)
Total	(42.50)	(42.00)	(47.00)	(43.83)
Mean (Yrs)	12.94	12.52	12.73	12.73
± S.E.	0.07	0.02	0.03	0.02
S.D.	0.73	0.24	0.33	0.40

Figures within parantheses indicate percentages.

Table 6.2 : Body height of menstruating and non-menstruating girls

Age at the time of recording height	Menstruating			Non-menstruating			
	No.	Mean (in m.m.)	S.D.	No.	Mean (in m.m)	S.D.	t Value
9.00 - 9.99	-	-	-	75	1247.35	68.58	-
10.00 - 10.99	-	-	-	75	1281.06	72.56	-
11.00 - 11.99	3	1489.00	35.05	72	1333.72	79.07	3.34*
12.00 - 12.99	17	1457.50	46.61	58	1393.96	60.84	3.93*
13.00 - 13.99	37	1476.30	52.56	38	1399.92	71.29	5.22*
14.00 - 14.99	64	1495.98	57.35	11	1425.91	57.51	3.76*
15.00 - 15.99	67	1493.25	58.31	8	1425.62	43.04	3.17*
16.00 - 16.99	75	1478.00	53.86	-	-	-	-

* indicates statistically significant at 5.0% level of probability.

Table 6.3 : Body weight of menstruating and non-menstruating girls

Age at the time of recording weight	Menstruating			Non-menstruating			t Value
	No.	Mean (in kg)	S.D.	No.	Mean (in kg)	S.D.	
9.00 - 9.99	-	-	-	75	20.96	2.76	-
10.00 - 10.99	-	-	-	75	22.90	3.50	-
11.00 - 11.99	3	37.16	1.31	72	26.54	4.66	3.89*
12.00 - 12.99	17	35.62	4.90	58	29.11	4.22	5.24*
13.00 - 13.99	37	37.91	5.81	38	30.17	4.33	6.40*
14.00 - 14.99	64	39.51	5.03	11	31.95	5.33	5.51*
15.00 - 15.99	67	42.05	5.35	8	33.87	2.02	4.11*
16.00 - 16.99	75	41.10	5.51	-	-	-	-

* indicates statistically significant at 5.0% level of probability.

Table 6.4 : Height-weight index of menstruating and non-menstruating girls

Age at the time of recording measurement	Menstruating			Non-menstruating		
	Weight (Kg)	Height (mm)	Height-weight index	Weight (Kg)	Height (mm)	Height-weight index
9.00 - 9.99	-	-	-	20.96	1247.35	1.68
10.00 - 10.99	-	-	-	22.90	1281.06	1.78
11.00 - 11.99	37.16	1487.00	2.49	26.54	1333.72	1.98
12.00 - 12.99	35.62	1457.50	2.49	29.11	1393.96	2.08
13.00 - 13.99	37.91	1476.30	2.56	30.17	1399.92	2.15
14.00 - 14.99	39.57	1495.98	2.64	31.95	1425.91	2.24
15.00 - 15.99	42.05	1493.25	2.82	33.87	1425.62	2.37
16.00 - 16.99	41.10	1478.00	2.78	-	-	-

REFERENCES

BALI, R.S.; M. RANDHAWA, 1979, Relationship between menarcheal age and body girths. *Indian Journal of Physical Anthropology and Human Genetics*. 5, 1 : 71 - 74.

BARDHAN, A., 1962, A short note on the relationship between menarcheal age and certain anthropometric measurements of physique of the age 11 to 25 years. *The Anthropologist*. 9, 1 & 2 : 25 - 30.

DAS, B.M.; S. SENGUPTA, 1984, Age at menarche among rural Assamese women. *The Journal of Assam Science Society*. 27, 1 : 6 - 13.

DAS, P.B.; B.M. DAS, 1967, Age at menarche of Kalita girls in Assam. *Man in India*, 47, 2 : 113 - 117.

DEKA, R., 1976a, Menarcheal age among the Kachar women of upper Assam. *Bulletin of the Department of Anthropology, Dibrugarh University*. 5 : 1 - 6.

DEKA, R., 1976b, Age at menarche and hemoglobin E among the Kachar women of upper Assam. *Man in India*. 56, 4 : 349.

FIRSCH, R.E.; R. REVELLE, 1969, Variation in body weight and the age of adolescence growth spurt among Latin American and Asian populations in relation to calorie supplies. *Human Biology*. 45 : 185-212.

FIRSCH, R.E.; R. REVELLE, 1970, Height and weight at menarche and a hypothesis of critical body weights and adolescent events. *Science*. 169 : 397 - 399.

FIRSCH, R.E.; R. REVELLE, 1971, The height and weight of girls and boys at the time of initiation of the adolescent growth spurt in height and weight and the relationship to menarche, *Human Biology*. 43, 1.

GOGOI, D., 1972, Menarche and menopause among women of an Ahom village in upper Assam. *Bulletin of the Department of Anthropology, Dibrugarh University*. 1 : 18 - 22.

JACOBSON, L., 1954, On the relationship between menarcheal age and adult body structure. *Human Biology*. 26 : 127 - 132.

JOSEPH, H., 1971, Physical growth and menarcheal age in Tanjanian school children and adults. *Human Biology*. 43, 3.

KAR, R.K.; S. MAHANTA, 1975, Menarche and menopause among the Singpho women of Arunachal Pradesh. *Indian Journal of Physical Anthropology and Human Genetics*. 1 : 51 - 57.

LIVSON, N.; D. Mc. NEILL, 1962, The accuracy of recalled age at menarche. *Human Biology*. 21 : 218 - 221.

MARTIN, R.; K. SALLER, 1957, *Lehrbuch der Anthropologie*. Stuttgart : Gustav Fischer Verlag.

PALMER, C.E.; L. J. REED, 1935, Anthropometric studies of individual growth, I. Age, height and rate of growth in elementary school children. *Human Biology*. 7 : 319 - 334.

RAKSHIT, S., 1960, A short note on menarcheal age of Assamese girls. *Man in India*. 40 : 52 - 55.

SRIVASTAVA, R.P.; M. GOSWAMI, 1968, The menarcheal age of Assamese girls. *The Anthropologist*. 15, 1 & 2 : 57 - 60.

TANNER, J.M., 1962, *Growth at Adolescence*. (2nd ed.). Oxford : Blackwell Scientific Publication.

TANNER. J.M., 1966, The secular trend towards earlier physical maturation. *T. Soc. Geneesk*. 44 : 524 - 539.

VALSIK, J.A.; R.S. STUKOVSKY; N. JANKU, 1973, Factors influencing menarche, In *Physical Anthropology and its extending horizons*. Edited by A. Basu, A.K. Ghosh, S. Biswas, R. Ghosh, R. Ghosh. pp 99 - 108. Calcutta : Orient Longman.

7

Biomedical Anthropological Approaches in North Eastern India : A Synthesis of the Tea Garden Population of Assam

R.S. Balgir

The North Eastern region of India comprises seven sister states, namely, Arunachal Pradesh, Nagaland, Manipur, Mizoram, Tripura, Meghalaya and Assam. It is blended with plains and hills and eye-catching scenic beauty with lush green vegetal mantle. The heterogeneous terrains include foothills, riverbeds, tea gardens, paddy fields and large thick forests and high mountain ranges.The climate is hot and humid with heavy rainfall. The people of the region are mostly tribals belonging to Mongoloid ethnic stock. Most of them are not the original inhabitants of the region but they have migrated from the neighbouring countries, i.e., Tibet, Nepal, China, Myanmar, Thailand, etc. They speak different languages and dialects, possess distinct socio-cultural heritages, religions, customs, dresses and ornaments, music and dances, values and beliefs and practices unique pattern of marriages, etc. They are economically backward and industrially under-developed people. The varied geographical, climatic and ecological niches have diversified their mode of subsistence, traditional habits and the life style as a whole (Balgir, 1992a). This region represents a sort of museum of different cultures and the people.

The state of Assam is the central-most part of the region which is surrounded by these seven recently carved territories (Fig 7.1). It is composed of mostly plains, plateaus and small hills, and cultivable land and paddy fields. The average temperature ranges between 24 and 30^{0}C with average relative humidity 74-95% and average rainfall of 551.8 mm. The tea, oil, coal and plywood industries of Assam play a significant role in the National Economy. The world famous Kaziranga National Park enriched with variety of natural fauna including one-horned Rhinoceros is well known on the International map for wildlife. The mighty Brahmaputra is the largest and the longest river of Assam which creates havoc every year during the monsoon season. Because of natural reservoirs of oil, gas, and coal, the area is prone to natural calamities like earthquakes, etc.

Biomedical Anthropology

Biomedical anthroplogy is a newly emerging discipline which combines the theoretical and methodological concepts of physical anthropology and medical anthropology in the study of disease and health of human populations. This includes the ideas of physical anthropologist with interests in human biology, growth and development, human genetics, nutrition, and human being as physical entity, and of a medical anthropologist whose interests are in the areas of health behaviour, medical care systems, health planning, psychosomatic illness including mental health, and demographic variables. The contention is that a biomedical anthropological approach functions best when it emphasizes the biological basis of health and disease, while at the same time actively incorporating and understanding the socio-cultural nature of the sickness process. The later component has also been designated as clinical anthropology. This whole focus encompasses the fields of medical ecology, medical anthropology, epidemiology, and human biology and human genetics.

Biomedical anthropology has its following major components:

1. Biomedical anthropology is based on the application of anthropological theory to problems of health and disease. It has both biological and biocultural aspects.

2. Biomedical anthropology is centred around disease and health in a structured manner and its investigations enquire into the impact of the disease (or condition) upon biological processes of individuals or the populations to which they belong.

3. The domain of biomedical anthropological study incorporates both biological and cultural explanations of the health, illness, and disease processes including integral approaches to health institutions.

Thus, both physical and medical anthropology contributes concepts of health and disease, and to the systems of health care by which individuals or populations seek to maintain their sense of physical and mental well-being. Biological traditions of physical anthropology focus the research efforts upon the ecological and evolutionary outcomes of disease or pathology in individuals and populations. Medical anthropologists focus their research upon the socio-cultural meaning and behaviour underlying the concepts of health and disease. While these issues have been studied by physical and cultural anthropologists working independently of each other, the synthesis of the two areas can provide a clear understanding of the role of disease and responses to it among human groups (Johnston and Low, 1984).

This study involves the above conceptual themes for the synthesis of a tea garden population of Assam in North Eastern region of India.

Tea Gardens and Labourers

Assam and West Bengal are the two leading tea producing states of India. In the state of Assam, the tea plantation covers 1,92,427 hectares of land which constitutes 52% of the total area of India under tea plantation, followed by West Bengal (25%) Kerala (9%), Tamil Nadu (9%), Tripura (2%), Himachal Pradesh (1%) as recorded in 1977 (Kar, 1981). In Assam, the tea industry has passed through different phases of boom and slump to reach the present stage which may be considered relatively somewhat steady. At present, there are more than 750 tea estates in Assam.

In Assam during the first half of the 19th Century (1840 AD), dense forests were cleared for the cultivation of tea. Local people being reluctant to take up employment in the tea industry, the incentives were given for recruitment of labourers from outside Assam belonging to various states of India. Herds of people who were unemployed, economically broken (weaker) and poverty stricken came from the states of West Bengal, Bihar, Orissa, Madhya Pradesh, Andhra Pradesh and Tamil Nadu in search of employment in the Tea Industry. They now form a major bulk of the labour force of the Tea Industry in the state of Assam.

In the beginning, being uprooted and alien people who can be easily controlled and exploited, suffered from various kinds of mal-adjustments in a new setup and entirely different atmosphere. These adjustments include biological, physiological, climatic, geographical, socio-cultural, and economical with entirely different people. A good number of people, thus, suffered from these mal-adjustments; some died, others went home after the expiry of the tenure (Balgir and Dutta, 1990). Despite their pathetic migratory history, a major section of these people (mostly tribal), however, survived that stage. The agro-based tea industry has accommodated the labourers more or less permanently within the respective tea plantations and encouraged them to settle down in the new habitat and economy leaving their original home permanently. The majority of these tribal people, namely, Savara, Ghasi, Lohar, Tanti, Gond, Kharia, Bhuyan, Kissan, Khond, Mirdha, Murrah, Orang, Gowala, etc., who are either Dravidian or Mundari speaking groups belong to the state of Orissa (Balgir and Dutta , 1990)

Tea Garden Population

While autochthonous (indigenous) populations of North Eastern region of India especially from Assam are extensively studied for various aspects of human biology and human genetics, the knowledge about certain emigrant populations of Assam is relatively limited. One little known population of the state of Assam is the tea garden tribal population. In view of the limited data generated on this population, the present study is directed towards this interesting biosphere. Although tea garden populations belong to various geographical, cultural, linguistic and ethnic heritages, but for the present purpose, it has been considered as a single group of people.

Human Ecology

Considering their geographical and ecological environment as compared to that of their homeland, there were drastic changes from dry and high temperature to high humidity and comparatively less hot climate due to absence of high radiation load, etc. in Assam. There were populations and environment interactions. Thus, the impact of human ecology in understanding the humans and their problems by studying the individuals and population as biological entities, profoundly modified by the culture, and by studying the effects of environment on man and those of man upon his environment is appreciable in Assam (Balgir, 1991). This has given rise to applied studies in health ecology, medical ecology, epidemiology, medical anthropology, and health and nutrition in the tea gardens. Integration of issues related to health and disease has brought about the nutritional anthropology on the forefront within the folds of human ecosystems.

The restriction of a population group to a particular niche depends on its structural adaptations, physiological adjustments and tolerances, and behaviour patterns. At the same time, living in a particular niche brings increasing evolutionary perfections of adaptations for living there rather than somewhere else.Usually the population group favoured by a given micro-climate has a higher rate of population growth at that particular temperature and humidity. This was the case with the tea garden population of Assam.

Medical Anthropology

With regard to the problems of housing, health, education and other welfare activities, both the tea garden management and workers assume it to be the responsibility of the Tea Company. In practice, it has been observed by us in Jokai Tea India Limited, Dibrugarh that many of the welfare schemes including those of health introduced by the management have not been responded favourably. Careful examination of the issues revealed that the schemes were introduced without proper motivation, awareness, and without taking the traditional socio-cultural background of the population. In medical anthropology, ideas about health and disease are based on culturally determined beliefs and values. Explanatory models of disease causation are embedded in beliefs reflecting each population's (culture's) theory of disease, regarding diagnosis, etiology, nosology and prognosis.

To improve the health status of certain at risk population groups, the role of biomedical anthropologist into the health field including the health care in the tea gardens is not only welcomed but is imperative. The failure of conventional health professionals (doctors) and conventional models in the tea garden require the intervention into the design and provision of health services by the medical anthropologists. People still believe that the diseases like cholera, chicken pox, etc. are the result of wrath of some malevolent spirit and annually organise ceremonies in its honour. Divine, protective and ameliorative magic, chants and spells are still employed to ward off disease and difficulty. Age old prescriptions of indigenous herbs are generally used for fever and other common ailments.

With the existence of a hospital and services of biomedical anthropologist in the tea garden has been considerably changing the attitude of the people towards the diseases and their treatment. Increasing use is now being made of modern medical and surgical aids. They still give sometimes traditional treatment at home for some minor ailments, otherwise, for serious problems, the tea garden doctor is now consulted. It is interesting to study how socio-cultural factors intertwine (interact) with morbidity and mortality, public health, excessive drinking and work output in the tea gardens of Assam.

Epidemiology

Frequent epidemics of diarrhoea and dysentry, malaria, parasitic infestations, hemolytic and nutritional anaemia and common infections including those of Japanese encephalitis and skin which are rampant all over Assam, have made them vulnerable as well as adapt to these immunogenetical health hazards for their survival. They now immediately follow the instructions of a medical doctor to prevent the spread of an epidemic in the tea gardens. Although due to the change in economy, the nutritional status of the people in general has improved, but still it is not upto the standard because of so many factors involved. Among the reasons, mention may be made of inadequacy of intake of food, quality of the food materials supplied to them is not upto the mark, selling of food supplied to purchase alcohol, use of various types of sedatives and drugs, etc.

Human Biology

The study of disease has received greatest impetus because of developmental focuses paticularly the emergence of human biology especially population genetics with conceptual approach to human variation. The concept that the normal range of human biological variability is not only subject to, but is evidence of operation of natural selection and consequently of adaptive significance (Balgir and Sharma 1988b; Balgir 1994). This led to intensive search for relationships between genetic polymorphisms and disease, i.e. knowledge of genetic factors in disease especially to explore the relationships between phenotypic and genotypic variation and disease (Balgir, 1991). The population biology examines the role of disease in channelling the evolution (elimination of lethal genes) and differentiation of human populations. the sickle cell hemoglobinopathy, glucose-6-phosphate dehydrogenase (G-6-PD) deficiency, incompatibility of blood groups serology, malaria, etc. are the common public health problems in the tea garden population of Assam (Balgir, 1991; 1992b).

Of the polymorphic inherited characters, the rarest of them cannot be maintained merely by recurrent mutation alone to replace a phenotype lost by selection. Human blood groups and sickle cell hemoglobin are two examples of red cell polymorphism in man. The sickle cell gene may be lost from the population each time a homozygote (who has sickle cell disease) fails to contribute to the next generation because of death before the reproductive age (Table 7.1). The sickle cell heterozygotes are, however, thought to be differentially maintained in the population because individuals with this phenotype are less likely to succumb to falciparum malaria and consequently survive to contribute genes to the next generation (Balgir and Dutta, 1990). This implies that there are different selective values to the several forms of polymorphisms. In some instances, the presence of a small amount of a material may be associated with one effect, and the presence of larger amounts of the same material may be associated with a very different effect. One gene for sickle cell hemoglobin (HbAS) protects against malaria, while the two genes (HbSS) result in the (often) fatal sickle cell disease (Tables 7.2 and 7.3).

Polymorphisms may produce antigenic differences. Antigenic variants of ABO and other blood groups may result in transfusion reactions (Table 7.1). Differences in Rhesus blood groups may cause life-threatening antigenic reactions between a mother and her child late in pregnancy and at the time of birth (Balgir, 1992b; 1993). Polymorphic antigens may have an effect when one human's tissues interact with those of another in blood transfusion, transplantation, pregnancy, intercourse, and possibly when antigens are carried by infectious agents.

Individuals with heterozygous sickle cell (HbAS) have less severe attacks from plasmodium malarial infections than the homozygotes (HbAA) who are free of sickle cell mutation. That means, the heterozygotes have a better change of survival in that environment where malaria is abundant than either of two homozygotes. Individuals with homozygous sickle cell genotype (HbSS) would die of sickle cell anaemia, irrespective of the malarial or non-malarial areas. Although heterozygotes (HbAS) are favoured by the selection against normal homozygotes (HbAA) but they can never breed true, that is, they always generate some offspring with homozygous genotypes. An over-dominant condition leads to genetic polymorphisms, i.e., the maintenance of two or more allelic varieties that persist in a population.

Genetics and Disease Interactions

The geographical distribution of serogenetic markers in different parts of the world is thought provoking and of immense importance to the geneticists working in medical and public health services. It is interesting to observe that in a particular geographic location, the frequency of certain genetic markers is relatively high as compared to the other localities. Similarly, certain diseases tend to confine only to a particular locality. It is now well conceived that genes and ecosystem in a particular situation interact in a very complex and subtle way so that the genetic variations of tissue factors and serum proteins influence the interaction (Balgir and Sharma, 1988a). These genetic variations may be considered at individual, family, and population level. Relationship between some human red cell genetic markers and diseases has been in the focus for understanding the disease susceptibility (Balgir, 1993).

In human population genetics, the study of distribution of sickle cell hemoglobin and of adaptability of tea garden population is an interesting one (Balgir, 1992b). It is also a landmark in the development of biomedical anthropology. By analysing the patterns of gene frequency distribution, it has been demonstrated that a deleterious allele responsible for sicklemia (sickle cell anaemia) and the deficiency of enzyme G-6 PD are important factors in adaptation to falciparum malaria (Balgir and Dutta, 1990; Balgir 1992b; 1993). The concept of balanced polymorphism could be seen in human gene pools of tea garden population, suggesting the harmonious interplay of ecological factors and genetics of disease. Both biological and cultrual adaptations result in biological and socio-cultural stability of the ecosystem in Assam.

The perspective of the present analysis and synthesis is a dual — ecological and functional one. It is ecological, emphasizing the close interactions for subsistence strategy (employment in the tea industry), increased incidence of the anopheles mosquito as a vector of malaria (Dutta et al., 1989) and culex mosquitoes as a vector of Japanese encephalitis, physiological adaptation and the harmonious and beneficial evolutionary response of the gene pools of the population. The effects of cultural practices and disease incidence make the biocultural linkages more thriving. This approach is also a functional one in that, how evolutionary mechanism works to restore an equilibrium condition. The increase in malaria prevalence (Dutta, et al, 1989) is accommodated by an increase in the frequency of the sickle cell allele, i.e. heterozygotes (Balgir and Dutta, 1990) which may be viewed as restoring or maintaining the groups involved as functional societies and populations, having population dynamics.

This has produced one of the first clear and detailed example of the close association between culture, biology, disease process and gene selection. This holistic model indicates that sicklemia and the distribution of the sickle cell allele, G-6-PD deficiency and blood groups serology in the tea garden population (Table 7.1) could not be understood without an understanding of the biocultural processes and migratory forces working historically in human ecosystems. This work can provide a model which can be followed in studying the harmonious and beneficial relationships (symbiosis) between genetic variation, disease, and cultural practices.

Conclusion

The biomedical anthropological approach is a new dimension out of the tradition of holism in anthropology. This approach is best suited to the study of health, disease and sickness behaviour encompassing the biological, biocultural and eco-environmental aspects of the human populations for maintaining a sense of physical and mental well-being. This contribution gives the glimpses of fore-mentioned approaches in the analysis and synthesis of a tea garden population of Assam in the North Eastern region of India.

Acknowledgements

The author is grateful to Dr. K. Satyanarayana, Director, R.M.R.C. (ICMR), Bhubaneswar for the permission, valuable suggestions and comments. Thanks are also due to Mr. P.C. Nayak, Senior Stenographer of this centre for typing this manuscript.

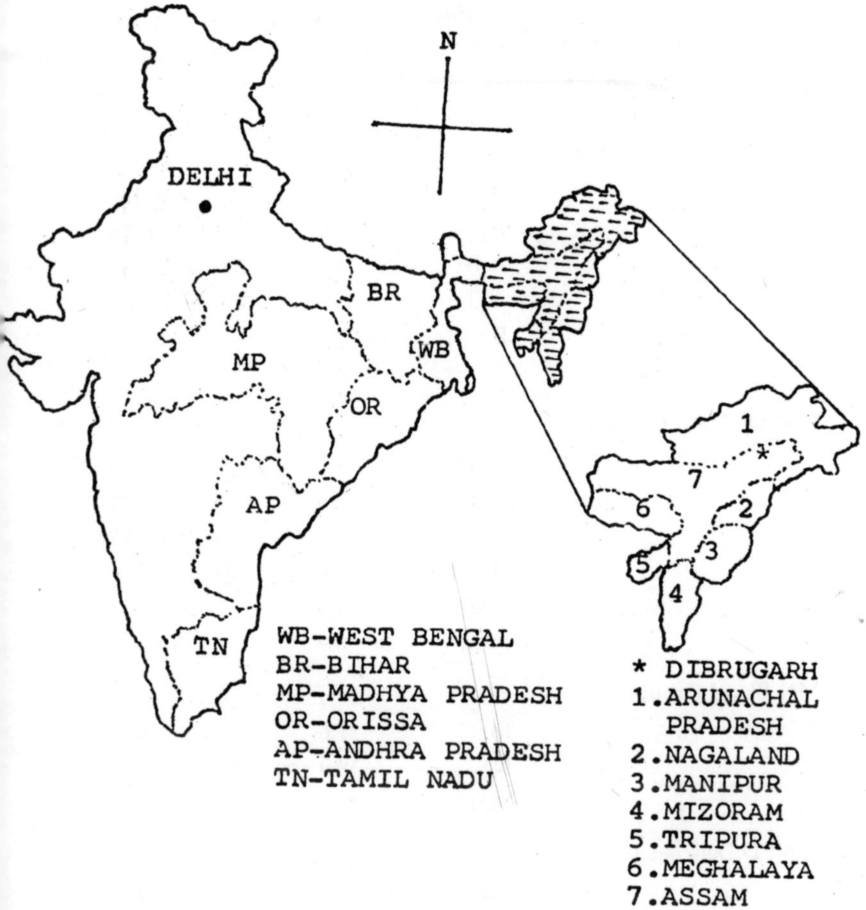

FIGURE 7.1
Map showing seven sister states of north-eastern region of India.

Table 7.1 : Distribution of serogenetic markers in Tea Garden population of Dibrugarh district, Assam*

Serogenetic System	Phenotype	%	Gene Frequency
A_1A_2 BO Blood Groups :			
	A_1	23.6	A_1 = 0.180
	A_2	2.7	A_2 = 0.028
	A_1B	9.1	B = 0.249
	A_2B	1.8	O = 0.543
	B	32.7	
	O	30.0	
Rhesus Blood Groups :			
	CCDe	64.5	CDe = 0.790
	CCde	0.9	cDE = 0.018
	CcDe	27.3	cDe = 0.113
	cDE	1.8	cde = 0.079
	cDe	4.5	
	cde	0.9	
MN Blood Groups :			
	M	31.6	M = 0.564
	N	18.9	N = 0.436
	MN	49.5	
G-6-PD Deficiency :			
	Gd^+	93.7	Gd^+ = 0.937
	Gd^-	6.3	Gd^- = 0.063
Hemoglobin Types :			
	AA	86.9	A = 0.933
	AS	12.8	S = 0.067
	SS	0.3	

* Data from Balgir and Dutta (1990)

Table 7.2 : Distribution of sickle cell hemoglobinopathy in different Tea Gardens of Dibrugarh district, Assam*

Tea Garden	Population with Sickle Cell Trait %
Barbaruah	11.5
Bokel	17.5**
Dikom	11.8
Mattack	10.2
Nudwa	17.4
Singlijan	9.5

* Data from Balgir (1992b)
** 1% of the cases were suffering from Sickle Cell Anaemia

Table 7.3 : Distribution of sickle cell hemoglobinopathy in different Tea Garden population groups of Dibrugarh district, Assam*

Population Groups	Sickle Cell Trait %
Karmakar**	32.3
Tanti	30.8
Das	28.6
Dusad	25.0
Naik	25.0
Lohar	23.0
Ratia	20.0
Ghatwar	16.7
Kharia	16.7
Mirdha	14.3
Murrah	11.8
Orang	11.5
Gowala	9.1

* Data from Balgir (1992b)
** 3.2% of the cases were suffering from Sickle Cell Anaemia.

REFERENCES

BALGIR, R.S., 1991, Genetic diversity among the six Mongoloid populations of North Eastern India. *Journal of Human Ecology*. 2 : 207 - 210

BALGIR, R.S., 1992a, Genetic markers in the tribal health, development and welfare of North Eastern India. *Proc. 79th Annual Conference of Indian Science Congress*, Baroda

BALGIR, R.S., 1992b, Distribution of serogenetic markers in the tea garden tribal population of Dibrugarh district, Assam. *Bulletin of the Department of Anthropology, Dibrugarh University*. 19 : 29 - 38

BALGIR, R.S., 1993, Sero-epidemiological profile of some selected populations in North East India. *Bulletin of the Department of Anthropology, Dibrugarh University*. 21 : 22 - 29

BALGIR, R.S., 1994, Age at sexual maturity among eight endogamous populations of North Eastern India. *Journal of Human Ecology*. (In press)

BALGIR, R.S.; L.P. DUTTA, 1990, Studies on genetic polymorphism in relation to Malaria in tea gardens of Dibrugarh district, Assam. *Indian Journal of Malariology*. 27 : 237 - 241

BALGIR, R.S.; J.C. SHARMA, 1988a, Genetic markers in the Hindu and Muslim Gujjars of North Western India. *American Journal of Physical Anthropology*. 75 : 391 - 403.

BALGIR, R.S.; S.K. SHARMA, 1988b, Distribution of sickle cell hemoglobin in India. *Indian Journal of Hematology*. 6 : 1 - 14

DUTTA, P.; D.R. BHATTACHARYA and L.P. DUTTA, 1989, Incrimination of Anopheles virus as a vector of malaria in Dibrugarh district, Assam. *Indian Journal of Malariology*. 26 : 149 - 152

JOHNSTON, F.E.; S.M. LOW, 1984, Biomedical Anthropology : An emerging synthesis in Anthroplogy. *Yearbook of Physical Anthropology*. 27 : 215 - 227.

8

Numerical Taxonomy and Group Divergence of the Khasi Population Groups

Pratap C. Dutta, Dipesh Chowdhury, Dipak Kumar Adak

Introduction

Das (1978) has compiled a small volume based on his own earlier published material, which indeed contains a wealth of information on the biological anthropology concerning four distinct Khasi population groups. The groups are : the Khasi proper, known also as Khynriam; the Pnar or the Jaintia, who are also called Synteng; the Bhoi; and the War. They inhabit different areas of the Meghalaya State, adapting to varied, smaller eco-zones. Inter-marriage among the four groups are permitted, and it occurs at the bordering zones of population groups. As a matter of fact, however, such mating is not frequent because of geographical and/or cultural barriers. As a competent physical anthropologist, Das had carefully generated largest series of data from those four groups living in the interior places where inter-marriage did not take place. Data comprise four different parameters—such as anthropometry, dermatoglyphics, ABO blood groups and taste sensitivity to phenyl-thio-carbamide.

As could be understood, Das's main focus was to observe variation in somatic characteristics among the four Khasi population groups. To achieve the goal, he critically analysed the material by taking recourse to the statistical treatment of the data based only on samples from *univariate populations*. And he did this in order to see how the four Khasi groups are related to each other. The other genetic markers were mainly utilised to ascertain the validity of the results obtained from anthropometric analysis.

As far as the character variation among the Khasi groups is concerned, it must be admitted that Das has successfully highlighted the situation of somatic variation among them. But to assess the inter-group relationships, utilising the data based on samples from *univariate populations*, is rather hard and any attempt towards this would simply amount to some informed speculation, for obvious reasons, however. Nonetheless, Das has attempted by stating that two of the Khasi groups, the Khynriam and the War, are very close to one another, while the others deviate from each other—furthest being the Bhoi and next to them stand the Pnar.

Biologically speaking, to attempt understanding such an anthropological problem, which is rather a core problem of biological taxonomy, we need necessarily to involve in a statistical problem—essentially multivariate in nature. The multivariate analysis would take recourse to a conjoint investigation of quantitative variates obtained from a set of characters of a given number of populations (for a detailed discussion see Dutta, 1967, 1983). The present paper attempts to estimate the group divergence of the Khasi, using the statistical constants of anthropometric data published by Das (1978).

Numerical Taxonomy and Group Divergence

Let us now explore the possibility of classifying the Khasi population groups and to order their respective positions in relation to one another. These two issues may be accomplished by evaluating numerically the morphological affinities or differences between and among the groups. And this can be done by analysing the overall distance differences and ascertaining mutual relationships between all possible pairs of the given Khasi groups from a matrix of all multivariate distances between the groups obtained utilising a suitable measure of taxonomic distance. In fact, we are here interested in group characteristics of population without concerning the individual character variations of the populations. The measure used is likely to reveal a picture of configurations of the Khasi groups involved by comparison, suggesting some pattern of group constellations and their mutual relationships. To resolve the problem, we are therefore obliged to fall back on a suitable coefficient, or measure, which must be capable of determining the anthropometric difference between any two Khasi groups, specifying a distance estimate between them.

Using the measure of Penrose (1947, 1954), it is possible to effectively approximate a generalised distance between any two $\underline{P}$ - variate statistical populations by $\underline{m}\ \underline{c}^2\ \underline{H}$ which is the sum of size and shape distances multiplied by the number of characters considered. The measure, denoted here as $\underline{D}^2{}_{p}$, is easy to calculate but reportedly with almost the entire accuracy of Mahalanobis's (1936 ; see also Rao, 1952) D^2. The Penrose distance has an advantage over other measure of taxonomic distance ($\underline{D}\ \underline{D}$ of Czekanowski, 1909; Coefficient of Racial Likeness of Pearson, 1926 ; D^2 of Mahalanobis ; g of Hiernaux, 1965), because it can be partitioned into two components of "shape" and "size" factors which are asymptotically and independently distributed.

For the purpose of distance estimation, common standard deviations for each character is agreed upon, and the group means are expressed in terms of standard deviation units. Assuming that $\underline{d}_1, \underline{d}_2, \underline{d}_3, \ldots\ldots\ldots \underline{d}_{\underline{m}}$ represent the difference between standardised means for $\underline{m}$ characters in two populations, Penrose has shown that

(i) Coefficient of Racial Likeness =

$$\underline{C}^2{}_H = (\underline{d}^2{}_1 + \underline{d}^2{}_2 + \underline{d}^2{}_3 + \ldots\ldots\ldots \underline{d}^2{}_{\underline{m}})/\underline{m}$$

$$= \overset{\underline{m}}{\underset{1}{\underline{S}}} (\underline{d}^2)/\underline{m}$$

(ii) Size distance =

$$\underline{C}^2{}_Q = (\underline{d}_1 + \underline{d}_2 + \underline{d}_3 + \ldots \underline{d}_{\underline{m}})/\underline{m}^2$$

$$= \sum_{1}^{m} (d)^2/m^2$$

(iii) Shape distance = $C^2_H - C^2_Q$

$$= \sum_{1}^{m} (d^2)/m \quad - \quad \sum_{1}^{m} (d)^2/m^2$$

$$= C^2_Z\, (m - 1)/m,$$

where C^2_Z is the "Zarapkin coefficient" (Zarapkin, 1934), which effectively performs the task of measuring the "shape distance".

Das has collected absolute linear measurements on 13 anthropometric characters relating to both the sex of the four Khasi population groups. For our present purpose, a panel of nine characters for males, out of 13, has been selected for investigation. The selected characters appear to be useful in effecting discrimination and also for providing reliable estimates of distance measures between any two Khasi population groups. Character means and standard deviations of the four Khasi groups to be compared are set out in table 8.1.

For calculating distance estimates, the values derived by expressing the means of the four Khasi groups in terms of pooled standard deviations, i.e., in standard deviation units, are presented in table 8.2. The procedure of computations employed to find out the difference between measurements and the derived mutual distances between the Khasi groups is illustrated in table 8.3. The results obtained are provided in table 8.4 through 8.6.

The mean size and shape distances have further been determined by calculating mC^2_Q and $(m - 1)\, C^2_Z$ for each comparison (six in number). This is essential in order to obtain an overall view about the size and shape factors involved in determining the divergence of the groups. The computed mean value of shape distance between all pairs of combination is found to be much larger, $(m - 1)\, C^2_Z = 2.01$, than the mean size distance, $m\, C^2_Q = 1.52$. This suggests that the Khasi groups tend to differ more in shape than in size. The shape distance thus becomes more important than size. And it follows that the groups can be classified by means of shape distance rather than size distance, because of a clean overall morphological dissimilarity and differences. To paraphrase Penrose (1954 : 338) :

> "It is normally the shape, or morphology, of the objects which enables it to be classified, not its size, except when the size differences are extreme .... . The general use of a coefficient of shape for estimating 'distance' between types of objects is thus a very natural procedure, and two objects with zero 'shape distance' from one another will be assigned to the same class."

The computed estimates of $\underline{m}\ \underline{C}^2_H$ test, which provides the values of $\underline{D}^2_P$, performed on all possible pairs of combination, are given in table 8.6. The values are arranged there in an increasing order of magnitude of $\underline{D}^2_P$ values. It immediately reveals that the Khynriam are closely related to the War, followed by the Pnar. The Bhoi are distantly located from the War and the Khynriam. Furthermore, the Bhoi are furthest apart from the Pnar, in order of distance.

Examining the values in table 8.6, it appears that these might be a pattern of relationship among the four Khasi populations, as just stated above. In order to provide a specific evidence in that regard, the values obtained from averaging $\underline{D}^2_P$ S within and between clusters, following the method prescribed by Rao (1952 : 362) are shown in table 8.7. To obtain a clear insight of the situation, both relating to classification and ordering of the position, Figure 8.1 seems to be useful. Here an attempt has been made to approximate the configuration and their mutual relationships, where the square root of the average $\underline{D}^2_P$ d_S as in table 8.7, represents the distance.

Further, the change in the average $\underline{D}^2_P$ within a cluster owing to the inclusion of an additional group has been computed. Rao (1952 : 363) tells us that if the change is appreciable one, then the group added there has to be considered as lying outside the cluster. The computations based on the values obtained for $\underline{D}^2_p$, as in table 8.6, are shown in table 8.8. It could be seen that there occurs a sharp rise in $\underline{D}^2_p$, when the Pnar and then the Bhoi groups are added to the Khynriam and the War groups. This implies that the Khynriam together with the War group forms a cluster, while the Pnar and, in a much greater magnitude, the Bhoi are lying well beyond the cluster.

Conclusion

This is the scenario of the Khasi population groups as far as their taxonomy, group divergence and the inter-group relationship are concerned. Briefly stated, the Khynriam and the War are very closely related, morphologically, suggesting that they may be assigned to the same class, taxonomically. On the other hand, the Pnar and the Bhoi, who are mutually widely apart from one another and each of which also clearly maintains a distant position from the former two Khasi populations, can well be classified into two distinct taxonomic categories, morphologically.

Table 8.1 : Mean and standard deviation of anthropometric characters of the Khasi populations

Measurements (in mm.)	Khynriam (n = 100)		Pnar (n = 100)		Bhoi (n = 100)		War (n = 100)	
(m = 9)	Mean	S.D.	Mean	S.D.	Mean	S.D.	Mean	S.D.
St.	1566.2	51.71	1573.5	58.90	1570.0	57.18	1556.8	55.59
S.H.	823.6	33.90	811.2	37.87	823.6	32.65	815.7	32.87
H.L.	188.2	5.43	191.0	6.21	183.4	5.54	186.7	6.28
H.B.	146.4	5.61	145.3	4.30	142.4	4.65	144.3	5.04
H.C.H.	564.0	16.12	545.9	13.02	517.9	16.06	541.6	13.53
Mx.BZB.	135.1	4.24	135.1	4.52	134.5	5.19	134.7	4.29
B.B.	101.6	5.54	102.2	4.97	99.5	5.06	100.5	5.51
N.H.	45.4	1.13	47.9	3.56	48.7	4.26	45.8	4.30
N.B.	39.2	3.55	37.2	2.44	39.5	3.01	38.0	3.32

Table 8.2 : Means of anthropometric characters of four Khasi groups in terms of pooled standard deviation unit

Population	St.	S.H.	H.L.	H.B.	H.C.H.	Mx. BZB.	B.B.	N.H.	N.B.
Khynriam (n = 100)	28.02	23.95	32.01	29.75	37.02	29.50	19.24	12.75	12.60
Pnar (n = 100)	28.15	23.59	32.48	29.53	37.01	29.49	19.36	13.45	11.96
Bhoi (n = 100)	28.08	23.95	31.19	28.94	35.11	29.37	18.84	13.68	12.70
War (n = 100)	27.85	23.72	31.75	29.33	36.72	29.41	19.03	12.86	12.22
Pooled S.D.	55.90	34.39	5.88	4.92	14.75	4.58	5.28	3.56	3.11

Table 8.3 : Differences between measurements and derived distances between any two Khasi population

Character	Difference	(K)-(P)	(K)-(B)	(K)-(W)	(P)-(B)	(P)-(W)	(B)-(W)
(1)	d_1	-0.13	-0.06	0.17	0.07	0.30	0.23
(2)	d_2	0.36	0.00	0.23	-0.36	-0.13	0.13
(3)	d_3	-0.47	0.82	0.26	1.29	0.73	-0.56
(4)	d_4	0.22	0.81	0.42	0.59	0.20	-0.39
(5)	d_5	0.01	1.91	0.30	1.90	0.29	-1.61
(6)	d_6	0.01	0.13	0.09	0.12	0.08	-0.04
(7)	d_7	-0.12	0.40	0.21	0.52	0.33	-0.19
(8)	d_8	-0.70	-0.93	-0.11	-0.23	0.59	0.82
(9)	d_9	0.64	-0.10	0.38	-0.74	-0.26	0.48
Sum of 'd' values S^9_1 (d)		0.18	2.98	1.95	3.16	2.13	-1.03
Sum of squares of 'd' values $S^9_1 (d)^2$		1.33	6.03	0.62	6.64	1.30	4.10
Size distance $C^2_Q = S^9_1 (d)^2/9^2$		0.00	0.11	0.05	0.12	0.06	0.01
Shape distance $\frac{m-1}{m}$ $C^2_Z = S^9_1 (d)^2/9 - S^9_1 (d)^2/81$		0.15	0.57	0.02	0.61	0.09	0.44
Mean square distance $C^2_H = S^9_1 (d)^2/9$		0.15	0.68	0.07	0.74	0.14	0.46
Size = m C^2_Q		0.00	0.99	0.42	1.11	0.50	0.12
Shape = (m – 1) C^2_Z		1.33	5.05	0.20	5.53	0.79	3.99
D^2_P = m C^2_H		1.33	6.03	0.62	6.64	1.29	4.10

Note : K = Khynriam, P = Pnar, B = Bhoi and W = War.

Table 8.4 : Values of size distance ($\underline{m}\ C^2_Q$) between any two Khasi populations

Population	Khynriam	Pnar	Bhoi	War
Khynriam	-	0.00	0.99	0.42
Pnar	-	-	1.11	0.50
Bhoi	-	-	-	0.12
War	-	-	-	-

Table 8.5 : Values of shape distance ($(\underline{m} - 1)\ C^2_Z$) between any two Khasi populations

Population	Khynriam	Pnar	Bhoi	War
Khynriam	-	1.33	5.05	0.20
Pnar	-	-	5.53	0.79
Bhoi	-	-	-	3.99
War	-	-	-	-

Table 8.6 : Values of $\underline{D}^2_P$ (based on 9 characters) between any two Khasi populations arranged in increasing order of magnitude

Khynriam	Pnar	Bhoi	War
0.62	1.29	4.10	0.62
War	War	War	Khynriam
1.33	1.33	6.03	1.29
Pnar	Khynriam	Khynriam	Pnar
6.03	6.64	6.64	4.10
Bhoi	Bhoi	Pnar	Bhoi

Table 8.7 : Intra and Inter-cluster average $\underline{D}^2_P$

Cluster	Population	A	B
A	Khasi War, Pnar	1.08	5.59
B	Bhoi	5.59	

Table 8.8 : Computational scheme for finding cluster

Population added to cluster	D^2_P	No. of terms (n)	$\frac{\text{Increasing in } D^2_P}{\text{Increasing in n}}$	Average D^2_P	Cluster
Khynriam, War	0.62	1	...	0.62	Khynriam, War
Pnar	3.24	3	1.31	1.08	Khynriam, War, Pnar
Bhoi	20.01	6	5.59	3.34	

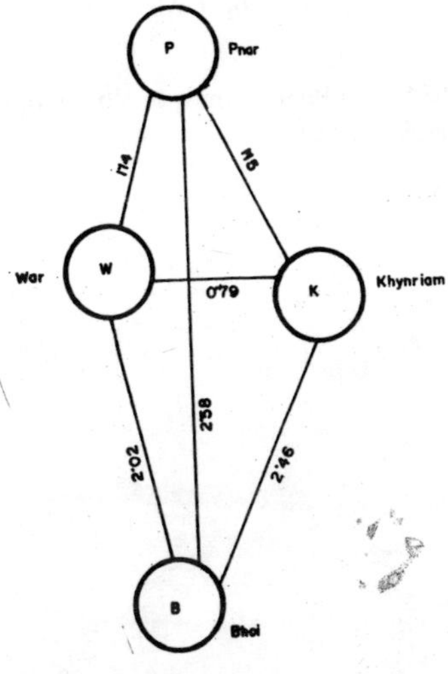

FIGURE 8.1
Clusters and their Inter-Relationships

REFERENCES

CZEKANOWSKI, J., 1909, Zur Differential diagnose der Neandertal gruppe. *Korr. bl. Dtsch. Ges. f. Anthrop. Ethnol.* Urgesch, 40 (6/7) : 44 - 47.

DAS, B.M., 1978, *Variation in Physical Characteristics in the Khasi Populations of North East India.* Guwahati : Dutta Barua and Co.

DUTTA, P.C., 1967, Physical Anthropology of the Gandhabanik and population variability in southern West Bengal. *Bulletin of the Anthropological Survey of India.* 16 : 343 - 377

DUTTA, P.C., 1983, *The Bronze Age Harrappans : A Bio-Anthropological Study of the skeletons discovered at Harappa.* Calcutta : Anthropological Survey of India.

HIERNAUX, J., 1965, Une nouvelle measure do distance anthropologique entre populations, utilisant simultanement des frequences geniques, des pourcentages de traits descriptifs et des moyennes metriques. *C. r. hebd. Seanc. Acad, Sci. Paris.* 260 : 1748 - 1750.

MAHALANOBIS, P.C., 1936, On the generalised distance in statistics. *Proc. Nat, Inst. Sci. India.* 2 : 49 - 55.

PENROSE, L.S., 1947, Some notes on discrimination. *Ann. Eugen. London.* 13 : 228

PENROSE, L.S., 1954, Distance, Size and Shape. *Ann. Eugen. London.* 18 : 337 - 343.

RAO, C.R., 1952, *Advanced Statistical Methods in Biometric Research* New York: John Wiley.

ZARAPKIN, S.R., 1934, Zur Phaenoanalyse Von geographischen Rassen und Arten. *Arch. Naturgesch.* 3 : 161.

9
Biological Distances Among the Three Muslim Populations of Manipur

M.L. Shah

Introduction

A large population is generally divided into isolated subpopulation as a result of geographical distance which helps to enhance various processes of micro-evolution. If the isolation is of high degree between the subpopulation, there will be enhance scope for random genetic drift and also inbreeding (Harrison and Boyce, 1972). Genetic drift will enhance the rate of selection in the total population. Such a typical situation is well represented by the composite population of the Manipuri Muslim, inhabiting in the valley of Manipur.

The present paper attempts to examine the direction, magnitude and trend of variations in respect of individual's somatometric characters and its indices within and between the three subpopulation applying univariate statistical techniques and the proximal relative biological distances between each pair of the population with the help of multivariate distances among the three Muslim male populations, representing each of Bishnupur, Imphal and Thoubal districts of Manipur valley.

The Manipuri Muslims are said to have migrated from Sylhet (now in Bangladesh) and Cachar district of Assam in 1606

A.D. (Singh and Khan, 1973; Constantine, 1981). Singh and Singh (1967) and Singh (1985) suggested that a large band of the Muslim sepoys from Sylhet entered Manipur during the reign of Khagemba Maharaj (1597-1652), King of the then Manipur and they came in the service of Sanongba who raised an army from Sylhet to take revenge against his step-brother, Khagemba Maharaj on an issue of a boat.

The Manipuri Muslims are known as *'Pangan'* among the other communities specially the Meiteis in the State and it is said to have a corrupt term of 'Bengal' (Hodson, 1908). Manipuri language became as their mother tongue. The main occupation of the Manipuri Muslim is cultivation and rice is their staple food. However, many of the Muslims of Kwakta and Sora villages of the Bishnupur and Thoubal districts which are situated at a distance of about 55 and 38 kilometres on the south-west and south-east of Imphal, capital of the State, subsist on fishing from the nearby lakes — Loktak and Lousi respectively. But, the Muslims of Khetrigao of the Imphal district which is lying at a distance of about 6 kilometres on the east of Imphal are mostly employed in governmental service and business. These three Muslim villages are said to have settled in Manipur valley more than 350 years from now (Fig. 9.1). The literacy percentage of the Manipuri Muslims is very low when compared to those of the other communities in the State.

The total population of the Manipuri Muslims was 99,327 individuals in 1981 census in the State. After their settlement at Imphal region for the first time, they are said to have received inflow of genes from the indigenous local population specially Hindu group of the State (Brown, 1873). Afterwards, they have started migration towards the Bishnupur and Thoubal districts of Manipur valley under different ecological niche (Fig 9.1). In due course, these subpopulation have become wide apart genetically from each other considering the relative distance of migration, socio-economic and ecological background etc.

Material and Method

A total sample of 300 Muslim male individuals representing 100 each from the Kwakta, Khetrigao and Sora villages of the

Bishnupur, Imphal and Thoubal districts of Manipur valley respectively in respect of 27 somatometric measurements (Table 9.1) have been scored for the present study. No individual who are physically deformed were included for the study. Moreover, closely related individuals have been excluded as far as possible with a view to include maximum extent of the genome.

The age composition of the individuals ranges between 20 and 49 years. The mean values of the age group of these individuals were 32.6 years, 27.5 years and 28.1 years in respect of Bishnupur, Imphal and Thoubal Muslims respectively.

Standard techniques which have been recommended by Martin and Saller (1956) have been employed for the collection of data. As many as 12 indices have been calculated from these metric characters following the usual formulae. The data on the metric characters and its indices have been analysed in two ways. The first one is the univariate comparison of each trait to examine the trend of variation of statistical constant and significant differences among each and between the pairs of these Muslim populations. The second one is the multivariate analysis of overall distance by obtaining T^2 value of generalised distance of Sanghvi (1953) to see overall biological distance between each pair of the three Muslim populations of Manipur.

Results and Discussion

I. *Univariate Comparison:*

In the univariate comparison of somatometric characters among the three Muslim male populations of Manipur valley, the Bishnupur Muslims have shown the highest mean value in 18 measurements (St, HT, HAC, HIS, AS, MHL, MHB, BZB, MFH, ND, EL, EB, HL, HB, FL, FB, and Bwt) out of 27 somatometric measurements as the maximum number of the traits. In contrast of the Bishnupur Muslims, the Imphal and Thoubal Muslims have the highest mean values in only 3 (SHV, BOB, IOB) and 4 (BACB, AH, BGB, NH) measurements respectively. Incidentally, the three populations show equal mean values in least frontal breadth (LFB) and nasal breadth (NB) only of all the measurements. The Thoubal Muslim shows equal mean values to that of the Imphal Muslim in ear breadth (EB) and Bishnupur Muslim in bizygomatic breadth (BZB) of the measurements respectively. The Bishnupur Muslim also shows homogeneous mean value to that of the Imphal Muslim in bigonial breadth (BGB).

The lowest mean values among the Bishnupur Muslims have been recorded only in 2 somatometric measurements (SHV, IOB). But, in case of the Imphal and Thoubal Muslims, the lowest mean values have been observed in 11 (BACB, AS, AH, MHL, MFH, MUFH, NH, HL, HB, FB, and Bwt) and 9 (St, HT, HAC, HIS, MHB, BOB, ND, EL, and FL) measurements out of 27 somatometric traits studied respectively.

In the statistical comparison of t-test between each pair of the three populations at 5 per cent level of probability, it has been observed that the Bishnupur Muslim shows significant differences in 11 measurements (AS, AH, MFH, MUFH, ND, EB, IOB, HB, FL, FB, and Bwt) with the Imphal Muslim and in 10 characters (St, HT, HAC, AS, HIS, ND, EL, EB, HB, and FL) with the Thoubal Muslim (Table 9.2). However, in between the Imphal and Thoubal Muslim population, t-test values of significant differences have been recorded only in 6 (AM, HIS, MFH, MUFH, ND, and FB) measurements.

From the univariate comparison between the mean values of 12 indices of the somatometric measurements among the three Muslim populations, it has been observed that each of the three population, shows the highest mean values in 4 each of different indices. The Bishnupur Muslim shows the highest mean values in 4 (MFI, MUFI, JMI, and HI) indices. Interestingly, the Imphal and Thoubal Muslims also show the highest mean values in 4 each of (CI, TFPI, JFI, NI and SHVI, LHI, BHI, EDI) indices of the somatometric measurements (Table 9.3). Statistical comparisons between the pairs of the population (Table 9.4) have revealed that the Bishnupur Muslim shows significant differences with the Imphal Muslim in 7 (SHVI, LHI, BHI, MFI, MUFI, JMI and HI) indices and in only 4 (SHVI, JMI, EDI and HI) indices with the Thoubal Muslim. In between the Thoubal and Imphal population, such type of significant differences have been seen in only 2 (LHI, BHI) indices of the somatometric measurements.

II. *Multivariate Comparisons:*

Overall distance measures based on Sanghvi's (1953) methods have been computed for somatometric measurements for comparing each pair of the three Muslim male populations for the present study.

The values of T^2 between the pairs of the three Muslim populations for the 27 somatometric traits used in the present study suggest a closer similarity between the Imphal and Thoubal Muslims (Table 9.5). The most distant relationship has been observed between the Bishnupur and Imphal Muslims while the distance between the Bishnupur and Thoubal Muslims lies in the middle. The proximal distance configuration is represented graphically (Fig 9.2) on the basis of the square roots of these values (Table 9.5).

It has been revealed from the multivariate distance measures that the results conform to the biological divergence of the Bishnupur and Thoubal Muslims from the Imphal Muslims who were the nucleous group of the Manipuri Muslims. This process of divergence has been widened more in due course between the Bishnupur and Imphal Muslims as shown by distance measures of T^2 which might be due to the pressure of both natural selection and genetic drift.

Conclusion :

The variations which have been observed of the univariate and multivariate comparisons between each pair of the three Muslim male populations of Manipur valley suggest the micro-evolutionary processes which have been taking place within a time depth of nearly four hundred years, due to the contributing factors of isolation by distance, random genetic drift, selection, admixture and inbreeding etc. under different micro-ecological background of these subpopulation.

The overall results of the univariate and multivariate analysis appears to lend a strong suggestion of closer biological distance between the Imphal and Thoubal Muslims and the increasing divergence of the Bishnupur Muslim from the Imphal Muslim. The trend of divergence between the pair of the Bishnupur and Thoubal Muslims lies in the middle among each pair of the three Muslim male populations of Manipur valley.

Table 9.1 : Distribution of the somatometric measurements among the Muslims of Manipur valley

Measurements	Abbreviations	Bishnupur Muslim		Imphal Muslim		Thoubal Muslim	
		Mean	± S.E.	Mean	± S.E.	Mean	± S.E.
Stature	St	163.41	0.60	162.54	0.56	161.65	0.54
Height Tragus	HT	150.51	0.53	150.04	0.53	148.75	0.53
Height acromion	HAC	132.62	0.48	131.86	0.60	130.85	0.52
Biacromion breadth	BACB	37.77	0.22	37.76	0.23	37.78	0.16
Arm span	AS	170.16	0.67	167.11	0.56	167.75	0.73
Height illiospinale	HIS	96.50	0.43	95.55	0.42	93.86	0.45
Sitting height vertex	SHV	82.73	0.38	83.67	0.36	83.44	0.30
Auricular height	AH	12.76	0.08	12.37	0.10	12.89	0.11
Max. Head length	MHL	18.08	0.06	17.94	0.06	17.99	0.10
Max. Head breadth	MHB	14.69	0.05	14.68	0.05	14.65	0.05
Least frontal breadth	LFB	10.23	0.04	10.23	0.04	10.23	0.04
Bizygomatic breadth	BZB	13.20	0.06	13.18	0.05	13.20	0.06
Bigonial breadth	BGB	10.25	0.05	10.25	0.05	10.36	0.06
Morphological facial height	MFH	11.25	0.05	10.98	0.06	11.15	0.05

Table 9.1 *(Continued)*

Morphological upper facial height	MUFH	6.75	0.05	6.55	0.04	6.68	0.05
Biorbital breadth	BOB	9.32	0.05	9.36	0.04	9.30	0.04
Inter orbital breadth	IOB	3.08	0.02	3.16	0.03	3.15	0.03
Nasal height	NH	4.67	0.03	4.65	0.03	4.72	0.04
Nasal breadth	NB	3.32	0.03	3.32	0.03	3.32	0.03
Nasal depth	ND	2.04	0.02	1.97	0.02	1.91	0.02
Ear length	EL	5.91	0.06	5.77	0.04	5.69	0.05
Ear breadth	EB	3.08	0.03	2.99	0.03	2.99	0.03
Hand length	HL	18.62	0.08	18.47	0.08	18.59	0.09
Hand breadth	HB	7.90	0.05	7.66	0.03	7.72	0.04
Foot length	FL	24.42	0.11	23.94	0.09	23.88	0.11
Foot breadth	FB	9.51	0.05	9.22	0.05	9.39	0.05
Body weight	Bwt	53.45	0.75	51.62	0.53	52.28	0.60

Table 9.2 : Test of significance : Somatometric characters

Measurements	BM × IM	IM × TM	BM × TM
St	1.06	1.14	2.13*
HT	0.63	1.72	2.35*
HAC	0.99	1.27	2.50*
BACB	0.03	0.07	0.04
AS	3.49*	0.70	2.43*
HIS	1.58	2.75*	4.24*
SHV	1.80	0.49	1.47
AH	3.05*	3.50*	0.96
MHL	1.65	0.43	0.77
MHB	0.14	0.42	0.57
LFB	0.00	0.00	0.00
BZB	0.26	0.26	0.00
BGB	0.00	1.41	1.41
MFH	3.46*	2.18*	1.18
MUFH	3.12*	2.03*	0.99
BOB	0.63	1.06	0.31
IOB	2.22*	0.24	1.94
NH	0.47	1.40	1.00
NB	0.00	0.00	0.00
ND	2.48*	2.12*	4.60*
EL	1.94	1.25	2.82*
EB	2.12	0.00	2.12*
HL	1.33	1.00	0.12
HB	4.12*	1.20	2.81*
FL	3.38*	0.42	3.47*
FB	4.10*	2.40*	1.70
Bwt	1.99*	0.82	1.22

* indicates statistically significant at 5.0% level of probability.

Table 9.3 : Distribution of somatometric indices among the Muslims of Manipur valley

Indices	Abbreviations	Bishnupur Muslim		Imphal Muslim		Thoubal Muslim	
		Mean	± S.E.	Mean	± S.E.	Mean	± S.E.
Sitting height vertex	SHVI	50.66	0.18	51.43	0.14	51.63	0.13
Cephalic	CI	81.35	0.31	81.91	0.38	81.13	0.38
Length height	LHI	70.67	0.49	69.00	0.56	71.41	0.62
Breadth height	BHI	86.89	0.55	84.26	0.63	88.10	0.75
Transverse Fronto Parietal	TFPI	56.66	0.24	57.03	0.28	56.67	0.29
Jugo-Frontal	JFI	77.55	0.30	77.60	0.33	77.56	0.33
Jugo-Mandibular	JMI	80.00	0.37	77.80	0.44	78.48	0.40
Morphological Facial	MFI	85.14	0.41	83.40	0.54	84.59	0.52
Morphological Upper Facial	MUFI	51.14	0.36	49.75	0.31	50.68	0.38
Eye divergence	EDI	33.15	0.22	33.85	0.29	33.86	0.25
Nasal	NI	71.45	0.73	71.52	0.75	70.96	0.71
Hand	HI	42.43	0.24	41.54	0.19	41.55	0.17

Table 9.4 : Test of Significance : Somatometric indices

Indices	BM × IM	IM × TM	BM × TM
SHVI	3.38*	1.05	4.37*
CI	1.14	1.45	0.45
LHI	2.24*	2.89*	0.94
BHI	3.15*	3.92*	1.30
TFPI	1.00	0.89	0.03
JFI	0.11	0.09	0.02
JMI	3.83*	1.14	2.79*
MFI	2.57*	1.59	0.83
MUFI	2.93*	1.90	0.88
EDI	1.92	0.03	2.13*
NI	0.07	0.54	0.48
HI	2.91*	0.04	2.99*

* indicates statistically significant at 5.0% probability.

Table 9.5 : Values of T^2 and their respective square roots for final values of overall distance

Population	T^2	T^2
BM × IM	4.63	2.15
IM × TM	2.05	1.43
BM × TM	4.14	2.03

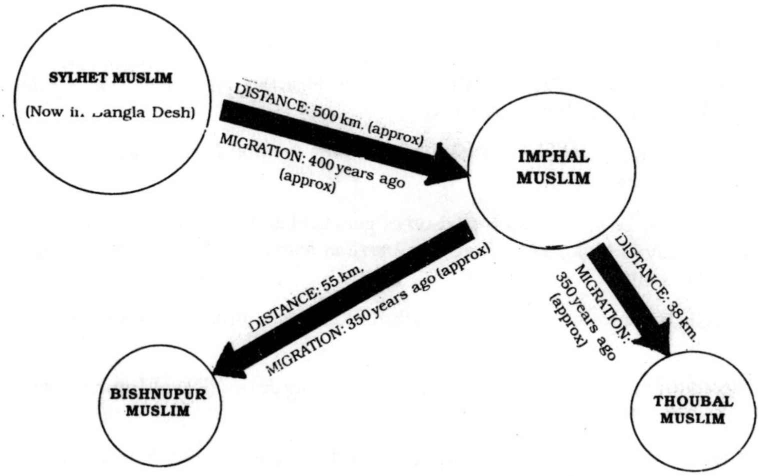

FIGURE 9.1
Migration pattern of Manipuri Muslims

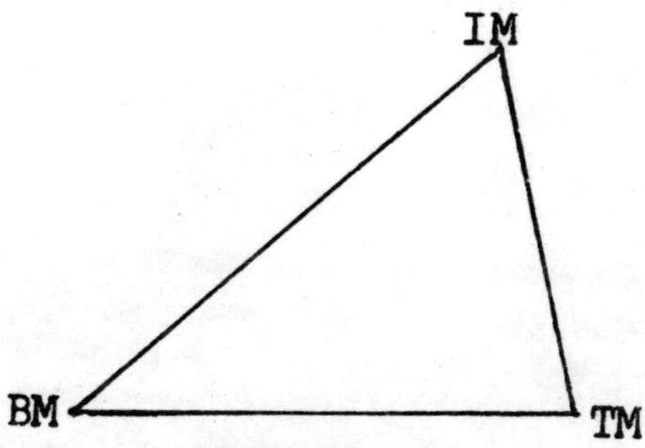

FIGURE 9.2
Diagramatic representation of distance configuration based on morphological distance

REFERENCES

BROWN, R., 1873, *Statistical Account of Manipur*, Calcutta.

CONSTANTINE, R., 1981, *Manipur : Maid of the Mountain*. New Delhi : Lancers Publications.

HODSON, T.C., 1908, *The Meiteis*. London : David Nutt.

HARRISON G.A.; A.J. BOYCE, 1972, *The Structure of Human Populations*. London : Oxford University Press.

MARTIN, R.; K. SALLER, 1956, *Lehrbuch der Anthropologie Band*. Stuttgart : Gustav Fischer Verlag.

SANGHVI, L.D., 1953, Comparison of genetical and morphological methods for a study of biological difference. *American Journal of Physical Anthropology*. 11 : 385 - 404.

SINGH, L; N.K. SINGH, 1967, *Cheitharol Kumbaba*. Imphal : Manipur Sahitya Parishad.

SINGH, O.B.; M.A. JANAB KHAN, 1973, *Nongshamei* (Puya) Imphal : M.J. Khan Hafij Hapta.

SINGH, R.K.S., 1985, *Pangal Thorakpa* (Muslim Immigration in Manipur) Imphal : Liberty Publishing Association.

10

Menarche and its Trend in North East India

Sarthak Sengupta

The age at menarche, which is defined as the occurrence of the first menstrual cycle indicates the sexual maturity of girls and marks the definite stage of uterine development. The reproductive life of women constitute by the period between menarche and menopause, i.e. complete non-occurrence of menstrual flow. The ovary probably sheds the first ovum about the time of menarche, but the process does not become established one until the age of 16 or 17 years (Jeffcoate, 1967). Such sterile period in human female after the onset of menarche is known as adolescent sterility (Montegu, 1957 ; Tanner, 1977). Results of research works reveal that both the onset of menarche and the period of adolescent sterility vary from population to population because of various factors like heredity, nutrition, ethnic, rural-urban living, latitude of the place, chronic disease etc.

There is considerable evidence indicating that the mean age at menarche of different ethnic groups varies. In North America, the average menarcheal age is 13.09 years, whereas in Middle and South America it is 13.80 years. The Asian girls (13.45 years) have a close approximation with the girls of the U.S.S.R. and Eastern Europe (13.42 years) as well as in Western Europe (13.63 years). It is interesting to note that there is considerable late onset of menarche among the girls of Africa (14.28 years).

A perusal of literature reveals that interest in the study on age at menarche of the Indian women dates back to 1845 when

Robertson made an investigation of puberty of Hindu women of Calcutta and Madras. Since then age at menarche has received considerable attention in all parts of our country and different investigators have studied this in different context. In North East India, studies on age at menarche have started very recently. In most of the studies the menarcheal age has been evaluated by retrospective method depending on recall and the number of subjects is sometimes very small. Recall age on menarche is subjected to unknown degree of bias. Comparable materials on the menarcheal age estimated by status-quo method are conspicuous by their absence.

The number of investigations already made in different states in India has been nicely summarised along with original data by Roberts et. al., (1977), Basu and Gupta (1979). Region-wise variation of menarcheal age in various Indian population as reported in these studies reveals that the lowest mean values of menarcheal age is observed by the population of Eastern region (12.83 years) who menstruate earliest of all. It is followed by the girls of Northern region (13.46 years) to Southern region (13.92 years) and finally to Western region (14.17 years) — the population menstruate later than the girls of the other three regions. Basu and Gupta (1979) observed a gradual rise in menarcheal age through Assam (12.61 years), Orissa (12.75 years), Uttar Pradesh (13.06 years), Bengal (13.13 years), Bombay (13.71 years), Andhra (13.82 years), Madras (13.89 years), Maharashtra (13.91 years), Punjab (13.93 years), Kerala (14.06 years) and Rajasthan (14.44 years). The menarcheal age at altitude in the Western Himalayas is more delayed (Singh and Thapar, 1983). It will be worthwhile to be mentioned here that the Rajput Bhotiya of Mana valley, Uttar Pradesh (16.38 years); Harijan (16.26 years), Rajput (15.78 years), Brahmin (15.37 years to 15.73 years) and Choudhury (15.26 years) of Shimla, Kangra and Kulu region; Tamang of North Bengal (15.90 years); Kabui of Manipur (15.15 years); Angami of Nagaland (15.00 years); Dawoodi Bohra of Rajasthan (14.88 years); Urban Gujarati girls (14.89 years); Christian Khasi of Meghalaya (14.60 years); Adi of Arunachal Pradesh (14.45 years) show a comparatively higher mean value of menarcheal age amongst the women of India.

In the present report an attempt has been made to present in details the mean age at menarche among females of various populations of North East India. This paper is the part of an extended study devoted to bio-anthropological investigation on people of North East India.

In North East India, population variation in mean age at menarche have been studied first by Rakshit (1960). Amongst the studies conducted in this field mention may be made of those by Nag (1965), Das and Das (1967), Srivastava and Goswami (1968), Duara (1969), Bhowmik et. al., (1971), Deka (1976), Das et. al., (1980), Jaswal and Jaswal (1981), Sengupta (1982, 1985), Devi and Singh (1982), Barua and Das (1983), Das (1983-1086), Das and Sengupta (1984), Devi (1984-1985), Devi (1985), Suri (1985), Das (1985) and Chakravarty (1986). There is a considerable variability among these samples.

The population of North East India may conveniently be grouped under the following categories, the basis for the grouping is on or the other factors like concept of purity and pollution among different castes, linguistic affinity, cultural similarity and common territory. Similar attempts were also made by Das (1970). The mean age at menarche increases from pooled sample of Manipuri Muslim (11.59 years) to Naga groups (14.58 years) through Other Backward Caste communities of Assam (12.40 years), Tai Mongoloid groups (12.69 years), upper caste Hindus of Assam (12.81 years), Tea Garden Communities (12.83 years), Baro and allied groups (12.84 years), Scheduled Castes of Assam (12.89 years), Arunachalis (12.90 years), Assamese Muslim (13.06 years), Metei (13.69 years) and Khasi population (13.88 years). It is evident that there is a good deal of variation between the two Muslim communities of Manipur and Assam.

A cursory glance at Table 10.1 reveals that studies on the population of Assam have received much attention in comparison to the population in other States of North East India. There is an identifiable tendency for the population of Brahmaputra Valley (both Indid and Mongoloids) to be comparatively early maturers. A good nutritional level plus avoidence of infections and other childhood diseases can lead to an early menarche.

Further work in this line would help to confirm the above fact. From the comparative table (Table 1) it is evident that among the populations of North East India, the Muslim of Manipur state (Chakravarti 1986) exhibit the lowest (10.73 years) average menarcheal age while, the same researcher (Chakravarti 1986) report the average age at menarche to be 15.15 years among the Kabui of Manipur, which happens to be the highest ever reported age at menarche in North East India.

The studies in the North Eastern region have shown that the females belong to Mongoloid groups (mostly tribes) experience menarche at a later age than the Caucasoid (caste) population. Das and Sengupta (1984) reported that the caste Hindus are similar to each other, but they differ significantly from low castes and Muslims. Same is also observed in case of low castes, who also differ from the Muslims. The difference in menarcheal age between rural and urban women are well known and has been reported from this part of India (Nag 1965, Barua and Das 1983, Das and Sengupta 1984, Das 1983-1986). In the rural area and poorer sample mean age at menarche is comparatively higher than in the urban richer. Socio-economic status is very closely linked with nutritional pattern of a population. Deficient nutrition may be attributed for such high menarcheal age. Important dimensions like socio-economic level of family, family type, birth order, family size and religion on age at menarche have also been considered in several studies reported from North East India.

The problem of relatively higher incidence of menarche in winter months and a lower incidence in summer as reported by Valsik (1934), Eagle and Shelesnyak (1934) has also been confirmed by Devi and Singh (1982) among the Meitei and Brahman population of Manipur. Deka (1976) reports late onset of menarche in women homozygous for haemoglobin E as compared to normal heterozygotes and homozygotes. The relationship between altitude and age at menarche has also been a topic of interest. Studies from North East India support that the women from plains had comparatively earlier age at menarche as compared to females of comparatively higher altitudes. A very interesting study is that of Das (personal communication) who in her investigation of Assamese girls from Lower Assam observed a close relationship between age at menarche and body build. Such observation however, is no longer debatable because it is a well established fact that the period of menarche is the age of maximal rate of growth.

There is a number of studies on adolescent sterility interval. It has been reported that (Bhattacharya, et al., 1977) the mean adolescent sterility among the Bengali is 25.98 ± 2.43 months. Sen (1953) reports that such period among the upper caste Bengali is 29.89 ± 1.96 months and among the Bagdi population as 2.70 years. Rakshit (1960) found it among the Maharashtrian Brahmin as 2.53 years. However, there are no such studies as yet to commence on it from the population of North East India.

Montegu (1945) is of opinion that menarche before 12 years of age is abnormal. However, his hypothesis was critically examined by different scholars. Many questions were raised later on. It has been reported that the range of such abnormality in eastern India varies from 3 to 14 per cent (Bhattacharya, et al., 1977) with an overall frequency of 7 per cent. They estimated the rate among the Banik (13.64%), Brahmin (10.20%), Vaidya (7.70%), Teli (8.30%), Muslim (9.50%) and the Kayastha (5.37%), population of West Bengal. In another study Sen (1953) observed such abnormality as 10-12 per cent in case of upper caste Bengali population. In Assam, Deka (1976) reported such trends in Kachari (18.50%) population. Studies carried out by Das and Sengupta (1984) provide such comparative information from Brahmin (4.94%), Kalita (3.74%), Kumar (7.26%), Jogi (16.35%) and Kaibarta (18.00%), while Das (1983-1986) reported the information again from Brahmin (16.75%), Kalita (16.33%), pooled Assamese Castes (22.64%) and Ahom (6.49%) population of Brahmaputra valley, Assam. Further, such abnormality rate is as high as 25.26% among the Ahom of Assam (Sengupta 1985), 15.00% among the Apatani of Arunachal Pradesh (Jaswal and Jaswal, 1981), 29.55% among the Muslim girls of Manipur (Devi 1984-1985). Thus, the population of North East India, exhibit a wide range of variation with regard to such abnormality.

It has been observed that there is a general trend of change in menarcheal age through time. Downward trend in menarcheal age is one of the most significant findings of the present era. A secular increase or decrease in age at menarche has been noted in many parts of the world. It is interesting to note that in Western countries the average menarcheal age is gradually decreasing. In Germany, a decrease of 1.7 years is observed within a period of 80 years (between 1860 and 1940). In Sweden the average rate is 10 days per annum, whereas in Japan the rate is 1 year in a period of 8 years. In India the same trend is also observed. Sarkar and Roychoudhury (1968), Banerjee and Das (1978) observe that the average age at menarche of Bengali girls of Calcutta is going down at the rate of 5 to 5.7 days per annum. Among the Brahmins of Maharashtra, in a period of 12 years (1962 to 1974) a decrease of 0.53 years was observed. On the contrary, as reported by Bhattacharya et. al. (1977) the mean age at menarche of the Brahmin, Kayastha and Vaidyas of Bengal have slightly gone up in comparison to the mean values of Sen (1953). However, while comparing with Curjels data (1920) on average menarcheal age among the Hindu and Muslim women, it indicates downward trend in the mean age at menarche. Further, secular trend concerning the menarche in Punjabi women is seen to exist between the mothers and their daughters (Bakshi et. al., 1978).

In North East India it is seen that only a few study of the same population is done after a lapse of some years. As in other regions, in North East India the mean age at menarche has shifted to higher ages and the increase is quite substantial in the Brahmin, Kayastha and the Kalita in between a period of 25 years (i.e. during the period 1960 to 1984). Increase in age at menarche has been noted in Brahmin (0.03 years per annum), Kayastha (0.02 years per annum). Kalita (0.03 years per annum), whereas, contrary to the above gradual decrease in the case of Christian Khasi (0.04 years per annum), Non Christian Khasi (0.03 years per annum), Kaibarta (0.03 years per annum) and Muslims of Assam (0.02 years per annum) are perceptible. This is in conformity with the study of Pattanayak (1971), who observed an increase of 1.30 years from mothers and daughters of three upper castes of Orissa, while a decrease of 0.77 years was observed in daughters from the study of Dawoodi Bohra Muslim mothers and daughters of Udaipur (Basu and Gupta, 1977). Similar type of survey in many more populations are yet to be screened in order to confirm the trend.

Menarche is a developing milestone. A knowledge of average age at menarche is essential for various reasons like growth and nutritional study, to understand the interplay between biogenetic endowment and environment, in formulating social laws relating to age at marriage and the like. In North East India, many of the populations are yet to be studied from this angle. These call for investigation on age at menarche indifferent populations for better understanding.

Table 10.1 : Mean age at menarche among various populations of North East India

State	Population	Number	Mean	± S.E.	Source
Arunachal Pradesh	Adi	109	14.45	0.98	Duara, 1969
	Singpho	95	12.59	0.15	Kar & Mahanta, 1975
	Apatani	219	13.40	0.08	Jaswal & Jaswal, 1981
Assam	Brahmin	60	12.46	0.12	Rakshit, 1960
	Brahmin	26	12.51	0.11	Das & Das, 1967
	Brahmin	26	11.85		Srivastava and Goswami, 1968
	Brahmin	170	13.59		Das et. al., 1980
	Brahmin	81	13.23	0.07	Das & Sengupta, 1984
	Brahmin	191	12.53	0.08	Das, 1983-1986
	Kayastha	32	12.45	0.20	Rakshit, 1960
	Kayastha	11	12.00		Srivastava and Goswami, 1968
	Kayastha	122	13.07	0.04	Das & Sengupta, 1984
	Kalita	17	12.12	0.25	Rakshit, 1960
	Kalita	172	12.61	0.14	Das & Das, 1967
	Kalita	20	11.32		Srivastava and Goswami, 1968
	Kalita	289	13.14		Das et. al., 1980
	Kalita	107.	12.79	0.04	Das & Sengupta, 1984

(Continued)

State	Population	Number	Mean	± S.E.	Source
	Kalita	300	12.51	0.07	Das, 1983-1986
	Baishya	35	12.97	0.12	Das & Das, 1967
	Kumar	55	12.49	0.08	Das & Sengupta, 1984
	Jogi	55	12.31	0.08	Das & Sengupta, 1984
	Kaibarta	30	12.89	0.12	Das & Das, 1967
	Kaibarta	245	12.98		Das et. al., 1980
	Kaibarta	50	12.44	0.10	Das & Sengupta, 1984
	Other Caste	106	12.28	0.09	Das, 1983-1986
	Muslim	29	13.35	0.14	Rakshit, 1960
	Muslim	319	13.09		Das et. al, 1980
	Muslim	74	12.84	0.04	Das & Sengupta, 1984
	Ahom	50	11.65		Srivastava and Goswami, 1968
	Ahom	264	12.96	0.60	Gogoi, 1972
	Ahom	66	12.29		Das et. al., 1980
	Ahom	194	12.60	0.12	Sengupta, 1982
	Ahom	77	12.83	0.12	Das, 1983-1986
	Mishing	82	12.68		Das et. al., 1980
	Mishing	355	12.26	0.08	Bujarbarua and Das (Unpub.)
	Mikir	52	12.75	0.18	Khatoniar, 1972
	Sonowal	200	12.77	0.12	Deka, 1976
	Moran	67	13.51		Das et. al., 1980
	Chutiya	62	12.54		Das et. al., 1980
	Deori	77	13.03		Das et. al., 1980
	Lalung	51	12.36	0.06	Das et. al., 1980
	Turung	32	13.06	0.20	Das, 1985
	Khamiyang	40	12.80	0.13	Das, 1985
	Santhal	200	13.24	0.12	Bujarbarua (Unpub.)
	Munda	200	12.42	0.10	Bujarbarua (Unpub.)

(Continued)

State	Population	Number	Mean	± S.E.	Source
Manipur	Brahmin	65	12.45	0.08	Devi & Singh, 1982
	Meitei	161	12.77	0.04	Devi & Singh, 1982
	Meitei	410	13.28	0.04	Devi, 1985
	Meitei	487	14.34		Chakravarti, 1986
	Muslim	450	12.35	0.04	Devi, 1984-1985
	Muslim	402	10.73		Chakravarti, 1986
	Kabui	484	15.15		Chakravarti, 1986
	Tangkhul	307	13.93		Chakravarti, 1986
Meghalaya	Christian Khasi	119	14.6		Nag, 1965
	Christian Rural Khasi	155	13.9	0.06	Barua & Das, 1983
	Christian Urban Khasi	161	13.8	0.06	Barua & Das, 1983
	Non-Christian Khasi	131	14.1		Nag, 1965
	Non-Christian Rural Khasi	160	13.7	0.07	Barua & Das, 1983
	Non-Christian Urban Khasi	165	13.6	0.06	Barua & Das, 1983
Nagaland	Zemi Naga	214	14.13		Bhowmik et al., 1971
	Angami	50	15.0		Suri, 1985

REFERENCES

BAKSHI, R.; R. SINGH; I.P. SINGH, 1978, Secular trend in age at menarche in Punjabis. *Proceedings of Xth International Congress of Anthropological and Ethnological Sciences.* (Abstract Number 11) Volume 1 : 5.

BANERJEE, A.R.; S. DAS, 1978, Menarcheal age in Calcutta. *Proceedings of Xth International Congress of Anthropological and Ethnological Sciences.* (Abstract No. 14) Volume 1 : 6.

BASU, S.K.; P. GUPTA, 1979, Menarche and its trend in India. *Indian Journal of Physical Anthropology and Human Genetics.* 5, 1 : 27 - 42.

BHATTACHARJEE, S; S. CHATTERJEE; S.K. BHATTACHARJEE, 1977, Menarcheal age in some endogamous groups of Bengal, India. *Journal of Indian Anthropological Society*. 12 : 60 - 68.

BHOWMIK, K.L.; M.K. CHOUDHURY; K.R. CHOUDHURY, 1971, *Fertility of Zemi women of Nagaland*. Calcutta, Institute of Social Change.

CHAKRAVARTY, R., 1986, *People of Manipur*. B.R. Publishing Corporation Vivekanand Nagar, Delhi.

CURJEL, D.F., 1920, The Reproductive life of some Indian Women. *Indian Journal of Medical Research*. 8 : 366 - 369.

DAS, B., 1985, Fertility and Mortality differentials among the Khamiyang and Turung population of Jorhat district, Assam. *Journal of Assam Science Society*. 28 : 14 - 19.

DAS, B.M., 1970, *Anthropometry of the Tribal Groups of Assam, India*. Field Research Project. Edited by Henry Field, Coconut Groove, Miami, Florida.

DAS, B.M.; P.B. DAS; R. DAS, 1980, *Biosocial Profile of the Five Mongoloid Populations of Assam*. (Mimeographed U.G.C. Sponsored Research Report), Anthropology Department, Gauhati University.

DAS, B.M.; S. SENGUPTA, 1984, Age at menarche among rural Assamese women. *The Journal of Assam Science Society*. 27, 1 : 6 - 13.

DAS, P.B.; B.M. DAS, 1967, Age at menarche of Kalita girls of Assam. *Man In India*. 47, 2 : 113 - 117.

DAS, P.B., 1983 - 1986, Variation in age at menarche of Assamese girls, *Gauhati University Journal of Science*. 29, 2 : 1 - 8.

DEKA, R., 1976, Age at menarche and haemoglobin E among the Kachari women of upper Assam. *Man In India*. 56, 4 : 349.

DEVI, S., 1984 - 1985, The age at menarche among the Muslim girls of Manipur. *Bulletin of the Department of Anthropology, Dibrugarh University*. 13 - 14 : 111 - 116.

DEVI, S.; K.S. SINGH, 1982, The age at menarche in the Meitei and Brahmin girls of Manipur. *Man In India*. (Cited from Devi, 1984 - 1985).

DUARA, A., 1969, *A study on certain aspects of demography among the Adi of Mirbuk Village, N.E.F.A.* (Unpublished M.Sc. dissertation), Anthropology Department, Dibrugarh University, Assam.

GOGOI, D., 1972, Menarche and Menopause among women of an Ahom village in upper Assam. *Bulletin of the Department of Anthropology, Dibrugarh University*. 1 : 18 - 22.

JASWAL, I.J.S.; S. JASWAL, 1981, Age at menarche among the Apatani of Arunachal Pradesh. *Bulletin of the Department of Anthropology Dibrugarh University*. 10 : 55 - 60.

JEFFCOATE, T.N.A., 1967, *Principle of Gynaecology*, Butterworth and Co. Ltd. (3rd edition) : 70.

KAR, R.K.; S. MAHANTA, 1975, Menarche and menopause among the Singpho women of Arunachal Pradesh. *Indian Journal of Physical Anthroplogy and Human Genetics.* 1 : 51 - 57.

KHATONIAR, A., 1972, *Demographic study of the Mikir of Assam.* Unpublished M.Sc. dissertation, Anthropology Department, Dibrugarh University.

MONTEGU, M.F.A., 1945, *Adolescent Sterility.* Charles C.Thomas, Illinois.

MONTEGU, M.F.A., 1957, *The Reproductive Development of the Female.* The Julian Press, New York.

NAG, M., 1965, Effect of Christianity on few aspects of Khasi Culture. *Bulletin of the Department of Anthropology, Government of India.* 14 : 1 - 34.

PATTANAIK, B., 1971, Age at menarche among the urban upper caste of Orissa. *Man In India.* 51 : 217 - 222.

RAKSHIT, S., 1960, A short note on menarcheal age of Assamese girls. *Man In India.* 40 : 52 - 55.

RAKSHIT, S., 1962, Reproductive life of Maharashtrian Brahmin. *Man In India.* 56 : 65 - 70.

ROBERTS, D.F.; S. CHINN.; B. GIRIJA.; H.D. SINGH, 1977, A study of menarcheal age in India. *Annals of Human Biology* 4 : 171 - 177.

ROBERTSON, J., 1845, On the period of puberty in Hindu women. *Edinburg Medical and Surgical Journal.* 64 : 156 - 159 and 257 - 264.

SARKAR, S.S.; J. ROY, 1968, The secular trend of menarcheal age in the city girls of Calcutta. *Man In India.* 48, 4 : 349 - 356.

SEN, T., 1953, Reproductive life of some Indian women. *Man In India.* 33 : 31-54.

SENGUPTA, S., 1985, Note sur les L'Age a la puberte des filles Ahom du Haut-Assam, Inde. *Bulletin et Memoires de la societe d'Anthropologie de Paris.* 2, 14, 1 : 55 - 58.

SINGH, L.; M. THAPAR, 1983, Age at menarche among the Bhotias of Mana Valley. *Anthropologischer Anzeiger.* 41 : 259 - 262.

SRIVASTAVA, R.P.; M. GOSWAMI, 1968, The Menarcheal age of Assamese girls. *The Anthropologist.* 15, 1 - 2 : 57 - 60.

SURI, R., 1985, *Physical Anthroplogy of the Angami Naga - A tribe of North East India.* Unpublished Ph. D Thesis. Anthropology Department, Gauhati University.

TANNER, J.M., 1977, 'Human Growth and Constitution'. In *Human Biology.* Edited by G.A. Harrison, J. S. Weiner, J.M. Tanner, N.A. Barnicot. Oxford University Press.

11
Development of Traditional Democratic Institution in Arunachal Pradesh

P.C. Dutta

Introduction

The vast landmass of nearly 84,000 Sq. K.M. in the North East of the country — now known as the state of Arunachal Pradesh, is the home land of some 25 major tribal groups who are included broadly in the racial classification of Indo-Mongoloid. They together contribute to the 69.82 per cent of the total population (6,31,339 as per 1981 census). The contributors to this population are the Monpas, Akas, Sherdukpens, Mijis, Khowas, Sulungs, Nishis, Apatanis, Hill Miris, Tagins, Nas, Adis (with 15 sub-groups), Khambas, Membas, Mishmis (with three groups), Khamtis, Singphos, Zakhrings, Tangsas, Noctes, Wanchos, Lisus, Mishings, Deuris and Mikirs. The last three groups are, however, yet to receive recognition as Arunachal Tribes.

Although the area remained as hidden land till the advent of the British in 1875, available sources of information indicate that Arunachal Pradesh is an ancient land. Testimony to this nomenclature is still borne by the existence of very many ancient ruins of monuments all along the foothill belt bordering the state of Assam. Parasuram Kunda in Lohit Valley, Bhismaknagar Forte and Palace, Padum Pukhuri, Rukmini Nati, Tamreswari temple in Dibang Valley, Malinithan, Basudevthan, Akahsi Ganga,

Ghagra-than in West Siang, Itafort in Lower Subansiri, Noksaparbat and Bhalukpung in East and West Kameng, Longput in Tirap and Buddhist stupa in Vijay Nagar are some of the archaeological monuments bearing testimony of ancient civilization dating back from ninth/tenth to 14th/15th Century. Authentic sources of information are although not very many, yet whatever materials are available amply justify the contention.

Due to lack of proper knowledge it was widely believed hitherto that the indigenous inhabitants of the area were aweful people without any civilization. But this general belief was entirely unfounded, because all the different tribes had their own civilization even prior to their interaction with people of the rest of the country. Under the scope of the subject matter in the present article an attempt has been made to trace how the present democratic setup has evolved in this part of the country, and whether there was any base on the soil itself for such innovation.

For the sake of convenience, the subject may be dealt broadly under two headings, i.e. (a) traditional or indigenous system and (b) the modern statutory system.

The Traditional or Indigenous System

The dictionary meaning of the word *'Democracy'* is "a form of government in which the supreme power is vested in the people collectively and is administered by them or by officers appointed by them, a state of society characterised by recognition of equality of rights and privileges". From this point of view we may say that 'democracy' is the fundamental characteristics of almost all the tribes of Arunachal Pradesh. Each tribal group of Arunachal Pradesh has their own traditional system of administration of the society, maintenance of law and order, and socio-cultural life of the people. The systems are in most cases institutionalised in the form of village councils of elders, called differently by different tribes such as *Tsorgens* of the Monpas, *Jung* of the Sherdukpen, *Mele* of the Akas, *Buliang* of the Apatanis, *Ging dungs* of the Nishis, *Kebang* of the Adis, *Abbala* of the Idu Mishmis, *Pharai* of Kaman Mishmis, *Mokchup* of the Khamti, *Ngothun* of the Noctes, *Wangsu-Wangsa* of the Wanchos and so on. We may make a brief survey of the various institutions of democracy of the people of Arunachal Pradesh.

The Monpas — one of the largest tribe inhabiting present West Kameng and Tawang districts have had well developed village self governing institutions almost similar to the *Kebang* of the Adis, in the shape of *Tsobla* and *Tsorgens*. The genesis of the system can be traced back to the 11th century when Tawang valley was converted to Buddhism. Some change to the system was made in the 16th century. As a matter of fact Monpa *Tsorgens* are elected chiefs for the maintenance of law and order and welfare of the people. The system underwent further change in the 19th century when the British -Monpa relations were formalized in 1844. Number of elected *Tsorgens* was increased and autonomous elected village councils established. Election of the *Tsorgens* is very systematic and can be well compared with the present day election system.

The Sherdukpen *Jung* is consisted of the village head man, as chairman, few members, one courier and a *chowkidar*. It decides cases by general consensus of opinion although the head man gives the final decision. Ultimate responsibility lies with the headman. The courier and the *chowkidar* have their own duties and responsibilities to be discharged for the village.

Aka *Mele* is popularly called *'Raiz'* (an Assamese term). Like the Sherdukpen *Jung* the *Mele* is constituted of *Gaonburah* (headman), his two juniors, *borah* and *gibba* and the members of the community. The function of the *Mele* is also similar.

The Bugun (Khowa) village council consists of the chiefs of the village, representative of the clans and two watchmen. The council meet in specified hall meant for the purpose. The chief of the village has all the powers and authority and represents the village in all matters and occasions.

The *Buliang* of the Apatanis is a council of clan representative but it does not have the centralized authority to wield power over all the inhabitants. The Apatani *Buliang* have three tier system—such as :

(i) *Akha Buliang* - Principal leaders.
(ii) *Yapa Buliang* - Middle aged men.
(iii) *Ajang Buliang* - Youngman.

Here the system is interesting in that while the *Akha Buliang* — consisting of the principal and aged members acts as the paramount consulting authority, the *Yapa* and *Ajang Buliang* on the other hand are somewhat subordinate to *Akha Buliang*. *Yapa Buliang* carry on the day-to-day affairs of the village and also decide disputes. It is however obligatory on the part of the *Yapa Buliang* to keep the *Akha Buliang* informed of all developments in the village. The *Ajang Buliang* are like messengers and assistants of the *Yapa Buliang*. They are also leaders and spokesman of the younger generation. The authority of the *Buliangs* is, however, limited. Complicated matters which may disturb the people's economy and pattern of living are always settled by formal treatise of friendship called *dapo*.

Unlike the village councils of other tribes — the institution of *Gingdungs* of the Nishis — is nothing but a middle man who tries to settle matters by peaceful negotiation on the basis of traditional customs matters and norms of the society. The *Gingdungs* do not have any power to exert while settling dispute but his wise counsel is universally accepted if found satisfactory by the parties at dispute. And in general the *Gingdungs* succeed.

Kebang of the Adis are well known indigenous institution of local self government. As Roy (1966) has described Adi *Kebang* "in true sense, a government by the people and for the people". The *Kebang* exercises the highest legal and judicial powers. While each Adi village has a *Kebang* (*Bango* = groups of villages). Similarly disputes between *bangos* is selected by another superior body called *Bogum-Bokang*, an institution formed at the instance of the Government. The system prevalent can be described as three-tier system.

Idu Mishmi *Abbala* — decides only judicial matters according to the customary laws. They however do not have any authority for village administration. Kaman Mishmis *Pharai* on the other hand is a council of elders — the members of which represent various clans.

Kmamti *Mokchup* also called *Mokchup-Khai-Kham* acts on the basis of laws, procedures and rules of morality and religion as laid down in their sacred text — *Thamasat*, and interpreted by the members of the council.

Ngothun and *Wangsu* — *Wangsa* of the Noctes and Wanchos are also well organised village council of elders. Although chieftainship is prevalent among both the tribes, the system of administration of justice and management of village affairs is quite democratic in the sense that the chiefs do not rule arbitrarily but not on the advice and counsel of the village elders.

Thus we have seen that the tribes of Arunachal Pradesh have their own system of local self government followed by them since time immemorial. The genesis of the system is almost obscure and no authentic source is available to trace and confirm it. But the fact remains that the peaceful way the various groups of people have been maintaining their socio-cultural, religious and political life ever since the time beyond memory amply justify existence of some system of local self government, adopted by the people and following through the ages.

The way of functioning of the councils of the various tribes is almost universal and some common features are inherent in all. Elwin (1965) has given a good account of the common features of the councils and their way of functioning. I quote -

"All the councils have certain features in common. They all derive their authority from ancient times and the fact that they are the expression of the will and power of the whole people. They are supported not only by social, but also by supernatural, sanctions and to give false evidence, for example, may call down the vengeance of the gods as well as excite the scorn of men. Sacrifices are commonly offered to avert supernatural dangers, to implore the devine blessing on the councils deliberations, and to bring peace between the contending parties."

"All the councils are informal in character and except for the Monpa councils and the Adi *Bangoes*, which seem to be more highly organised, the conception of regular membership, committees, secretaries and so on has not yet come in. The people composing the councils are the accepted leaders of a village and always include the local priest, whose services are often required, and, of course, the officially appointed headman who are issued with red coats."

Anyone, unless he is excommunicated, can attend and speak, though there are some tribes, such as Nishis (Daflas) who do not allow their women to do so.

Decisions are not taken by a formal vote but discussion continues until general unanimity is achieved.

The idea of 'electing people' is not yet familiar, though the Monpas are reported as having some sort of election.

Some tribes have what may be called a junior branch of the council. The *Ajang Buliang* of the Apatanis, the *Moshup* or *Dere* boys of the Adis, the *Morung* boys of the Wanchos and Noctes have always played an important part in looking after their villages, maintaining paths, helping in cultivation, providing simple relief service: the northern Adis have a sort of fire-protection unit, staffed by these boys.

Describing the nature of function, Elwin further writes—"the function of the village councils are threefold—judicial, administrative and developmental. On the judicial side the councils settle the disputes within the village boundaries and considerable powers have been given to them under the Assam Frontier (Administration of Justice) Regulation of 1945. Even serious crimes against tribal society (but not against Government) have been and are being settled, generally to the satisfaction of all concerned, by these councils. Probably, to the tribal mind, this is the most important of the council's functions.

On the administrative side, the councils deal with the maintenance of paths and bridges; they see to the water supply and sanitation of a village; they fix the dates of communal hunting and fishing and decide when the main agricultural operations should take place and when festivals should be held. Some of them make it their business to care for the poor and the disabled. There is no rule about this, and much depends upon the nature of leading men of any particular council.

Similarly with regard to development, this depends largely on the extent to which the local officials have worked through the local councils in planning all the many-sided work of developing the country. There is endless scope for this and generally, when the council as such is approached by an official the response is enthusiastic.

Roy has also recorded how the proceedings of the Adi *Kebang* is started with a traditional speech. It runs like this—

"Oh villagers and brethren, let us strengthen our customs and our council, let us improve our regulations; let us make the law straight and equal for all. Let the leaders who can speak best stand up and speak out for our betterment; let them speak out in a bold voice unabashed and undaunted like a cock crowing. Let our laws be uniform; let our customs be the same for all. Let us not decide differently for different persons; let us be guided by reasons and see that justice is done and a compromise reached that is acceptable to both the parties. Let us keep nothing pending, let us decide while the dispute is fresh, lest small disputes grow big and continue for a long time. Let the fine be levied reasonably. Let it be commensurate with the guilt and be just. Poverty should have compassion and justice be tempered with mercy. We have met in this sacred place of justice; we have come together for a council-meeting and let us speak in one voice and decide on one verdict. Here are the iron pots and brass pots brought by the accuser and the accused; here stands the mithun. So let us decide and met our justice so that all these go to him who is in the right."

From the excerpts quoted above it is quite evident that the institution of village councils as prevalent among the various tribal groups of Arunachal Pradesh are really democratic in the true sense of the term. They function in a very systematic way according to the norms, rules and procedure laid down by tradition. I have the opportunity of witnessing Wancho and Nocte village councils in session when I did my field study among them some thirtytwo years ago. Almost the same procedure as that of the Adi *Kebang* narrated by Roy is followed by the Noctes and Wanchos also in conducting the sessions. Among both the tribes the chief of the village preside over the meetings of the village council. They, however, have specific functionaries for specific duty in the council such as messenger, deviner, *handique* (equivalent to Minister), priest and so on. On the basis of the consensus of opinion of the members of the council the chief pronounces his final verdict. As has been believed by many people — Nocte and Wancho chiefs are not autocratic rulers but they are quite democratic in their attitude, behaviour and functioning.

With this background of the traditional system let us now examine how the modern (i.e. statutory) system of democracy found its way into Arunachal Pradesh.

Modern or Statutory System

Unlike some other tribal areas of the country — introduction of the modern system of democracy in Arunachal Pradesh was not very difficult. The foundation was already there inherent in the various societies of the people. It was only a matter of some marginal changes here and there and adjustment to suit the necessary requirement. Introduction of Panchayat Raj was felt necessary for building up an administrative infrastructure of an all India pattern. At the initial stage recommendation was made some time in 1960 by the Committees for Special Multipurpose Tribal Block for revival of the existing council of the people, instead of imposing statutory Panchayat for very many reasons. The Dhebar Commission (1960-1961) also made similar recommendation. But afterwards the Committee on Plan Project — constituted by the Government of India under the chairmanship of late Daying Ering, had recommended for introduction of Panchayat Raj in Arunachal Pradesh.

The Ering Committee recommended a representative form of government through establishment of four-tier Panchayat system. This committee also suggested for retention of the indigenous system and to conduct the election according to tribal custom. The four-tier system of Ering Committee includes—

(i) Village council at village level
(ii) Anchal Samity at circle level
(iii) Zilla Parishad at District level and
(iv) Agency Council at the top with 20 elected members.

The Ering Committee's recommendations were accepted and Panchayat Raj was introduced in Arunachal Pradesh under a regulation entitled "North East Frontier Agency—Panchayat Raj Regulation 1967. The inauguration of the system was, however, done on the third day of December, 1969 by the Governor of Assam at Shillong. Thus the edifice of an indigenous representative government was built up in Arunachal Pradesh.

This system through passage of time underwent some changes according to the necessity of time and situation. The former North East Frontier Agency was converted into an Union Territory with a new name Arunachal Pradesh — on the 20th day of January, 1972 following promulgation of the Act entitled North Eastern Areas (Reorganization) Act of 1971. Alongwith this change the Agency Council was also renamed as Pradesh Council. It was headed as Chairman by the Chief Commissioner. The administration of the area was vested on the Chief Commissioner. The Act also provided one seat each in Rajya Sabha and Lok Sabha respectively for the Union Territory to be filled by nomination by the President of India. Some changes were made afterwards in the manner of selection of members for the two supreme bodies of the country.

In the Pradesh Council — the executive counsellors nominated by the Chief Commissioner got opportunity to function as chairman in some sessions of the councils, which was a new innovation made by the Chief Commissioner, with a view to provide opportunity and scope for participation and training in decision making by the representatives of the people.

In 1975, the Pradesh Council was converted into a Provisional Legislative Assembly for Arunachal Pradesh. The Independence Day of 1975 brought a new change to the highest decision making body of the Union Territory. The Pradesh Council was converted into a Legislative Assembly with provision of or 30 elected members and three nominated members. The office of the Chief Commissionership was replaced by the Lt. Governor. The Executive Councillors were constituted into a Council of Ministers headed by a Chief Minister who is also the leader of the House.

This accelerated development in the political history of the areas began only after the Independence. The people for the first time directly participated in the general election in February, 1978 to elect their representative to the Assembly.

Chowdhury (1982) observes— "The apprehensions expressed by certain scholars about possible adverse impact of the quick administrative and political changes on the tribal societies of Arunachal Pradesh have not been fulfilled. The people have responded to the democratic process enthusiastically, and have shown enough maturity in adopting to rather speedy constitutional changes. Arunachal has already gone through two general elections alongwith the rest of the country and has already witnessed smooth and democratic changes of governments". The third general election was held in 1984 and the government formed and Assembly constituted with the elected members are still continuing. During this period another significant development is conversion of the Union Territory into a fullfledged State on the 20th February, 1984 with a provision of 60 elected members. The spectacular changes in the socio-political and administrative aspects in Arunachal Pradesh is unique in the whole country.

It may be noted that there in Arunachal Pradesh tradition and modernity, old and new, are marching hand in hand in the path towards progress, peace and prosperity. The traditional village councils are not finding a strong rivalry in the statutory system. Instead it has become a source of inspiration for continuance. It may however be said that the field of operation of the traditional institutions has undergone some changes due to introduction of the new system. The people of Arunachal Pradesh are tradition bound and they regard and respect their traditional system. It is a universal truth that tradition die hard, and this maxim is well applicable in respect of the people of Arunachal

Pradesh. The modern institutions of democracy may takeover some of the fields of operation such as administration and development, but the socio-cultural traits inherent in the society will always remain within the period of the traditional councils.

Arunachal's march on the path of progress from merely a frontier tract to a fullfledged State within a short span of time must be said to be unparallel in the history of civilization of any people.

REFERENCES

BARUAH, T.K.M., 1960, *The Idu Mishmis*, Shillong : North East Frontier Agency Administration.

BARUAH, T.K.M., 1977, *The Singphos and their Religion*. Shillong : Directorate of Research, Government of Arunachal Pradesh.

CHOWDHURY, J.N., 1973, *Arunachal Panorama*, Shillong : Directorate of Research, Arunachal Pradesh.

DUTTA, P.C., 1959, *The Tangsas*, Shillong : Directorate of Information and Public Relations, North East Frontier Agency.

DUTTA, P.C., 1978, *The Noctes*, Shillong : Directorate of Research, Arunachal Pradesh.

ELWIN, V., 1965, *Democracy in N.E.F.A.*, Shillong : Directorate of Research, Government of Arunachal Pradesh.

FURER HEIMENDORF, C. VON, 1980, *A Himalayan Tribe : From Cattle to Cash*. New Delhi : Vikas Publications.

MOHANTA, B., 1984, *Administrative Development of Arunachal Pradesh*.

ROY, S., 1966, *Aspects of Padam Minyong Culture*. Shillong : North East Frontier Agency Administration.

SHARMA, R.R.P., 1961, *The Sherdukpen*. Shillong : Research Department, North East Frontier Agency Administration.

SHUKLA, B.K., 1959, *The Daflas of the Subansiri Region*, Shillong : Research Department, N.E.F.A. Administration.

SINHA, R., 1962, *The Akas*, Shillong : Research Department, North East Frontier Agency Administration.

12

Enforced Change Resulting a Break in Highland Trade : A Study on the Tawang Monpas of Arunachal Pradesh

Bibhash Dhar

Social change and modernization is a subject which is relatively new among the studies in anthropology in the developing countries. The plural society of India has allured the scholars and investigators from the country as well as from outside to study and record the aspect of change leading to modernization under various impacts. The real strength of the country was on its innumerable villages and the economy largely based on agriculture. Even two hundred years of colonial rule in India failed to change the basic structure of the Indian society.

Cohn (1968 : 3) made a similar observation, "Relatively speaking, British domination until the middle of the nineteenth century had little direct effect on Indian social, economic and cultural life". However, it was only after the entry of forces like industrialization and the urbanization factor of modernization in the later part of the colonial rule changes were visible and felt in the different aspects of the socio-cultural life of the people. This, however, does not mean that the Indian society was not changing at all. Society in India, as elsewhere is neither static nor stagnant. Change is sometimes slow and thus relatively less perceptible. In the pan-Indian region, Sanskritization, as conceived by Srinivas played a major role in bringing about changes in the different aspect of the socio-cultural life of the people. As observed by Srinivas (1966 : 23), "Sanskritization has been a major process of cultural change in Indian history, and it has occurred in every part of the Indian sub-continent. It may have been more active at some periods than at others, and some parts of India are more Sanskritized than others; but there is no doubt that the process has been universal".

Factor affecting change and modernization are many. Changes are often caused by the new political development, economic situation, technological advancements, demographic change, the wave of modernization and industrialization, improved communication, new administrative reforms and various other factor. Cultural contact is a major factor affecting change in communities. The causes of change as observed by Hogbin (1958 : 3) are the sudden modification of the natural environment as a result of flood, drought, volcanic eruption and the like. Migration of group of people to a new country and invasion by foreigners possessing superior tools also cause change. Sometimes changes are brought about as a result of new political situation. In such situations people in fear of punishment often modify their age-old habits and practice to match the situation. Hogbin (1958 : 96) has termed this type of change as 'enforced change'.

To concentrate in the north-eastern region of India could be safely said that the study on the aspect of change is still a virgin field. In the pre-Independence period the tribal people of this region practically had no contact with the outside world beyond the periphery of their own. Whereas the tribal lot in the other regions of India came in contact with various communities since the early periods of history. In this context Majumdar (1978 : 2) observed, "In India, contact of tribes with the Aryan or Aryanised neighbours started from the proto-historic times, or even earlier. We find mention of tribes in the epics". First ever work on the aspect of contact and change in the north-eastern region was, however, done in 1931 when J.P. Mills wrote about the effects of contact on the tribes of Naga Hills in the Indian Census Report. Contact of the people of the erstwhile NEFA (North East Frontier

Agency), present-day Arunachal Pradesh, was even more restricted as the entry of the people from the other regions of the country was prohibited by *Pax Britannica* during the British rule in the country. The wave of Sanskritization also could not influence the people of erstwhile NEFA as the tribal people of the region managed to keep themselves aloof from the broader cultural system of the country.

II

The Monpas are a group of tribesmen found inhabiting the sierra in the districts of Tawang and the West Kameng in Arunachal Pradesh. They are highland people and are mostly found at an altitude ranging from 6,000 to 12,000 ft above the mean sea-level. A group of Monpas who have made the plateau of Khalegthang (Kalaktang) as their habitat are of course found in a relatively lower altitude. The people returned a total population of 27,818 as per the Census of India, 1981, forming a major population in the state. The sex ratio is 972 per 1000 males. The country of the Monpas is an area of rugged terrain with relatively steep sierra and deep gorges. The higher reaches remain snow-covered throughout the year. Economy of the people is agriculture which they do by cutting terraces all over and supplemented by the indigenous highland trade of indigenous items in the trans-Himalayas and in the plains of Assam. Unlike the other tribes of the state the Monpas were known to the outside world through their caravan trade since time immemorial. The people, long ago, since the twelve century voluntarily changed their traditional religion of *Bon* to the Buddhism of the Tibetan Lamaist form.

The indigenous trans-Himalayan trade links that the Monpas established was mainly with the Bhutanese, the Tibetans, the Assamese and other communities in the mountains. From Tibet, in the pre-Independence period the Monpas used to obtain the items like *churpi* (a hard cheese-like substance), dried meat, wool, yak, mineral salt in exchange of the articles of bamboo and cane, the indigenously woven mats, chilli, orange, apple, maize, vegetable dye, wooden bowls and handmade paper. From Bhutan they used to bring yak, *churpi*, wild tea-leaves, clothes, etc. From the market of Assam the people used to collect iron implements, bell-metal utensils, silk cloth and many other items of their use. It is through this indigenous highland trade the people were able to establish ample scope of interaction with the various tribal communities in the Himalayas. These indigenous contacts of the Monpas could not usher in the aspects of either modernization or change mainly because the communities were as homespun and traditional as the Monpas themselves were. In the context of the indigenous highland trade of the people, Furer-Heimendorf (1982 : 146) observed, "....in the westernmost part of Arunachal Pradesh there are climatic and geographical conditions which favoured the opening of trade-routes linking the territory both with Tibet and with the plains of Assam... . Along with these trans-Himalayan trade-routes Tibetan cultural elements and ultimately Buddhist monks and nuns infiltrated in the mountain region lying between the easternmost part of Bhutan and southern border of Tibet". Tawang area, as such, always enjoyed importance because of its strategic location. It was this strip of land known as Tawang tract that acted as a bridge in linking Tibet with the plains of Assam in the olden days. Observation made by Gupta (1974 : 30) has made it further clear, "Also through the Tawang Tract, which extended from the Tibetan plateau right down to Assam plains, just north of Udaguri, ran an important trade route between India and Tibet". As this was an established trade route, possibility is there that the Monpas of Tawang cultivated the idea of indigenous trade as they used to see and meet the caravans passing through their country on way to either Tibet or Assam.

The traditional and relatively stereotyped life of the Monpas suffered a jolt following a terrible political turmoil coming from beyond the border in the form of the Sino-Indian border conflict in the year 1962. This, beyond doubt was a traumatic experience for the people inhabiting this strategic location. However, it was immediately after the conflict that the socio-cultural life in the Monpa country started to undergo a rapid transformation. The Government of India soon extended its socio-political strategy among the border people. Modern communication means and other infrastructure facilities were rushed in the Monpa country. The wave of modernization made it entry in the land of the

Monpas. The people were yet benefited as everyday they met new Westernized Indian people from the pan-Indian region who came to Tawang and other Monpa areas on posting in the different office establishment of the Government.

The other outcome of the Sino-Indian border conflict was a series of political changes leading to strict vigil on the international borders. The sealing of the borders was something new, sudden and relatively 'abnormal' situation the people faced. This new development has applied a sudden brake in their flourishing indigenous highland inter-ethnic trade. To cope up with this situation of ambiguity an unpredictability the Monpas stressed on establishing greater economic links with the market in the plains of Assam. Soon the people realised that they had to establish closer links with the markets in Assam and elsewhere in India to market their production and obtain the items of their necessity. This particular transformation may be termed as enforced change. This particular transformation may be termed as enforced change. This enforced change on the one hand brought the Monpas close to the people of India and on the other hand benefited the people as the waves of westernization and modernization entered the exotic border land. At present the people grow apple and other fruits in abundance as cash crops. These items are marketed in the various centres in the country. This had been made possible with the construction of the modern arterial link of 343 kilometres that connect Tawang with the rest of the country. The Monpa trade is continuing but in a modern and universal way.

REFERENCES

COHN, B.S., 1968, Notes on the history of the study of Indian society and culture.

FURER-HAIMENDORF, C. VON, 1982, *Highlanders of Arunachal Pradesh.* New Delhi: Vikas Publishing House.

GUPTA, K., 1974, *The Hidden History of the Sino-Indian Frontier.* Calcutta.

HOGBIN, I.H., 1958, *Social Change.* London: Watts.

MAJUMDAR, D.N., 1978, *Culture Contact in Two Garo Villages.* Calcutta: Anthropological Survey of India.

SRINIVAS, M.N., 1966, *Social Change in Modern India.* Bombay: Allied Publishers.

13
Vaishnavism Among the Noctes : An Ethnographic Study

K.C. Mahanta

Since time immemorial the entire North East India comprising primarily the northern sub-Himalayan forest belts and the snow and rain-fed river system of the Brahmaputra and the Barak with their sprawling narrow valleys has formed the homeland of diverse socio-ethnic and socio-linguistic communities. Amidst these diverse landscapes, the valley of the Brahmaputra has since formed the fountain-head of great traditions (Redfield, 1956 : 42) radiating various socio-cultural norms to the outlying peripheral regions mostly inhabited by multiple tribal folks in the North East. The process of interpersonal contacts between the people of the valley and those of the outlying highlands over the last more than two millennia has been constantly at work bringing in a good deal of enculturations and assimilations of the people's norms and material components in the hills as also in the valley. Apart from material components for day-to-day use, there has been a constant flow of aesthetic ideas from the valley region to the highlanders over the last more than two thousand years. From time to time the ideological components entering the tribal lands brought in refinement and awakening in the tribal life process to a certain degree amidst a host of age-old traditional norms. It might be noted the Brahmaputra valley region received most aesthetic socio-cultural components from the heartland of the Indian sub-continent ever since Vedic times. The pan-Indian caste system, the various Vedic faiths and rituals and observances, family patterns and marriage systems, the kinship systems, etc., all developed and get nourished over several millennia in the heart of the vast sub-continent. All these basic socio-cultural traits get percolated through the length and breadth of the country including the far-off Brahmaputra valley. Most of these pan-Indian norms got consolidated and eventually assimilated amongst the basically non-tribal population of the valley. Some of these select pan-Indian norms came to be imbibed by the tribal population of the region. One such specific aesthetic component of socio-cultural life was the Vaishnavite faith that was cherished and adopted by a singular tribe of the North East, namely, the Noctes of Arunachal Pradesh nearly three hundred years back. The age-old beliefs and practices among them were far from being organised into any creed or ideology. Personal and group safety and welfare could then be realized through magico-religious performances and worship and control of nature and natural phenomena. The people were largely animistic, having beliefs in multitude of supernatural beings.

The paper is based on both literary work and field survey. The socio-historic outlines incorporated in the paper have been derived from various sources on Assam history, chronicles, folk-tales and folk-stories. Unstructured interviews for a little more than three months over a period of four years since 1979 were undertaken for understanding the present day functioning of the neo-religion adopted by the people.

The People and the Habitat

The Noctes form one of the major tribes of the Tirap district of Arunachal Pradesh occupying the central region of the district. The habitat is most undulating with hills ranging from 2500 ft rising to 6000 ft in altitude towards the Burmese (Myanmar) border. It is a country full of luxuriant evergreen commercially important vegetation. A rich variety of wild and domestic animals and birds comprises the fauna of the area. The Nocte land is criss-crossed by three rivers, namely, the Saṭjo, the Baraf and the Tarat all joining the mighty river Dihing in the plains of Assam. The Nocte land is fortunate enough to have some brinewells and saline springs from which salts are produced.

The Noctes are generally called the Naga by the people of the adjacent plain area. They are a homogeneous group of people having their own language, customs, traditional faiths and rituals. They have all along been referred to as the "Nagas of the eastern region" in old administrative reports. Since known historical times, the Noctes have been known as Namsangia, Borduria, Paniduaria, Kolagongia and Khuragongia Nagas among the neighbouring Assamese people of the plains. These tribesmen have long had close connection with the plains people especially for the purpose of trade transaction. Items like salt, ivory, Assamese *Endi*[1] and metal articles formed the chief goods for transactions since the early days of Ahom sovereignty. And since the days of the Ahoms inception in Assam, the Noctes had maintained very cordial relations with the people of the plains.

Ethnic Characteristics

No detailed scientific study of the physical characters has yet been made on the Noctes. Dutta (1978 : 18) reports, "In 1954 a field party of the Department of Anthropology, Government of India (now known as the Anthropological Survey of India) investigated A-B-O, M-N blood group and A-B-H secretor factor only among the Noctes of Khonsa, Lapnan, Barkhuma (Khela) and Borduria villages". The Noctes as a group belonging to the general Naga as a tribe come in the dolichocephalic Mongoloid type. Guha (1937 : 138) says, "The tribes in the hills on the northern and eastern frontiers of Assam represent a separate type with a head shape wither wholly or with a tendency to be dolichocephalic".

From the recent study of some physical anthropological variables by Goswami and Das (1990 : 103), the somatometric and other physical characters of the Noctes could be fairly understood. The work reveals the variables of the Noctes as follows: the Noctes are short-statured people. But they are tallest of all the three other groups of tribesmen of the district of Tirap, namely, the Wangcho, the Tangsa and the Singpho. Concerning the head size, the Noctes are predominantly dolicho to mesocephalic, their head being the shortest and narrowest of all the three other groups of tribesmen. Also the Noctes possess the smallest head circumference of all the other three groups. The Nocte face is of mesoprosopic and mesene type. While the Noctes possess the longest nose of all the three groups, in mean nasal index, the (the Noctes) come under mesorrhine class. Concerning occurrence of ABO blood groups, the frequency of A blood is higher than B. With regard to finger ridge pattern among male Noctes, whorl, and loop occur almost in equal frequencies, the whorl and loop ratio being more or less 1 : 1. Among female Noctes, loop predominates.

Intercourse with the Brahmaputra Valley

Ever since the inception of Ahom sovereignty in Assam, the Noctes had maintained close relations with the Assamese of the Brahmaputra valley. The evidence of the early relations could be had from some of the material possessions preserved by some Nocte chiefs since the days of the Ahom kings. The Noctes who were called the Nagas by the Assamese people used to come down to the plains for trade. The Ahoms had control over them, and this control was mainly for the possession of the brine springs. The British since around fourth decade of the last century recorded various events among the Noctes in their annual administrative reports.

There are many Nocte villages adjacent to the plains of Assam; the people of these villages have long been accustomed to the plains for trade and seasonal work in the tea gardens of Assam. Ever since long past, the Noctes were in the habit of paying regular visits to a number of upper Assam towns like Naharkatiya, Joypur, Margherita, Dibrugarh, etc., especially in the winter months of December to February. These visits were undertaken for procuring certain essential commodities like salt, match boxes, iron tools, bell metal dishes, bowls and buckets and beads and bangles from the plains. Such visits by Noctes to the plains have become few and far between since the onset of the eighties as Khonsa, the district headquarters town, and other townships developed by leaps and bounds over the years. Prior to the development of vehicular surface traffics to the Nocte country till late fifties of this century, the river Buridihing which has its source from the Tirap mountains flowing northward to join the Brahmaputra served as a water way to take the Nocte entrepreneurs to the areas in the lower reaches of the river. It can well be perceived that free intercourse and movement of men and material, long before the British period, actually laid the foundations socio-cultural relationship between the Noctes and the people of Brahmaputra valley in the past. One may note that this relationship was most outstanding in the field of socio-religious interaction. The Vaishnavite movement in Assam had direct effective influence on the Noctes of Tirap and was instrumental in converting a large section of the population into Vaishnavism.

Traditional Religious Features

By far all tribesmen the world over appear to be polytheists. The tribal people of North East India also have not been an exception to this universal norm. Animistic beliefs and practices involving the worships and propitiation of various gods and tutelaries have since time immemorial formed the core of the religious ideology among the Noctes, as among other North-eastern tribesmen. Most of these beliefs and practices are based on, or emanate from, the worship of nature. The people thus worship and propitiate multitudes of gods and spirits for personal as well as group welfare and for averting untoward events of life. Despite being a polytheist people, they also manifest faiths in the existence of a high god or creator god, who is conceptualized as being an omniscient, omnipresent and omnipotent, benevolent supernatural being. Supernatural beings are attributed anthropomorphic value and quality. The all powerful high god manifests its existence and power as a guardian deity of the tribe as a whole. Propitiation of the supernatural beings through idoltry is certainly a development that has come to be superficially added to, but not incorporated in, the animistic beliefs and practices, after the tribesmen came into contact with Vedic people. Besides having a belief in the existence of the creator god, the tribal communities perform various rites and ceremonies and make offerings to their respective spirits and spiritual beings that are believed to be the presiding deities of the household, of the village, the forest, the river and the stream.

Popular Traditional Belief

The Noctes' conceptualization concerning the existence of the high god and the tutelary supernatural beings is a highly variable one. No two Nocte villages manifest identical ideology in respect of the nature and attribute of the high god or the supernatural beings. Nevertheless, the Noctes in general believe in the existence of a high god whom the call *Jauban, Jongban* or *Tesong*. He dwells in the earth being the cause and effect of all happenings in the life of an individual. He manifests a duality of character — both good and evil. His benevolent temperaments brings in happiness and prosperity and his evil disposition is accompanied with miseries and misfortunes. These two aspects are referred to as *Kat Jauban* and *Wang Jauban* respectively. In some villages the two aspects are manifested by *Rang Jauban* and *Ha Jauban* the former dwells in the sky and the latter in the earth looking after and protecting the village.

The Noctes also believe in the existence of many other spiritual beings dwelling in the jungles, ditches and rivers and streams and causing various ailments like fever, cough, dysentry, etc. The soul of a person dying unnatural death is believed to turn into a dreadful spirit. People are mortally afraid of such a spirit. In order to avoid the dreadful spirit of a person dying an unnatural death, the body of the deceased is highly mutilated with a view to immobilizing the spirit.

Apart from the belief in a array of spirits and demons, the Noctes performs a variety of rituals that are believed to be efficacious for the welfare and well-being in the life of man. The Nocte believes that proper performance of rituals can bring about economic betterment and prosperity in the life of an individual. Further performance of certain rituals whenever occasion demands can avert the incidence of death, disease and misfortune.

Having had a cursory study of Nocte traditional rituals and beliefs, it is pertinent to *gauge* the salient features of the Vedic cults that prevailed in Assam prior to Vaishnavite florescence in the sixteenth century.

Vedic Cults

It is fact of history that immigration of the pre-Aryan groups of people from the Indo-Gangetic basins to the Brahmaputra valley continued ever since the Rigvedic period that dates back to 3000 years B.C. The flow of immigrants from the Indus basin that was obviously a slow and steady process over the centuries continued down to the reign of Pala Kings in Assam in the tenth and the eleventh centuries A.D. By this time, the pan-Indian immigrants came to be a formidable and perceptible force in the Brahmaputra valley region. The successive immigration over the centuries brought forth a hardcore pan-Indian religious system in the form of Vedic ritualistic ideology during the pre-Vaishnavite period in Assam. The Vedic ideas consisted of the cult of fertility, or the worship of the phallus, that came to be symbolized in the form of Mother Goddess Durga, Manasha or Kali. Ever since this proto-historic time of Naraka and Bhagadatta of the Mahabharata fame, the seat of the Sakti cult symbolized by Mother Goddess Durga, alternately, also called Mother Goddess Kamakhya in Assam has been in existence at a temple atop a hillock called Nilachal to the west of the city of Guwahati. The Kamakhya temple as it is called is "famous for its practices in magic and sorcery in the medieval history of India" (Goswami, 1960 : 37). The cult of fertility that developed eventually had its basis of Saktism and Tantricism that flourished and had its sway all over Assam. Gogoi (1976) is of the opinion that the Kalikapurana of the eleventh century A.D. gives us a vivid account of Kamrup, as pre-thirteen century Assam was known, as being the land of Tantric worships and ritualism. Apart from the Kamakhya temple, many temple relics in various parts of Assam show that Saktism was embraced as a popular faith by the common masses, especially in the valley region. Gogoi (ibid) also opines that the ancestors of Sankardeva and Madhabdeva, the two chief Vaishnava abbots of Assam in the fifteen and sixteen centuries, were the ardent followers of Saktism with animal sacrifice and offering of blood, a practice that sharply contrasts with the tenets of Vaishnavism.

The enormous popularity of the Tantric and Sakti cults in the pre-Vaishnavite Assam proved to a fragile one eventually at the advent of the Vaishnavite faith with its lofty but simple thematic appeal. The esoteric cults of the pre-Vaishnavite are could hardly act as a unifying integrative force as they lacked any soft and gullible elements that the common man especially the illiterate tribesmen could imbibe and practice. The pre-Vaishnavite doctrinaire religious conceptions that characterised the successive waves of the pre-Aryans and the Aryans, could hardly have any impact whatsoever on the people other than those of the valley region. Consequently, the tribesmen of the outlying hilly areas remained outside the pole of the pan-Indian dogmatic esoteric cults. The complex philosophy involved in these cults could hardly be imbibed by the preliterate primitive tribesmen of the North East. The Tantric forms of religious beliefs and practices of the Hindus were structurally akin to the animistic belief and practices of the tribal inhabitants of pre-Vaishnavite greater Assam. Notwithstanding this similarity, the pre-Vaishnavite tenets of Hinduism, on account of having rich literary medium of expression, could have no impact upon the illiterate tribal folks of the region. A high extraneous sense of caste superiority coupled with a sense of religious and socio-cultural chauvinism on the part of the pan-Indian immigrants probably acted as a barrier against spread and penetration of socio-religious ideas among the tribal masses of greater Assam. Prior to the advent of Vaishnavism in the sixteenth century, there was no proselytising mission of any kind in Assam, nor was there any direct contact between the immigrant neo-settlers in the Brahmaputra valley and the tribal masses of the region. Lack of continuous day-to-day direct contact between the valley-dwellers and the highlanders practically precluded any exchange of socio-cultural norms and ideology among the two sets of people. It is through the egalitarian spirit and a sense of humanism and fellow feeling on the part of the Vaishnavite exponents in the sixteenth and seventeenth centuries that the neo-faith could penetrate into sections of certain tribal groups of people of the region. The Nocte of present day Arunachal Pradesh form one of the outstanding tribal groups of people that embraced Vaishnavism long before western proselytisation came into vogue in this part of the country around early nineteenth century.

Eka Sarana Bhagavati Dharma

In this connection it is worthwhile to look into the pristine ideological tenets of Vaishnavism called Eka Sarana Bhagavati Dharma as enunciated by its exponents Sankardeva and Madhavdeva in the sixteenth and seventeenth century and subsequently modified into more than one form by their followers. Sankardeva's creed was based on equality and brotherhood. Its philosophy was founded on the monistic theory of God and *Awatara* (incarnation), Lord Sri Krishna, as the ultimate source of refuge of the initiated. The doctrine "with its allegiance to one Supreme God (*Adwaitabad*), its abhorrence of animal sacrifice, its freedom from esteric rites and its simple ceremonial consisting only of hymns and prayers" form the salient features of the Eka Sarana Bhagavati Dharma in Assamese (Barua, 1933 : 308). The followers of the Vaishnavite School of Mahapurusha Sankardeva are called Mahapurusiyas after the epithet "Mahapurush" meaning the "sublime soul". The initiated ones called the "Saraniyas" are expected to observe a strict code of socio-ritual discipline and are supposed to pass through a strict code of restrictions in eating, drinking and in pursuing the socio-religio-cultural life. They are strictly forbidden to offer animal sacrifice and drink and are prescribed to live an austere, pious and puritanical life performing regular worships and singing and reciting of devotional songs and saying prayers in the morning and evening. The ritual offerings of the Vaishnavites consist of unparaboiled rice, gram, fruit, curd and molasses. With the advent of Sankardeva's monistic doctrine, the age-old idol worship of the Sakti cult waned and its place was steadily taken over by certain far-reaching innovations in Hinduism in the Brahmaputra valley in the form of congregational prayer and devotional songs to the accompaniment of the playing on the *Khol*[2] or *Mridong*[3] and *Tal*[4]. Sankardeva's most remarkable unique innovation in the preaching of Vaishnavism is manifest in the introduction of dance and music and dramatical performances called *bhaonas* as media of propagation. These unique devices were adopted in order to enthuse devotional feelings in the mind of the common people who got motivated adopting the neo-faith in no time. The essence of Sankardeva's Vaishnavite philosophy was derived from the Bhagavatgeeta, the holy scripture of the Hindus, to propagate it among the masses. At the same time Sankardeva brought about a large-scale socio-cultural metamorphosis by introducing among the Assamese masses another innovation in the form of monasteries or *Satras* that were modelled after the Naimisharanya *Satra* depicted in the Bhagavatgeeta. The *Satras* came into existence in the first part of the sixteenth century as an indispensable part of the Assamese socio-cultural life. In the early years of neo-Vaishnavite propagation a *Satra* served as a house for religious discourse. Ever since their inception *Satras* have become an institution for imparting and cultivating a distinctive way of life in the Assamese socio-cultural milieu. The traditional Assamese socio-religio-politico life revolved round the *Satra* that acts as the pivot of an individual's total personality. The institution of *Satra* has helped the Assamese become a god fearing, devout, ritualistic, humanitarian, tolerant, non-violent, non-aggressive, non-individualistic, group-centered community as they known to be.

With the propagation and spread of Vaishnavism Satras sprang up everywhere in the Assam villages. A *Satra* is normally named by prefixing it by the name of the place of its location. A *Satra* has its tentatively defined jurisdiction over a number of villages that may vary from a few to as many as one hundred or more. The traditional typical *Satra* is constituted of a *namghar*[5], a *manikut*[6], the *hati*[7] and a *batchara*[8]. At present many of the *Satras*, save the prominent ones such as the Barpeta Satra, the Auniati Satra, the Kuruabahi Satra, the Dakhinpat Satra, etc., have lost their traditional basic socio-cultural features and parted with their manifold socio-cultural activities and norms. In many cases, *Satras* are seen to have only the namghar and another feature like the *manikut* or the *batchara*. In this connection it is worth mentioning that the *namghar* besides being attached to a *Satra* complex, is a common feature of the Assamese villages that has developed as an offshoot of the Vaishnavite movement. Apart from being an assembly house for congregational devotional prayer and recitation of scriptures a *namghar* is a symbol of unity, solidarity and cooperation in every village community in Assam, subserving multifarious purpose as a prayer house, a venue of village assembly, a cultural school, a village court or as an agency of social control. A *namghar* is, in fact, a mini parliament in every single village in Assam.

A *Satra* as a socio-religious institution functions under the religious and spiritual authority of an executive cum religious head called Mahanta or Satradhikar who is assisted by a deputy known as Deka-adhikar. A Satradhikar holds office for life. After his demise, the office is succeeded by his deputy, the Deka-adhikar. A Satradhikar is a spiritual guide and a teacher of spiritual knowledge. He is one who is supposed to be well versed in most spiritual literatures and legends. It is the Satradhikar who is also called *Ata* provides spiritual teachings and guidance to the devotee-disciples called *bhakata* or *sishyas*. The process of imparting this spiritual value to devotees under a Satradhikar is called *Saran*, that is, initiation into the order of the Vaishnavite faith. *Saran* as a life long effective process introduced by Sankardeva brings about discipline and serenity in the material pursuits of life of the initiated. It is the spiritual recognition of a devotee or an adherent of the faith. Sankardeva formulated *Saran* as constituting the following elements: *nam* (simple utterance of the name of Sri Krishna as God incarnate in devotional songs, prayers and recital of scriptures), *deo* (Sri Krishna), *guru* (spiritual guide) and *bhakat* (congregation of devotee-disciples or self individual). Sankardeva by his extraordinary skill and intellect, devised diverse methods through the use of self-composed songs, verses and couplets and instrumental music, tune, art, dance and dramatical performances to inculcate the intent of surrender to God incarnate, Lord Krishna. He made diverse aesthetic elements of culture as adjuncts to the spread of the Vaishnavite faith among the Assamese masses, preaching the creed of *Eka Saran*, that is, surrender to one Supreme God Almighty, Lord Sri Krishna. The missionary and proselytizing activities of Sankardeva and his closest disciple Madhavdeva brought about an era of great Vaishnavite movement and religious transformation among the downtrodden and low caste backward people. Himself a great poet, playwright, composer, artist and thinker and philosopher of the devotional or *Bhakti* school, Sankardeva shaped the Assamese personality[9] as what it was till the fag end of the eighth decade. The bhakats under the Saran system represent a class of devotees who relinquish the mundane aspirations and desires and lead the life of celebates within, or outside the precinct of the *Satra*. Some *bhakats* devote themselves to ecclesiastical work of the *Satra*. Common village folks turn into *Sishyas* as and when they are initiated into the Vaishnavite order through the medium of *Saran*. *Sishyas* reside outside the *Satra* and lead a domestic life. The economic sustenance of the *Satras* is borne through annual contributions of the *Sishyas*. It is the *Sishyas* who under a system of what is called *Sidha-bhojani* and *Guru-Kar* contribute for the maintenance of the *Satras*. The system consists in the annual voluntary payment of some amount of money in cash as *Guru-Kar* and packets of rice, pulse, potato, salt, etc., as *Sidha-bhojani* which are treated as gifts. Gift-giving is considered as morally imperative on the part of every Vaishnavite family head in Assam. *Saran* on the part of the every adult Assamese Hindu is obligatory as the belief goes that the life of an *asarania*, as the uninitiated one is called, is doomed to be in jeopardy and hazard, the individual having to face all sorts of spiritual deprivations in the other world. Remaining *asarania* is sinful. Also the *asaranias* are treated as outcastes and impure and debarred from taking part in religious and social functions of the community.

In the context of the pro-Vaishnavite brain storm prevailing in the sixteenth century Assam, an attempt is made in this paper to examine the extent of Vaishnavite impact and influence upon a tribal community, namely, the Noctes of the district of Tirap in Arunachal Pradesh. The data for this work are basically derived from the peoples' anecdotes and folk tales and folk stories. Further certain works on verses especially the biographies of the religious heads and preachers have served as valuable source material. Besides these documentary evidences, with a view to making a first hand enquiry about the practice of Vaishnavism by the Noctes, a month long enthnographic study of a Nocte village, namely, Lapnan near the district headquarter town of Khonsa was undertaken by the ethnographer in 1978 and again in 1992. In course of these studies, a number of knowledgeable persons were interviewed. It could be learnt from a cross-section of village elders that their forefathers some 15 generations ago adopted the Vaishnavite faith from the Ram Dev Ata of Chaliha Bareghar Satra of Mezenga near the town of Nazira in Upper Assam.

The Noctes are a singular tribe and a lone people to embrace Vaishnavism nearly two-and-a half centuries back amidst a large number of tribal groups inhabiting the sprawling whole mountainous territory to the north and east of the Brahmaputra valley. It is not that the Noctes adopted pure undiluted pristine Vaishnavism. By the time the Noctes came to practise Vaishnavism, it underwent a good deal of modification especially after the demise of the prime abbot Sankardeva and his close associate and follower Madhavdeva. It might be noted that Sankardeva introduced neo-Vaishnavism in Assam with the prime objective of weaning away the lowly so-called low-caste and untouchable people. Being in the lowest rung of the socio-cultural hierarchy, they were in fact the downtrodden section of the population who professed the age-old Vedic *Varnashrama* dharma[10]. The pursuit of the Vedic norms has ever since created the highly rigid caste-based social stratification in the Hindu society as a whole, paving the way for breeding atrocious discrimination between the so-called high castes and the low castes. Sankardeva's neo-Vaishnavism threw a ray of hope for ending this age-old social discrimination. It enthused a sense of equality and brotherhood among all adherents of the neo-faith. The change over to the new behavioural socio-cultural ideology is manifest in the Vaishnavite scriptural epithet *"Kukkura-Gardabha-Chandalaro-Aatma-Ram"*, meaning literally and freely "even the scavenger, the dog and the ass have the similar sublime souls". The faith ordains it adherents simply to utter the name of Sri Krishna and to listen to His name being uttered and sung and to follow a puritanical teetotal life. A large section of the Assamese people regardless of caste, creed, language or faith, got converted into the new order of life. Sankardeva himself initiated a large number of Brahmins and Sudras including Kaibarttas and other low caste people besides a Muslim, a Garo, a Bhutiya, a Mishing, a Naga, a Kachari and an Ahom. During the life time of Sankardeva the Eka Saran Bhagavati Dharma flourished and remained intact. After his demise, controversy arose concerning the succession of the Abbotey. The question of succession took an acute form after the demise of Madhavdeva, the closest disciple of Sankardeva, leading to the emergence of four sectarian divisions or *Samhatis*, namely, Bhahma Samhati, Purusha Samhati, Kala Samhati and Nika Samhati under the stewardship of different dissident preceptors.

The Vaishnavism propagate by Ram Deva Ata of Chaliha Bareghar Satra, as outline above, is of Kala Samhati school. This *Samhati* comprises elements of Saktism and Tantricism that abounded in Assam as already discussed, since pre-Vaishnavite times. The adherents of the Kala Samhati school being devoted to esoteric rites are accustomed to performing nocturnal rituals accompanied with mid-night dinners containing unorthodox items like liquor, pork and certain types of forbidden fish. The cult of night eating is known as *Rati Khowa.*

The Eka Saran Bhagavati Dharma or pristine Vaishnavism that is more or less equated with Brahma Samhati following sectarian division, is invariably and very scrupulously associated with the conduct of orthodox system in the sphere of eating, drinking and other day-to-day pursuits of life. Its followers are most scrupulous to avoid excessiveness in life in all respect. Strict observance of norms is the hallmark of pure Vaishnavite faith. Contrary to this puritanical life, the followers of Kala Samhati cult are usually referred to as *aritiyas,* that is, non-followers of orthodox system. The tribal people who are habitually far from being teetotallers could in no way be fitting to the puritanical way of life. On the other hand, the Kala Samhati cult with esoteric rituals and habits did go well with unorthodox pursuits in the day-to-day life of the people. The tenets of the Kala Samhati cult are so prescribed by its exponent guru Ram Dev Ata that they fit well with the socio-cultural norms of the Noctes. Adoption and practice of Vaishnavism as such by the Noctes are thus not attended with any conflict or disharmony in social life. As meat and drink form the primary items of food in the Nocte day-to-day menue the Vaishnavism adopted by the people displayed a good deal of flexibility in relaxing the restrictions on the use of the dietary items. Unhampered by any restrictions on the consumption of traditional food items, the Noctes by and large underwent initiation into the order of the reformed Vaishnavite sect of Kala Samhati under the spiritual leadership of Ram Dev Ata.

Conclusion

The Noctes are a turbulent warlike tribe. The history of almost every one of the villages in the Nocte country is replete with treacherous head-hunting raids. Apparently the tenets of Vaishnavism with its serene sublime philosophy of surrender to one God, *Eka Saran*, in the person of Sri Krishna could hardly be fitted with the socio-cultural ethos of the people. The people being obsessed with the annual ritual of head-hunting drive, Vaishnavism certainly stood out as an anti-thesis of the people's age-old norms. Despite this social incompatibility, Vaishnavism could make headway among the Noctes on account of two inherent factors of the new faith. One, the people are impressed not much by the concept of surrender to one Supreme Almighty God in the person of Sri Krishna meaning *Eka Saran* but by the egalitarian spirit of the *dharma* or faith. Second, the people developed a fascination, or rather an inclination, for undergoing *Saran* under a preceptor in order to earn what the Noctes call *dharam*, that is, religious merit. The people treat *dharam* as immensely valuable; it can avert various mishaps and misfortunes. Whenever there arises an individual or collective sense of crisis or untoward happening, the Nocte make it a point to visit the *Satras*, especially the Chaliha Bareghar Satra of Nazira, for the purpose of acquiring *dharam*. It could be learnt from the Noctes themselves that their *Guru* of Chaliha Bhareghar Satra also used to visit the Nocte villages quite regularly till the fifties of this century. In the second half of this century the visits of the *Guru* have become few and far between. Yet the people have never parted with the faith. They are seen to aspire after *dharam* which they believe gives them healthy life, good harvest, plenty of wealth and abundance of games in the forests and many children.

As in Assam, some Nocte villages also have miniature *namghars* that serve as a place of congregational worship at the time of the Satradhikar's visit. The visit of Satradhikar provides the people with an occasion for unusual religious activity accompanied with great merriment and rejoicings. It is an occasion for novices for undergoing *Saran* by accepting religious codes of conduct from the Satradhikar. *Sisyas* or the disciples offer the Satradhikar *Sidha-bhojani* and *Guru-kar*, their annual ritual liability, and thereby, believe, they earn *dharam*.

The Nocte Vaishnavite faith is conspicuous by the absence of any devotional song, dance or staging of any religious drama, called *bhaona,* the cardinal features of the Eka Saran Bhagavati Dharma. These were all extra-religious devices to popularise the Vaishnavite faith among the Assamese masses. In accordance with Assam's puritanical Vaishnavite observances, recital of scriptures and singing of religious chorus called *nam kirtan* by a congregation of devotees is held at the *namghar* on every *gurubar* or Thursday. The Noctes who live a very hard and arduous life are very much preoccupied with foraging for day-to-day food from morning till evening. Concern for sheer survival negates most aesthetic diversions including congregational assemblage and prayer. Further certain extra-religious devices like dramatical performances never got into the community at all as there was no systematic missionary effort at mass-proselytizing the people through their use as media for religious teaching. What Vaishnavite traits are seen at present among the Noctes were all chosen and acquired by the people themselves on their won accord. It is through choice that the Noctes have since adopted and practised certain select traits of the Eka Sarana Bhagavati Dharma. And these traits are those that serve the people's immediate purpose most.

In recent years the Noctes evinced interest in adopting some new features like holding and practising of *nam-kirtan, bhaona,* etc. Datta (1978 : 253) reports that since 1966 Nocte disciples were imparted training in performing *nam-kirtan* for running *namghars* and that Sri Sri Gopal Krishna Dev Goswami, the Satradhikar of Chaliha Bareghar Satra, performed *bhaona* of *'Ram Bijoy', 'Kalkunj Badh', 'Khatasur Badh', 'Laba Kusar Yudha', 'Khudrakar Yudha 'Yatra'* and *'Dimba Kunja Badh'* in the *namghars* at Namsang, Borduria and Khonsa. Traditional aspirations for material prosperity and individual and group well-being have since kept the people attached to some superficial features of Eka Sarana Bhagavati Dharma in conjunction with the traditional animistic beliefs. In view of the acceptance of some new feature of Vaishnavite faith in recent years, as noted above, it could well be anticipated that the Noctes will veer round the pure and pristine form of Vaishnavism in the foreseeable future.

Notes:

1. *Endi* : A kind of silk cloth, normally used as a wrapper in the winter time as warmer, obtained from species of silk cocoon that feeds on the leaves of the castor plant. It is alternatively called as *'Aree Kapor'*.

2. *Khol* : A kind of drum, made of earth burnt and fitted with animal hide on either extremity to be played with bare hands to produce rhythmic sound.

3. *Mridong* : A kind of drum, like a *Khol*. It is somewhat more slender and longer than a *khol*.

4. *Tal* : Cymbal, made of brass.

5. *Namghar* : is a house traditionally built of thatch and wooden posts on ground plinth, presently being replaced by cement concrete pillars and C.I. sheet roofings. The structure is meant for congregational prayer besides occasionally serving as a village assembly.

6. *Manikut* : is the temple where the Bhagavat Geeta is placed on a holy pedestal.

7. *Hati* : is hutment to serve as residence of permanent celebate devotee-employees of the *Satra*.

8. *Batchara* : is a guest house.

9. *Assamese personality* : was what has been described at page 199. The Assamese personal-

ity narratives have undergone considerable metamorphosis ever since the post eighties.

10. *Varnashrama dharma* : concern the duties of persons towards both the *Varnas* and the *ashramas* in their interrelationship with each other.

REFERENCES

BARUA, RAI BAHADUR K.L., 1933, *The Early History of Kamrup*, Shillong.

DATTA, P.C., 1978, *The Noctes of Arunachal Pradesh*, Shillong: Arunachal Pradesh Administration.

GOGOI, P., 1976, *Tai Ahom Religion and Customs*. Guwahati: Publication Board, Assam.

GOSWAMI, M.C., 1960, An annual shamanistic dance (*Deodha Nach*) at Kamakhya, Assam. *Journal of University of Gauhati* (Science), 11, 2 : 37 - 58.

GOSWAMI, M.C.; P.B. DAS, 1990, *The People of Arunachal Pradesh: A Physical Survey*. Itanagar: Directorate of Research, Government of Arunachal Pradesh.

REDFIELD, R., 1956, *Peasant Society and Culture*. Chicago: University of Chicago Press.

14

Religious Trends and Identity Crisis : A Cross-Cultural Study Among Three Plain Tribes of Assam

Chandra Jyoti Sonowal

Tribes all over the world are witnessing forces of detribalization in different magnitudes. The tribal situation in India shows a similar trend as well. Facets of detribalization are affecting the economic, political, socio-cultural and religious life of the tribesmen. Religion is one of the most important social institutions of all tribal societies. It operates as an important agent of socialization.

Tribals witnessed their absorption into Hinduism mainly during pre-British period. Such absorptions were accompanied with certain refinement of tribal socio-cultural life relating to food habit, ceremonial observances, etc. The motive behind such conversions was mainly to attain higher social status. Srinivas (1952) described this process mainly as 'Sanskritization'. By Sanskritization he means mainly a process by which a low caste or tribe or such other groups take over the customs, rituals, beliefs, ideology and life-style of a higher caste, especially the twice born. Bose (1946) also forwarded a model of proselytization into Hinduism which he called the Hindu mode of tribal absorption. According to him Aruans had evolved stable regional, economic and social units in which the relatively isolated and backward ethnic groups (tribes) also found a place in terms of corporate social status and economic and political functions. In this process while ensuring cultural autonomy to the newly integrated tribes ultimately came into existence a cultural process by which the age-old dominated a lowly ranked tribe gradually emulated the cultural pattern of the dominant Hindu upper castes.

Vidyarthi (1977) observes that the tribes in India are blended with other faiths of non-tribal neighbours and those of erstwhile British rulers. Effective among all these are Hinduism and Christianity which have put their religious beliefs in the melting pot. Evidences of Hinduisation are evident in almost all the tribal areas of the country. The Tharus (Srivasta : 1958) and the Khasas (Majumdar, 1962) have succeeded in getting themselves accepted as Kshatriyas and/or as Brahmins. In Central India, the Cheros, Kharwars, Pahariyas of Chotanagpur, Gonds, Bhumij have declared themselves as Kshatriya. Sachidananda states (1964) that there is a great deal of influence of Vaishnavism over the Mundas and Oraons of Chotanagpur. Sahay (1962) again observes that many Oraons have accepted worship of Hindu deities like Shiva, Parvati, etc. In some places they employ Brahmin priests and have given up beef eating.

During colonial period, the tribals encountered Christian forces. The tribes coming under proselytization first were the Khasis of Meghalaya (in 1813), the Oraon of Chotanagpur (in 1850) and the Bhuts of Madhya Pradesh (in 1880). Dubey (1972) has confused Christianization with Westernization in the North-east. He states that the Nagas, the Kukis and the Mizos have professed Christianity while the Mikirs, the Kacharis, the Boros and the Mishing, etc., have adopted Hindu rituals and their ways of life have been partly 'Sanskritized'.

Sanskritization in the plains of Assam is an altogether different phenomenon from the other parts of the country as the notion of dominant caste does not exist in Assam. Thus no tribes wanted to emulate a higher caste to achieve an enhanced status. The *Satra* institution attached with Vaishnavism did not acknowledge caste hierarchy. The main orientation of the tribes to emulate Hinduism, therefore, was to get a notion of 'pure-ethnic group' and the notion of Sanskritization can be ascribed to the detribalization process in Assam.

The Problem

The tribal people of Assam, especially the tribes of the plain area were exposed to various detribalization forces of which the spread of neo-Vaishnavism religion was one of the strongest one. The people, prior to the acceptance of Vaishnavism were animistic in nature and practice. Advent of the Ahoms, a Tai-Shan tribe, in Assam and consequent disintegration of pre-existing tribal political authority and exposure of the tribesmen to non-tribal influx of caste Hindu population in the valley region were the helping factors for growth of Vaishnavization and detribalization of these tribes. Interestingly enough, the tribal people did not try to leave their identity as a tribe and yet they were attracted towards the liberal policy and relatively easy norms and practices of neo-Vaishnavism. The extent of acceptance of new religious ideas led the people to a state of peculiar social environment. The people have not got a relatively high position, nor did they partially or totally avoid their tradition, rather they became an admixture of both. Introduction of several new religious ideologies seems to have created intra-tribal conflicts. Loss of several age-old traditional practices is leading the people to the loss of socio-cultural identity and hence identity crisis is arising there.

The People

The Sonowal Kacharis : Endles (1881) describes the Kacharis as the earliest known inhabitants of Brahmaputra valley. Waddel (1901) says that the title 'Kachari' is usually interpreted as being the Indian term denoting an inhabitant of the Katch or submontane marshy tract. He says that the section of the Kacharis that live in upper Assam is the Sonowal or *Sadiola* who were mostly gold-washers in erstwhile Lakhimpur district of Upper Assam. The Sonowal Kacharis believe that there were twelve clans among them when they came to this land. One of these clans, namely, *Badu Hunalaya* clan, gave rise to the Sonowal Kacharis in course of time.

It is believed that the Kacharis had a wide spread territory in Upper Assam under several chiefs. They lost these chiefdoms to the Ahoms who entered Assam in the early part of 13th century. Towards the later part of 14th century, the Kacharis lost their easternmost land — Sadiya, to the Chutiyas. The common people did not follow the royal group and remained in their homeland. Now, the Sonowal Kacharis are distributed in Dibrugarh, Lakhimpur, Dhemaji, Tinsukia, Sibsagar, Jorhat and Golaghat districts of Assam.

The people being animistic believe in supernatural powers. They worship their own multiple Gods and Goddesses. Their supreme God is *Khiring* or *Bathow* and Goddess is *Bhoroli*. In each village they have the chief settlement deity — the *Gatigiri*. Besides him they believe in several other deities, some are benevolent, some others are manevolent, the people appease them through worships. The Sonowals also believe in soul. Ancestor worship is a common practice among the people.

The people indulge in drinking country liquor. It is made from rice. They eat pigs and fowls. Rice-beer (*saaz*) and meat, etc., are essential items to worship deities and ancestors. The people have in some villages worshipping places called *thaan*. At one time *'thaans'* were places where fowls, ducks and goats, etc., were sacrificed.

The Mishings

The Mishings are popularly known as 'Miri' among the common Assamese people. But for the Mishings, a Miri is one who performs the role of a priest. They prefer to call themselves Mishing — meaning a noble person. Once the Mishing were the inhabitants of the hilly areas of East Siang and Lower Subansiri districts of Arunachal Pradesh. The folk literature of the people shows that they migrated down to the plains of the Brahmaputra river and to its tributaries years before the advent of the Ahoms in Assam.

The people speak their own dialect. They speak Assamese also. They usually live near the river banks constructing bamboo made platform houses. They rear cattle and pigs in an extensive manner. The people now live in Dibrugarh, Lakhimpur, Dhemaji and Sibsagar districts of Assam.

Traditionally, the people are animists. They believe in spirits or supernatural beings called *Uie* which are hostile to men. *Uie* are responsible for diseases, sickness, death and destruction, etc. They believe that the spirits possess the same desires as human beings and therefore, people offer them food, meat and drink. They believe in soul-substance of dead persons. The *Urom Uie* is the departed soul which lives in a world of spirits — *Uie aamong*. Each year they perform ancestor worship sacrificing pigs and offering drinks. Every family perform *Urom aapin* ritual which lets free the ninth ancestor to live in *Sumin soin* to become a benevolent deity. People also worship *Taleng Uie* for rain and to protect them from natural calamities. *Dobiur Uie* is offered enormously to protect them from flood, landslide, destruction of crops, etc. The traditional priest — *Mibo* perform the rituals. A *Mibo* is initiated to priesthood by a kind of spirit called opom which looks like a sub-human being living a family life in the deep forest. A selected child is abducted by the opom and after its adulthood it becomes a *Mibo* — the traditional priest.

The Deoris

According to a popular belief the Deoris were the priest group in Chutiya kingdom in Sadiya of Upper Assam. The Chutiya kingdom was in existence in Sadiya till it fell to the Ahoms by 1535 A.D. Some scholars also believe that the Deoris are a branch of the Bodo tribe of Assam who once dominated the entire Upper Assam.

Being the priest group, the people remained closed-knit even after the dethronement of their client king. The invaders, i.e., the Ahoms did not disturb them. Instead, the people were honoured and offered privileges to construct *thaan* (temples) for ritual practice and worship. The Ahom king Dihingia helped them a lot. Their migration to the plains of Assam took place after Burmese invasion between 1822-25 A.D. and subsequent Singpho (a tribe of Arunachal Pradesh) raids to that place. They came down to the south-western part of Assam by the Brahmaputra. They stayed a few days on the south bank of the Brahmaputra and made a *thaan* as a memory of cordial relations between hills and plain tribes. They used to have their meals under the *'chois'*, i.e., roof-cover over the open boat built of bamboo and cane for protection of boat inmates from rain and sun. The place where the *choi*-fitted boats were anchored came to be later known as *Choikhua* (*choi* meaning roof-cover and *khua* meaning eating).

The Deoris have three sub-groups, namely, Dibongia, Tengaponia and Borgonia. The Dibongia only speak their own tribal dialect whereas the other two groups speak the Assamese language with certain admixture of local words.

The people are cultivators and also rear herds of cattle, pig, fouls and ducks. Usually the Deoris prefer to live near the river-banks making wooden or bamboo platform houses (*michong*). They have a habit of drinking rice-beer. Traditionally, the people follow animistic religious beliefs. They recite religious hymn during worship and sacrifice pigs and fowls. The people believe in supernatural power. *Kundi-Mama* or *Burha-Burhi* or *Gira-Girachi* are prime God and Goddess. They are also known as *Boliya Baba* and *Tamreswari*. Among the three sub-groups of the Deori, the Dibongias worship *Kundi-Mama*, the Tengapanias worship *Boliya Baba* and the Borgonias worship *Tamreswari*.

They have their own common place of worship and sacrifice called *thaan*. Besides the Supreme God and Goddess they worship several other traditional gods and goddess. For example, they worship *Saragdeo* for rain, *Minuchi-Nidura* for crops and wealth, *Gorokhia* for the well-being of cattle, *Burha Dangaria* to cure disease like fever and severe headache, *Jolshai* and *Tholshai*, *Gang-Rokhia* (village protector), *Gatial* and *Medi-Khukuri* (protector of cattle), *Sachaya* (Sun and Moon god), *Rongachon* (for cure of stomach pain and blood vomiting) *Apreswari* (fairy) and *Aai* (pox deity), etc.

During the *Bohag Bihu* festival (new years) a distinct ritual is observed in the *thaan*. One or more male persons are behold by the deities. The person then starts dancing and singing and through his or her medium the supernatural reveals itself and convey messages. The Supernaturals are also believed to forecast about the happenings of the coming year. It is seen that people from both tribal and non-tribal communities visit the *'thaan'*, during *Bohag Bihu* to know their fate in the coming year or to pray for the well-being of their families.

Socio-Cultural Background and Acceptance of Vaishnavism

All the three tribes accepted Vaishnavism to different degrees of practice and belief. Among them the Sonowal Kacharis are the most openly exposed and also the most highly detribalized group of people. There is hardly any recorded history regarding the conversion of the people. The ethno-historical data focus light to delineate the socio-cultural background under which such conversions took place.

The Sonowal Kacharis became the subjects of the Ahom rulers after they had lost their chiefdoms. But religiously the people were not exploited. The spread of neo-Vaishnavism became rapid after Sankardeva's demise as several of his disciples were separated from the mainstream and started to initiate tribal and low-caste people in Situ. They offered several incentives to attract the attention of tribal people. They assured them of higher social status and economic upliftment in social life. These religious preachers did not denigrate the tribal traditional practices. They only added some Vaishnavite religious elements into the tribal tradition. These diversified religious sects are known as *Kala Samhati, Mahapurusia, Kevolia* and *Mayamora,* etc.

The Sonowal Kachari on the contrary did not take initiation from these religious preachers. They became the disciple of the famous *Aoniati Satra* which was in the mainstream of the original neo-Vaishnava religion.

There is no reason or evidence to say that the Sonowal Kacharis entirely were initiated to Vaishnavism during Ahom rule. It is stated elsewhere in this work that the Sonowal Kacharis were not exploited by the ruling group religiously. The socio-cultural condition in those days did not compel them to leave their religious practices en masse. It was only after the Burmese invasion, especially the last one in 1822 A.D., which was so devastating that the Sonowal Kacharis had to run for life to different places. The clan-clustered villages were broken up and hetero-clan clustered villages emerged openly exposing them to non-tribal counterparts in new settlements.

The Burmese invasion badly affected the other plain tribes also. The Mishings too had to flee to different places. It was stated elsewhere in this paper that the Deoris came down to the valley of the Brahmaputra as a consequence of Burmese invasion. The Burmese invasion was followed by colonial administration in 1826 A.D. Inflow of job-seekers, introduction of fullfledged monetary economy and emergence of new elite groups was a landmark of this period. Class mobility was accompanied with caste mobility and the high caste people were able to get hold of policy-makers and implementers' position. The tribal people not being familiar to the new emerging situation felt incompatible. They did not get honourable place in society. Specially those who had to come out of the traditional cluster found the outside world inconsistent. In order to get social privilege and dignity they had to change their social identity. Disregarding of tribal people by the elite group is evident from several case histories and verbal chronicles. In such a situation acceptance of Vaishnavism served as an adaptive mechanism to the tribal people. The *Satras* offered a peculiar means of purification to the Sonowal Kacharis. The novice had to abstain from drinking and eating pork for two generations then the third generation was assumed to be pure enough for such jobs as dragging water to the *Satra* and becoming *Saru Koch* — the low-caste people. In this process the Sonowal Kacharis gave up their original surnames and instead adopted caste-surnames like Das, Bora, Dekaborua, Hazarika, Saikia, etc. In lower Assam a group of the Kachar is completely gave up tribal tradition and became caste-like society, now known as Saania Kachari (one who paid obeisance to the religious master). The easier and simpler practices of Vaishnavism attracted most of the tribal people and in course of time they gave up their age-old traditions. The Vaishnavite group came to be known as the *Hinduria* whereas the non-convert traditional followers are known as the *Behari*. The *Hinduria* group does not use country liquor and pork in their rituals and does not worship many traditional deities that need liquor and meat. They use milk in place of country liquor. The Beharis observe almost all the traditional rituals. The people irrespective of the new affiliation recite the *Kirtan* and the *Bhagawata* — two holy books in Vaishnava religion at household rituals and also in the *Namghar* (village monastery). The *Namghar* that is the outcome of neo-Vaishnavism is also used for community-feasting and traditional rituals. The chief deity of the *Namghar* instead of being the Vaishnavite God is the *Gati-Giri* who is a traditional god of the people. The people use liquor and pork at the *Namghar* premises.

Nowadays people take initiation not to raise their status outside the community but to get the recognition as novices for active participation in religious ceremonies. The people have to offer religious tax (*Kar var*) to the Satra annually. The *Satra* gives the people of each village a clay-bar (*Mrittika*) where the symbol of the foot of the *Gosain* (religious head of the *Satra*) is engraved. The religiously impure people of the family drink holy water consecrated by mixing a little clay of the bar in the water.

The mourning rituals are performed by traditional priest called *Medhi*. The other rituals are performed by any of the novices. They do not use religious hymns in sacrifice and very little religious skill (knowledge) is required for performing rituals.

The Mishings, who came to the plains of the Brahmaputra and its tributaries also faced the same condition. They accepted the *Kalasamhati* and the novices are called the *Kevolia Bhakat*. They took initiation under the religious preachers in their own locality. The people did not leave most of their age-old traditions despite the imposition of neo-Vaishnavite religious tenets. The people allow to incorporate foreign religious practices only for having outlet to economic upliftment and raise of social status. Most of the Mishings are now Vaishnavite. The most crucial change indiced by Vaishnavism is the replacement of the *Mibo*, the traditional priest, by the Vaishnavite *Bhakat* or *Sadhu*. *Bhakats* recite the *Kirtan* in ritual and the head *Sadhu* performs side by side animistic observances. Interestingly the *Dobiur Uie* ritual is never performed by the *Bhakats*. It is always performed by the traditional priest, the *Mibo*.

The Deoris were exposed to non-traditional religion very late in comparison to the other two tribes. Being a priestly group they were able to maintain isolation from other tribes or non-tribals. Vaishnavism appeared to them in lesser intensity, and the people took initiation haphazardly. Sri Sankardeva, the preacher of neo-Vaishnavism in Assam, visited Sadiya region twice. But he did not try to convert the Deoris to Vaishnavism. After him, several Vaishnava preachers tried to proselytize the Deoris but failed. It was only after *Gosain* Krishna Kanti and Jadava Ray (Religious head of *Satra*) who agreed that in rituals the Deoris would recall the *Satras* with reverence and would also offer some tribute to the Satras and the *Satra Gosain* on his turn would offer prayers for the well-being of the Deoris. Though there is no written document the verbal information showed that people accepted Vaishnavism towards the early part of the current. The people were converted to *Mahapurusia Pantha, Anukul Pantha* and so on. It is learnt that the preachers gave incentive of economic upliftment basically because the people were poor in most cases. They practised cultivation only. Case data on the event of conversion nearly 60 years back state that in some Deori villages of Sibsagar district there appeared a couple of novice from outside. They tried to initiate people to their faith. They advised the people to worship God everyday offering a *Sarai* consisting of uncooked food items. People invariably did it. They asked the people to construct a granary in their place. One day the pair of novices declared that two bundles of paddy came spontaneously to their granary at night. People believed it. They were told that their granaries would also be filled like this. The people started worshipping the couple. But it did not last long. Their falsehood was revealed and the people reverted to the original way. There are certain such hearsays for which the people had to pay a lot for their innocent nature and ignorance. Religious preachers who were travelling by boat could by simple effort convert the uninitiated. Sometimes several families in a lot were converted to Vaishnavism. But it is reported that they are always bound by obligation to the *thaan*. And the people befall the curse of the *thaan* spirit and they suffered a lot. Most of the people then reverted to traditional life way. But still, there are several families who are Vaishnavite with certain admixture of traditional elements.

Conversion among the tribal people is still going on. For instance, in the village of Kolowloa in the district of Dibrugarh, a preacher of Vaishnavism (*Sankari Pantha*) is converting people to *Sankari Pantha*. He teaches the Deori people that sacrificing pigs and fowls, use of huge amount of liquor in rituals and ceremonies are the primary cause of their economic backwardness. He also advises the people to adopt and practise monotheistic notion and not to participate and contribute to the *thaan* rituals. Several families took initiation from him, and now there is a strong conflict between the neo-converts and the traditionalists.

Impact of Vaishnavism

Acceptance and spread of Vaishnavism has multi-dimensional impact on the life of the tribal people. Once the tenets that were adopted and practised as a means of social and economic mobility are now thought of as rules of life.

At present the Sonowal Kacharis have several sects among the converts. Whatever the past socio-cultural condition might be, the people underwent a lot of change in this process. Most of them gave up traditional titles and forgot ways of several rituals and oral traditions. On the contrary, who did not forego their tradition, retained a dual form of religious beliefs—Vaishnavism and animism.

Nowadays all people, irrespective of *Hinduria* or *Behari* affiliation, undergo initiation. But one cannot say much about refinement of life ways of the people. Because they have not given up the drinking habit and eating pork, etc., which was initially forbidden by the religious master — the *Gosain*. Surprisingly enough, it is reported that when the *Gosain* or his disciples initiates the novices to certain principles (*mantras*) such as forbidding to drink liquor or eating poor or ritually impure things. However, after returning home the newly initiated group drink country liquor and eat forbidden meat along with other elder novices of the village. The only thing they follow is that they behave each fellow novice of that group as an intimate friend, show affection and never call by his real name, instead, they use a name given by the *Satra*.

There are some adverse and negative impacts also. Within the *Hinduria* group, as mentioned earlier, there are several other sub-sects like *Sankari, Nirgunia, Bhakatiya, Malajopia,* etc., who contrast themselves with others following some distinctiveness without any practical value. The *Bhakatiya*, for example, do not prepare country liquor at home. But they indulge in having unsqueezed country liquor. Sometimes they prepare it outside home or even taken wine from wine shops. The *Sankaris* and the non-*Sankaris* make the difference greater between them regarding the ways of observing rituals and funerals, etc. Several conflicts have been reported from different villages regarding such distinctions.

The Mishing people are still bound by a distinct dialect and rich tradition which unite them all. Amidst the non-tribal neighbours they are able to maintain most of their religious beliefs and practices. But it is not that they are without conflict in religious spheres. There are certain conflicts between *Bhakats* (Vaishnavite devotees) and non-Bhakats regarding the performance of rituals. There are some families who especially live in urban areas and have given up most of their age-old traditions and see the fellow people in a denigrating manner. But the community as a whole not changed totally. It has only accepted a few elements of Vaishnavism to get recognition from the higher caste or *Satra* authority. Though the people accepted Vaishnavism, the Bhakats have not given up most of their age-old beliefs and practices.

The case of the Deoris is significant in the sense that the proselytization is going on among them and it is creating a lot of socio-cultural problems among the people. Because the non-converts are numerically strong and have maintained emotional attachment to the *thaan*; they are strongly socially boycotting the converts. No non-convert is allowed to attend any kind of ceremony held by any convert. The converts refuse to contribute to the *thaan* ceremony and have parted with their age-old religious practices.

Role of Vaishnavism

Introduction of neo-Vaishnavism was an echo making event in the socio-cultural history of Assam. Sri Sankardeva was a great religious and socio-cultural reformer in Assam and he gave a distinct shape to the Assamese society. The reforms introduced by Sri Sankardeva properly guarded the Assamese people from entering directly into the domain of orthodox Hindu caste oriented religion. His religion did not recognise caste and class. All were welcomed with equal status. But his liberal view was not maintained by his followers. There appeared instead of moral teaching, a trend of expansionism.

The tribals were never the gainer in the sphere of social mobility and economic development. Refinement in religious practices did not give the people a status equal to the high caste people. Because the high caste people did never recognize them as to be of pure society. Moreover, the people did not totally part with their habit of eating and drinking so-called impure things. Nor did they leave the traditional ways of performing several religious rituals. People on the other hand never liked to mix up with the non-tribal people whatever their social status might be.

Though there was the promise that new religion will uplift the people's economic and social condition, the *Satra* authority actually did nothing. It never tried to equate the people. It also never noticed the day-to-day life ways of the people. The only thing — the beneficial one for the *Satra* — was that preachers tried their best to increase the number of followers and the *Satras* were able to collect the amount of *Kar-Var* (religious tax) from the disciple villages. Perhaps this was the reason for which the *Satra* authority did not impose strong restriction on traditional practices of their tribal followers.

In totality, neo-Vaishnava religion served to a great extent to form a harmonized Assamese society with certain common religious and socio-cultural aspects. There are certain tribal gods and goddesses which are equated with the Hindu gods and goddesses. There are certain legends and mythical stories regarding the relationship of these tribes with Hindu deities or heroes of epic ages. For example, the *Khring* or the *Bathow* and the *Bhoroli* of the Sonowal Kacharis are equated with the Hindu god and goddess *Shiva* and *Parvati* respectively. *Dobiur Uie* of the Mishings is equated with the *Shani*, and *Taleng Uie* with *Indra*. The Sonowal Kacharis consider themselves as the descendants of the legendary *Ghototkos* who was a son of great hero *Bhima* of the Mahabharata. The Deoris say that they are related to Lord Krishna because he eloped Rukmini from Sadiya (Kundil). There are several other such myths and stories which show that the Hindu escatology acted steadily to absorb the tribal tradition within its wide folds. Such a process became very fast under the patronage of neo-Vaishnavism, because the scholars of this age translated the Hindu religious books to Assamese and created stories taking the local background. The spread of such propaganda helped to absorb the tribal tradition into Hinduism—or more strictly speaking, into Vaishnavism.

Though the formation of Assamese community was a great achievement, intra-tribal conflicts were raising day by day. The roles of *Satra* were not satisfactory in such spheres. Instead, day by day, new sub-sects were emerging and changing the tribal lifeways. For instance, among the Sonowal Kacharis, when a ritual is performed in a family, or in village level ceremonies, there appears to have more than one heath — one for the non-converts and other for the converts or *Bhakatiyas*. The *Bhakatiyas* eat in a separate place covering the place with white cloths signifying purity.

Such examples clearly show that the role of *Satra* authority among the tribal people is somewhat confusing. Proselytization in the hill states show that Christianity has done a lot for the development of the tribal people. It guarded the people from orthodox Hindu domain and exploitation. Though not economically, educationally the Christianized tribes of north-east India gained a lot and raised their literacy rate higher than national literacy rate. But such a trend is not found in the case of Vaishnava proselytization at all.

Recent Trends

Revivalism and retribalization is an emerging event in these days. Especially, entire north-east India is experiencing with the strong blow of revivalism of tribal norms and tradition and also for autonomy. These three tribes too are no exception.

The Sonowal Kacharis have formed an organization to revive their age-old traditional practices. They have already revived the *Bathow Puja, Gojai-Monai, Haidung Songs* and such other certain forgotten folk traditions. In socio-cultural life also they have restructured the clan organization.

Among the Mishings *Takam Mishing Parin Kebang* has revitalized several ago-old tradition, performing some popular rituals at community level with wide advertisement and rich participation. They are also collecting folk tales, folk songs, etc., for reformation of Mishing culture.

The Deoris, though they are facing problems arising out of proselytization in current years, their students' organisations are trying to re-establish socio-cultural harmony and to develop their own script and dialect and for the eradication of evils of the society so that general upliftment of the population takes place.

Conclusion

The study and discussion above show that refinement sought to be brought in the socio-cultural life of the three tribal groups cannot be properly equated with the process called 'Sanskritization'. There was no evidence of caste mobility or transition from tribalism to casteism in the communal way. Though in the past people accepted Vaishnavism to raise their status, they were not ready to detach themselves from tribal identity and sentiments. Nor did they forego the main traditional religious practices.

It is seen that political, economic and socio-cultural conditions of the tribal people helped in the process of detribalization through religious means. As there was no caste mobility and no transition, we cannot say in the same vein as observed by Dube (1972 : 283) that Sanskritization occurred among plain tribes of Assam; rather we may assert that a distinct mode of proselytization occurred in the Brahmaputra valley under the patronage of neo-Vaishnavism. We can call this movement as 'Vaishnavization' of the tribal people of Assam.

The tribal people contributed a lot in the process of the formation of Assamese community. They always preferred to identify themselves as Assamese people and religiously as Hindu (Vaishnava). Therefore, Vaishnavism served a lot in community formation. But in this emerging process the tribal people underwent a good deal of changes. Their internal social harmony took a new shape leading almost to disharmony, as the Vaishnavite religious leaders introduced several sectism and sub-sectism among the people. These resulted in chronic conflicts among fellow persons. Moreover, those tribes especially the Sonowal Kacharis parted with most of their age-old traditions. At present, they find nothing special to stand for their distinctiveness as a unique and distinct tribal group. The new generation has emerged being conscious of and worried about the extinction of their own unique identity. At present, they are trying to re-establish and revive their age-old traditions to get back their socio-cultural identity. Rightly or wrongly their view is that in the process of Vaishnavisation and also in community formation, they were betrayed by higher castes and classes and they remained at the same level of social status and development. Instead of gaining a new life, they have lost their own cultural life-ways. Therefore, a movement of revivalism is new going on among all the tribal groups.

It is, therefore, seen that though religious ideas are introduced for the well-being of the tribal people, it led the people to a social state of social disharmony and imbalance in social life and thus it created the problem of identity crisis due to detribalization and tribal absorption.

The view of the preachers is questionable. The tribal people rear pigs and fowls and only a small portion of them are used in rituals. Rearing pigs and fowls cost nothing because these are fed on waste products of crops, etc. Moreover sacrificial animals are those that are easily available at hand. Rarely the people buy a pig or fowl for rituals. Use of liquor is not a matter of inconsistency to economy as traditional people have a limit and timing of drinking. They are in the habit of drinking after a day's hard work to refresh their body, to kill their pain and to make merry. As such drinking liquor is not a bad habit. Without understanding the socio-cultural and physical environment of the tribal people, preachers' denigrating involvement cannot gain a logical acceptance.

REFERENCES

BOSE, N.K., 1941, The Hindu Method of Tribal Absorption. *Science and Culture*. 7 : 188-194.

DUBEY, S. M., 1972, The Tribes of North East India. In *Tribal Situation in India*. Edited by K.S. Singh. Simla: Indian Institute of Advanced Studies.

MAJUMDAR, D.N., 1972, Tribe-Caste Continuum and the Process of Sanskritization. In *Tribal Situation in India*. Edited by K.S. Singh, Simla: Indian Institute of Advanced Studies.

MAJUMDAR, D.N., 1962, *Himalayan Polyandry*. Bombay: Asia Publishing House.

ROY BURMAN, J.J., 1988, Christianity and Development Among the Hill Tribes of North East India. *Journal of Indian Anthropological Society*. 23, 3 : 203.

SACHCHIDANANDA, 1964, *Culture Change in Tribal Bihar*. Calcutta: Bookland Private Limited.

SAHA, R.K., 1989, Impace of Non-Tribal Religion Among the Bhtra of Baster. In *Acculturation and Social Change in India*. Edited by S.C. Panchbhai and M.K.A. Siddiqui. Calcutta: Anthropological Survey of India.

SAHAY, K.N., 1962, Trends of Sanskritization Among the Oraons. *Bulletin of Bihar Research Institute*. 4, 2.

SINHA, S., 1972, Tribal Solidarity Movement in India. In *Tribal Situation in India*. Edited by K.S. Singh, Simla: Indian Institute of Advanced Studies.

SRINIVAS, M.N., 1952, *Religion and Society among the Coorgs of South India*. London: Oxford University Press.

SRIVASTAVA, S.K., 1958, *The Tharus*. Agra: Agra University Press.

VIDYARTHI, L.P., 1977, *The Tribal Culture of India*. Delhi: Concept Publishing House.

15
The Assamese Sikhs : The Samurais of Assam

Birinchi Kumar Medhi

Introduction

On historical, linguistic and certain socio-cultural grounds, the Sikh population of Assam may broadly be divided into two categories — the Assamese Sikhs and the migrant Sikhs. The mother tongue of the Assamese Sikh inhabitants of Assam is Assamese. They were the descendants of the early Sikh settlers during different historical times between 17th and 19th century. Besides language there are many other points of cultural identity between the Assamese Sikhs and the Assamese of the Brahmaputra plains. The overwhelming majority of the Assamese Sikhs are rural inhabitants and they are agriculturists. There are also Sikhs in Assam who have originally and primarily migrated from undivided Punjab. These Sikhs are mainly to be found in no-agricultural occupations in urban areas.

The total Sikh population of Assam as of 1971 census is 11,920 and they constitute 0.08 per cent of the State. Since the census enumeration does not take into consideration language as a criterion to count population of different religious groups, the total population of the Assamese Sikhs is not available. According to the estimate of the Assamese Sikhs themselves, their population is around 4,000.

The Assamese Sikhs are to be found in almost all the Brahmaputra valley districts of Assam. Small concentrations of the urban Assamese Sikhs are to be mainly found in Dibrugarh, Diphu, Guwahati, Nagaon and Tangla. They are also to be found in rural areas who live in forming small hamlets like Helem in Sonitpur district, Hatipara, Chaparmukh, Lanka and Barkola in Nagaon district and Rampur in Kamrup district. The rural Sikh situation in the district of Nagaon is unique compared to the other districts of Assam in that the overwhelming majority of the Sikhs of this district are the Assamese Sikhs. The village Barkola in Nagaon district has the largest concentration of the Assamese Sikhs.

Historical Background

Kamrupa or ancient Assam came into contact with the Sikhs when the founder of Sikhism, Guru Nanak, visited Assam during the 16th century. It is held that Guru Nanak visited Dhubri, now the district headquarter of Dhubri district, and the Kamakhya temple situated on Nilachal hills of Guwahati. Ever-since Guru Nanak visit Dhubri the place was held sacred by the people belonging to different religions.

The ninth Guru of the Sikhs, Guru Teg Bahadur, visited Assam in the 17th century. He accompanied Raja Ram Singh. Raja Ram Singh was deputed by Aurengzeb to make an expedition in Assam. There was a contingent of Sikh soldiers along with Ram Singh. Guru Teg Bahadur, along with the Sikh soldiers, camped at Dhubri. Guru requested all the soldiers to bring five shieldful of earth to raise a mound in memory of Guru Nanak, the founder of Sikh religion, who visited Dhubri. This mound was erected on the top of a hillock. Guru Teg Bahadur then had erected a pavilion on the top of the mound. This place has come to be known as Gurdwara Damdamia Sahib. Recently this holy place of Sikhs have been renovated and renamed as Gurdwara Sri Teg Bahadur Sahibji. This historic Gurdwara is considered as the first Gurdwara in this part of the region. Some of the Guru's disciples are stayed in Assam and their descendants are found in Dhubri. Historical accounts say that Guru Teg Bahadur also visited Kamakhya temple. A *panda* (priestly Brahman) of the Kamakhya temple had preserved a fragment of historical record which describes Guru Teg Bahadur's visit to Assam. The *panda* claims that his ancestors had come from Amritsar, the birthplace of Guru Teg Bahadur, in Punjab.

Following 100 years after the visit of Guru Teg Bahadur, a batch of Sikh soldiers came to Assam. They were recruited along with some other soldiers by two brothers, Hardatta and Birdatta, in connection with a secret manoeuvre to expel the Ahoms from Guwahati.

In the early part of the 19th century, a group of 300 Sikh soldiers under Chaitanya Singh proceeded to Assam from Punjab to help the Ahom king Chandra Kanta Singha to fight against the Burmese army who invaded Assam. In the fierce battle of Hadirachaki, Chaitanya Singh and a number of Sikh soldiers were killed. Chaitanya Singh's wife (according to some scholar mother) and the Sikh soldiers who survived in the battle did not return to Punjab. They proceeded from Goalpara on boats up to Brahmaputra river and finally reached Chaparmukh. They decided to live at Chaparmukh. Chaitanya Singh's widowed wife founded a Gurdwara at Chaparmukh. This gurdwara is now known as Gurdwara Mataji. The Sikhs who came to Chaparmukh gradually spread over to other places of Assam.

The visits of the Sikh Gurus to Assam in the 16th and 17th centuries and those of the Sikh soldiers in the 19th century gradually contributed towards the strengthening and propagation of the religion of the Sikhs in Assam and also led to the gradual growth of the Sikh population of Assam. The earliest Sikh settlers in Assam had chosen to marry here and their descendants act in many respects in the manner of the Assamese.

Socio-Cultural Life: Some Aspects

The Assamese Sikhs try to conduct their life according to the laws of Sikhism. But this does not imply that all of them have clear perception of the basic tenets of Sikhism. Because of their isolation from their co-religionist from a considerable period of time, the ancestors of the present-day Assamese Sikhs were more associated with Hindu neighbours. This has also happen for the fact that the early Sikh settlers married locally. The Assam

Vaishnavism has many parallels to that of Sikhism for which the earliest Sikh settlers of Assam were absorbed into the local population.

The present-day Assamese Sikhs have not been able to completely wane themselves away from the Hindu social life. The Assamese Sikh practised many rites and rituals and observed taboo prevalent among their Hindu neighbours. The religious life of the Assamese Sikhs is broadly guided by the principles of Sikh religion. However, some of these principles appear to be the own interpretation of the Assamese Sikhs of the principles of Sikh religion. Elements from both Hinduism and indigenous folk beliefs and practices have appreciable influence on the religious life of the Assamese Sikhs. In the context of the Assamese Sikh concentrations, it is the Gurdwara centering which their religious life evolve.

The presence of the Assamese Sikhs in the context of the Assamese villages is made felt by the attire of the male-folk who wear turban and keep their hair and beard long. Their womenfolk invariably wear *mekhela* and *chadar*, the traditional garb of the Assamese women. The attire distinction of the male and their clustering mainly in one hamlet in the Assamese villages where they reside make them clearly distinguishable from their non-Sikh neighbours. The Sikhs are also noticeable because of their having gurdwaras which can be recognised from a distance. For each of the Gurdwaras has tall flag poles wrapped in silken shocks and triangular flags with *Khanda*, the Sikh religious symbols, consisting of quoit (*chakra*) with double edged dagger (*khanda*) in centre and two swords (*kirpan*) crossing beneath. The Assamese Sikhs have been able to maintain their identity largely through their religious organizations and attire distinctions.

The Assamese Sikhs familial life exhibit a peculiar synthesis of Sikh, Hindu and Assamese folk traditions. The kinship terminologies of the Assamese Sikhs is comparable and bears close affinity to that of the Assamese Hindus. The marriage customs of the Assamese Sikhs are characterised by a curious mixture of the Sikh, Hindu and indigenous folk rituals.

Among the Assamese Sikhs several other factors play decisive role in selecting a male for marriage other than caste consideration. Compared to the Sikhs and the Hindus this is somewhat unique because both among the Sikhs of Punjab and among the Hindus in general one comes across endogamous caste groups. Caste is not prevalent among the Assamese Sikhs. One of the important consideration among the Assamese Sikh is that a Sikh should marry a Sikh. But this consideration among the Assamese Sikhs appears to be partially effective when they select a girl for marriage. Because a large number of marriages have taken place between the Assamese Sikh males and Assamese Hindu girls. The Assamese Sikhs try to find out a girl from among their community and whenever it is difficult to locate a Sikh girl, then they go for a Hindu girl. As pointed out earlier Assamese Sikh is a small community of around 4,000 people only. Therefore, the young people often find it difficult to find out a spouse from among themselves. But a sort of system appears to have been evolved to tie over such situation. The Sikh boys marry non-Sikh local girls, mostly Hindus, who adopt their husbands' faith. There are also instances of marrying away Assamese Sikh girls to non-Assamese Sikhs and this is resorted only as 'distress-deal'. Another important point needs to the mentioned here is that the Assamese Sikhs in general consider at par with the Kalitas and Koches, two agriculturist castes of Assam, and that they mostly select girls belonging to these two castes for marriage.

An analysis of 500 marriages of Assamese Sikhs has shown that in the case of fifty per cent marriages, the wife's community of origin is Assamese who belong to various Assamese castes. Of the total marriages (500), 26 per cent wives are Koch and 12 per cent wives are Kalita.

Conclusion

The expansion of social horizon of the Assamese Sikhs has taken place through their religion, matrimonial relations, educational achievements, occupational mobility, and so on. Like other Indian communities the Assamese Sikhs are also organized in terms of various social groupings and territorial affinities. They are organized in terms of various social groupings like family, descent group, affinal and consanguineal relatives and their religion. They are also organized in terms of territorial affinities like family, local settings, intra and inter-village organizations, religion and so on. They are thus a part of the net work of neighbouring localities and the region.

There are a number of villages in the Brahmaputra valley of Assam where the Assamese Sikhs and the Assamese non-Sikhs belonging to various religions and castes live together. Similar situations are also to be found in some of the towns of Assam where besides the Assamese Sikhs and other Assamese people the non-Assamese Sikhs, and other religious communities and linguistic groups live side by side. In such situations, however, one comes across more day-to-day interactions between the Assamese Sikhs and their Assamese non-Sikh counterparts compared to the contact and communication between the Assamese Sikhs and non-Assamese Sikhs. This may be viewed as a result of the sharing of a large area of socio-cultural life in common by the Assamese Hindus and the Assamese Sikhs. Besides language, there are many other points of socio-cultural identity between the Assamese Sikhs and the Assamese people of the Brahmaputra valley. The sharing of a large area of socio-cultural life in common by the Assamese Sikhs and the Assamese in general has facilitated contact and communication between the Assamese Sikhs and the other Assamese people across the religious boundaries. In this regard the Assamese language and the participation of the Sikhs and the other Assamese people in a common culture have played an important role. The long established traditions of the Assamese Sikh relations had made it possible for the Assamese Sikhs to identify themselves with the Assamese society closely. Thus it has become easier for the Assamese Sikhs to think themselves as Assamese Sikhs than only as Sikhs.

The Assamese Sikhs, the Assamese Hindus, the Assamese Muslims and the other Assamese people are engaged in the same kind of rural and urban occupations. Like their non-Sikh Assamese counterparts the Assamese Sikhs are the participants in the same socio-cultural and economic fields of Assam.

While viewing the Assamese Sikhs as a part of the Assamese society, some references should be made to the emergent pattern of identity awareness among the Assamese Sikhs. A small section of the educated Asssamese Sikhs feels that if adequate protection and opportunities are not offered to them, which they consider as a backward and minority community, they are sure to suffer. Over the years the educated and articulate sections among the Assamese Sikhs have tried to bring all the Assamese Sikhs together under a common formal forum. As a result of the effort of the educated and articulate section of the Assamese Sikhs an association in the name and style of *Asamiya Sikh Sanstha* (Assamese Sikh Association) was formed in the first half of 1980. The primary objective of this association to organize developmental works with regard to their religion, culture, society and economy, publication of Sikh religious books, and so on.

The Assamese Sikhs are well aware of the important happening within the State and in parts of the country. The awareness of the Assamese Sikhs of the important happenings is mostly expressed through the association, the only wider community forum of the Assamese Sikhs.

One often encounters views expressed by non-Assamese Sikhs about the society and culture of the Assamese Sikhs which invariably reflect a fear that unless the Assamese Sikhs learn Punjabi language and understand more about Sikhism, there lies the danger of the community as a whole and the question of their sustaining. But the Assamese Sikhs do not put emphasis on learning Punjabi language because they consider that the *granthis* (keeper of the gurdwara) will take care of that aspect. They put emphasis on knowing the Sikhism which has handed down through generations rather than the formal Sikhism. The religious situations obtaining among the Assamese Sikhs is, by and large, similar to that of the Sikhs of Deleke, a small village, situated at a distance of nearly eight km. from Tarn Taran in Amritsar district in Punjab which is known as the 'Cradle of Sikhism'. Singh (1961 : 191-219) has observed considerable impact of different religions on the Sikhs of Deleke. They worship different tribal and Hindu gods and goddesses and Muslims *pirs* and *faqirs*.

It is held by some scholars that Guru Nanak met Sankardeva, the founder of Assam Vaishnavism, during his visit to Assam. Almost all the *janam-sakhis* (birth evidences, biography) describe the meeting of these two great saints. However, the *charit puthis* (biographies of the Vaishnava Gurus of Assam) have not referred to the meetings of the Guru Nanak and Sankardeva. It has been already pointed out that the philosophy and doctrine of Assam Vaishnavism and Sikhism exhibit many similarities. To quote Neog (1984 : 173) :

> "....Sikhism and Assam Vaishnavism are parallels. That is why the earliest Sikh settlers in Assam were observed into the general population and those who came within the last two centuries had no difficulty in living in great amity with the local people."

The ideological convergence of Sikhism and Assam Vaishnavism has helped in reducing the inter-group social distance.

The Assamese Sikh community do not exist in Assamese society as separate and isolated entities. The socio-cultural life of the Assamese Sikhs operate within segment of a composite social framework.

Acknowledgement

I would like to express my appreciation to Dr. A.N.M. Irshad Ali, Professor and Head, Department of Anthropology, Gauhati University, for his comments on earlier drafts of this paper.

REFERENCES

ALI, A.N.M. IRSHAD; B.K. MEDHI, 1993, Sikhism in an Assamese Village. *Bulletin of the Department of Anthropology, Gauhati University*, 7 : 1 - 11.

ALI, A.N.M. IRSHAD; B. K. MEDHI, 1993a, The Assamese Sikhs: An Ethnographic Profile. *Bulletin of the Department of Anthropology, Dibrugarh University*, 20-21 : 1-11.

ALI, A.N.M. IRSHAD; B.K. MEDHI, 1993b, The Assamese Sikhs: Profile of a Minuscale Community. In: *People of India*, Edited by S.B. Roy and A.K. Ghosh, pp 277-287, New Delhi: Inter India Publications.

NEOG, M., 1984, *Religions of North East*. New Delhi: Munshiram Manoharlal Publishers Pvt. Ltd.

SINGH, I.P., 1961, Religion in Deleke: A Sikh Village. In: *Aspects of Religion in Indian Society*. Edited by L.P. Vidyarthi, pp 191-219. Meerut: Kedar Nath Ram Nath.

16
Traditional Political System : A Case Study of the Karbis of Assam

R.P. Athparia

Introduction

The Karbis who call themselves as the Arleng inhabit mostly in the Karbi Anglong district of Assam, formerly known as Mikir Hills District. It is located at the junction of the two geographically undemarcated segments of Assam popularly referred to as Upper Assam and Lower Assam. The Karbis are also known as the Mikirs. The ethnic name Karbi connotes brotherhood. It is the custom of the Karbis to keep fire alight in the hearths and offer portions of all eatables to the ancestral spirits before consuming. Another term used by the people to refer to themselves is 'Arleng' meaning 'man'. In the present note an attempt has been made to describe the traditional political system of the Karbis of Assam.

Following the classification of political systems presented by Fortes and Evans — Pritchard (1940) in 'African Political Systems', the Karbis could be said to fall into the category of 'State' society. When a society possesses a governmental structure, we have a class of political system to which the authors give the name 'State'; when such a structure is non-existent, we have a residual category called 'Stateless' society. We feel that judging from our empirical experience the above two categories along with their defined characteristics cannot be applied as fixed models to societies in this part of the country. However, the above classification helps us to understand the mechanism of internal political systems.

Among the Karbis, particularly the Karbis of the Hamren Civil Sub-division, a state like organisation is found. The State is a territorial as well as an administrative unit, the political rights and obligations are territorially delimited. The Karbi State or *Karbi Rajya* is divided into three broad territories called *Alongris*. The three *Alongris* are: Rongkhang, Chinthong and Amri. These are, again, divided into sub-territorial divisions called *Longris*. In all there are twelve *Longris* or sub-territorial divisions. The *Longris* are Habepi, Sangkheli, Umaha, Rapati, Umlarang, Rongkhang, Rongcheicho, Rongpi, Nokberi, Dera, Kiling and Umchera. Each *Longri* controls a number of villages which are known as *Arong*.

Regarding the demarcation of a Longri, there are controversies among the Karbis. Some claim that all the twelve *Longris* are found only in the Rongkhang Alongri, while others speak of *Longris* to be in existence only in the areas that were under the Jaintias. Besides these, regarding the line of demarcation of different *Longris* there is a good deal of confusion. Sometimes, a given area is claimed to be under the jurisdiction of more than one *Longri*. Therefore, the overall result as regards *Longri* is that none is sure of a fixed line of demarcation between adjacent *Longris*. But all conform to the view that there are twelve *Longris* in the Karbi land.

Lyall (1908 : 15) also referred to the *Alongri* territorial divisions of the tribe, but he is silent about the *Longri* divisions. According to the author, these territorial divisions are as follows: (i) the hilly portion of the Mikir Hills referred to as Chinthong, (ii) North Cachar Hills and the hilly parts of Nowgong referred to as Rongkhang, and (iii) the Khasi and Jaintia Hills called Amri. The natives, however, say that the Umtru river, a tributary of the Dhansiri divides the territories of Chinthong and Rongkhang, while the Langsang river of the Kopili is the demarcation boundary of Rongkhang and Amri.

Of these, the Amris are found mainly in westernmost hilly areas of Amri Block — the westernmost part of Mamren sub-division, Ri-Bhoi area of East Khasi Hills and foothills of Southern Kamrup.

The Rongkhang section of the Karbis are found to inhabit the entire area covering the eastern part of Hamren sub-division, particularly the plain areas of the Rongkhang Block. Rongkhangs are also found in parts of North Cachar hills falling within the Kopili valley.

The Chinthong Development Block of Hamren and those of Diphu sub-division, particularly the Lumbajong area including Diphu town, are said to be the Chinthong.

Seat of Traditional Authority

The Karbi chief, known as *Karbi Recho,* is the administrative and judicial head of the entire state. The centre of the Karbi traditional organisation is located at Nij Rongkhang or the village inhabited by all the *Pinpomar* (councillors) of greater Karbi society. This village situated in the Hamren sub-division is also known as Baruagaon on Pinpo-Arong where all the traditional *Pinpomar,* the councillors, reside or are expected to reside. Lyall (1908 : 5) mentions, "they have dim traditions of a king of their own in the good old days, whom they call *Sot Recho...* His seat is said to have been in Rongkhang (or Rong - hang), perhaps connected with Ni-hang (Rang - village)". By physical verification it was found that some popularly chosen office-bearers hesitated to go and reside in the inpo-Arong permanently as some of them thought that such a life did not encourage personal economic improvement of a family by limiting the scope of the traditional mode of earning a livelihood. It could be noted that under the system of *Pinpomar* a large number of offices have been created for the smooth functioning of the traditional Karbi State. It has also been noted that they were reluctant to hold an office under the *Karbi Recho* for the simple reason that the incumbent was to reside at *Pinpo Arong* far away from the own household. The office of the *Bor Senot* (councillor), for instance, to be filled by a chosen incumbent remained vacant till March 1977, the period of my enquiry, in Rongkhang area. The incumbent Sri Rong Bong Pator, aged 45 years, preferred to remain as Bor Gaonbura instead of accepting the traditional office due to him. Enquiry revealed that the said incumbent was a contractor under the Local Public Works Department besides continuing the office of Bor Gaonbura. Had he preferred to accept the office due to him he would not have been able to earn as much as he did by regular contract with the Government at Hamren. The case shows that economic motivation is a greater driving force than the traditional office. The *Pinpomar*, the councillors, are the chosen or selected representatives of the *Kur-Abang*, i.e., the council of the clan elders serving as ministers or advisers to the Karbi Chief, i.e., *Karbi Recho*. Tradition demands their living away from their wife and children. They are expected to live on the contribution made by the respective members of each clan-cluster which they represent in the chief's council. For each principal clan there is a *Deng Achar* who is the most elderly and experienced man along the members of his clan; it was his duty to collect rice or paddy from each household for the maintenance of the *Pinpomar*. The goods collected are then distributed by the *Deng Achar* to the *Pinpomar* in the *Pinpo Arong*, i.e., the seat of the tribal Government. This practice was in fullswing up to the time of Rongbonghom, during whose period the great legendary Karbi hero Thong Nokbe was killed by the Jaintias. Rongbonghom was a Karbi chief belonging to the Ronghang sub-clan. He was popular and kind hearted. It was he who abolished the capital punishment and instituted the custom of propitiating of gods by sacrificing goats, fowls, or pigs. The present day Karbi marriage system was said to be introduced by him. For his manifold accomplishments, he came to be known a *Phu Rengbonghom* meaning 'father Rengbonghom'. That was the period when the *Pinpomar* had the real and effective powers in running the overall affairs of the entire state.

Structure of Alongri Council

Each of the *Alongris* is administered by a council of elders known as *Lindoks*. Administratively, each *Alongri* is autonomous but it functions under the direct control of the *Karbi Recho*. The recruitment principle of the *Lindok* is kinship-based. The distinct sub-clans have provided the *Lindoks* with distinct obligations and privileges. In all there are nine *Lindoks*, out of which the Ranghang sub-clan provides the Karbi society with the *Karbi Recho* on a strictly hereditary principal.

There is a legend how the Ronghang sub-clan became the Karbi Chief. It is as follows:

In the Karbi capital, there lived a chief belonging to the Timung clan. He had two daughters. They were married off and the son-in-laws were Ingleng and Ronghang. It is said that the elder son-in-law, Ingleng was mean and treacherous and he had an ambition to become the chief of the Karbis. The younger son-in-law, Ronghang was good and well behaved. The machinations of the eldest son-in-law forced his father-in-law to vacate the throne and take shelter in the neighbouring Jaintia kingdom. This prompted the younger son-in-law to oppose the elder. A bloody fight ensued and the younger son-in-law won the battle and he became the king of the Karbis. From that time onwards the Ranghang sub-clan became the powerful king in the Karbi traditional political system.

The other eight *Lindoks* are the representatives of the eight sub-clans which enjoy equally prestigious position. The distribution of *Lindoks* in the three *Alongris* of Rongkhang Chinthong and Amri is noted below: the Rongkhang consists of four sub-clans, namely, Ronghang, Rongcheicho, Kiling and Rongpi; the Chinthong *Alongri* comprises the sub-clan of Hanse, Rongpi and Timung-Rongphar; and the last one, namely, Amri have Hanse and Teron sub-clans. Thus, there are more than one *Lindoks* in every *Alongri* council and each *Lindok* has specific duties and responsibilities being the organisation of religious ceremonies like the erection of megaliths and arranging of last rites and so on; or judicial functions connected with the maintenance of social norms and customs. The *Recho* (Raja) himself represents the Ronghang sub-clan and practically the Rongkhang Alongri council functions as the *Rechomei* or royal council through which the Recho controls the entire state.

The *Pinpomar* offer this office to the man who is considered to be honest and of unquestionable character and above all with leadership capability. The man if unwilling is persuaded to accept the office when the *Pinpomar* meet for the appointment of *Lindok.* If a seat of *Lindok* falls vacant of a particular sub-clan anyone from that particular sub-clan can propose a name. If the proposal is not objected to on any valid ground the proposal is accepted.

The qualification attributed to the office of *Lindok* are that the prospective candidate must be aged between forty and fifty, physically he must be healthy and energetic and mentally sound. Other required qualities are truthfulness and nobility. A *Lindok* is expected to be the custodian of social norms and customs; he should have a fair knowledge of social norms prevailing in the society.

When a man accepts the office of the *Lindok,* he is ceremonially inducted into the office. The *Pinpomar* and the villagers call at the house of the *Lindok*-designate. It is obligatory on the part of the *Lindok*-designate to treat the visitors to rice, rice bear, betel nuts and betel leafs. Then all of them worship the God Hemphu-Mukrang. A feast arranged by the Lindok-designate follows the worship. The same feast is repeated the following day. On the third day, a good deal of revelry takes place and the young and able-bodied men dance in a great congregation of applauding people. The *Duihidi* (the professional drummer) beats his drum vigorously and the dancers move to the tune of the beats. This dance is locally known as *Chachirikekan* (a dance in honour of the Lindok-designate). The appointment of the Ronghang Lindok is always attended with mirth and gaiety. The official residence of the Rongkhang Lindok is at the village of Nij Ranglhong or Pinpo Arong. A Rongkhang Lindok is invariably expected to reside at this village during the tenure of his office.

The grand old man of Hamren and Panbari village could remember the Karbi Recho right from Kiting Ronghang to the present-day. He reigned from 1909 to 1911. The ethnographer could learn that Kiting Ronghang was a man of Langlongda village of Rongcheicho Longri. This village was located on the western side of the Hamren sub-divisional headquarters. He was chosen by the Ronghang Deng Achar because he had fulfilled all the qualifications to become a *Recho*. During this time, the other officials of the Rechomei were as follows: Ram Teron, the Lindok of Rongcheicho sub-clan, woking the Lindok of Kiling sub-clan, Lik, the Miji, Sarset, the Rongpi Lindok of Rongpi sub-clan and Amri Terang, the Dili. It is said that Kiting was not a good administrator, and the *Pinpomar* of his council named above asked him to vacate the office of the Ronghang Lindok in the year 1911. Accordingly, Kiting left the office. After him, the Deng Achar of Umaha-Rapati Longri met the elderly members of the Ronghang sub-clan and chose Pagalang Ronghang for the office of the *Recho*. Pagalang had continued the office up to his death in 1936. Bura Ronghang succeeded Pagalang in the year 1937. Bura was the eldest son of Pagalang. Bura died in the year 1952. As the sons of Bura Ronghang were minor, the Deng Achar searched for the successor of Bura Ronghang. At that time, Bura's wife advised the Deng Achar to choose one Sarthe Ronghang of Borpu village of Hamren for the office of the Recho. The Deng Achar accordingly offered the office to Sarthe Ronghang. He assumed the office of Recho in the year 1953 and continued till 1978. As Harsing Ronghang, the eldest son of Sarthe Ronghang, was suffering from an incurable disease locally known as Chipru (skin disease), Sarman Ronghang, Sarthe Ronghang's father's brother's son succeeded to the office of Recho after Sarthe Ronghang. He belonged to Molahin village of Kiling Longri. It may be noted that Sarman Ronghang was not a member of the Umaha-Rapati Longri from which normally the Recho was to be selected. The *Deng Achar* was then under obligation to 'purchase' a man from any of the *Longris*. In the instant case, the *Deng Achar* of Umaha-Rapati Longri had to 'purchase' Sarman of Kiling Longri. This procedure is locally known as *Lindokop Kenam*. In this connection, the *Deng Achar* of Umaha-Rapati provided the necessary articles like pillow, bed cover, quilt, etc., to Sarman Ronghang. An amount of rupees one hundred and fifty was given to the *Habekethe*, the seniormost officials of Kiling Longri. Sarman was the *Recho* up to 1985. He vacated the office at his own will and settled in Kolonga Road village. At present, he is holding the office of the *Bruteman*, a village civil functionary next to the village head-man in position and rank. The same year, i.e., in 1985, the office of the *Recho* was taken over by one Mansing Ranghang of Umaha-Rapati Longri. Though Sarman gave up the office willingly his sons could no be considered to succeed him, as they were too minor to hold the office. Mansing also vacated the office at his own will and handed over the charge in March 1990 to the *Kathar Bura*, the religious head functionary of the *Recho*. The charge was perhaps handed over to *Kathar Bura* as he was the seniormost official of the *Recho* at the time. When Mansing handed over the charge, the *Bor Senot* and *Bor Miji*, civil officials of the *Recho*, met Hedsing Ronghang, the *Deng Achar* of Umaha-Rapati Longri and conveyed the message of the *Pinpomar* to select a man for the *Recho*. Hedsing Ronghang then met the elderly people of his *Longri* and chose Kat Ronghang of Linchika village of Umaha-Rapati Longri for the office of *Recho*. After completion of selection, Hedsing informed the *Pinpomar* of the *Recho* of the matter through the *Habe*, the head of the *Longri*. The *Pinpomar* discussed this issue on 7th March, 1990 and finally approved of the choice of Kat Ranghang. Kat Ronghang assumed office of the Recho from Kathar Bura on 8th March, 1990 is still continuing the office.

In case of Chinthong and Amri, it could not be established for lack of authentic information if the Lindoks of Chinthong and Amri had their official residence village. Presently, however, the Lindoks of Chinthong and Amri reside in their own parental villages. The work could well be followed by some ethnographers before the whole picture vanishes into oblivion.

The *Pinpomar* retain their hold over a *Lindok* and reserve the right to dismiss him if he is found to be inefficient and partial. A *Lindok* holds the office for life time. If a *Lindok* is dismissed, he forfeits all his rights and privileges.

It may be presumed that the numerical strength of the *Lindoks* in an *Alongri* symbolises the rank — the larger the number of *Lindoks* the higher is the position. But it may also be presumed in other way round. It may be said that an *Alongri* might enjoy higher rank on account of having large number *Lindoks* in its fold. The real position, however, could not be ascertained. From the field investigation it is revealed that while Rongkhang has four *Lindoks*, the Chinthong has three and the Amri two. Thus, Rongkhang, Chinthong and Amri represent three different ranks. On ceremonial occasions, the official of Rongkhang has the highest rank followed by Chinthong and

Amri. This is symbolised through presentation of four bottles of *Arak* (country liquor) to the Rongkhang, three to the Chinthong and two to the Amri. On the occasion of *Chomankan* also the same distinctive treatment is observed. During this occasion, the Rongkhang receives four pieces of *Jambili Anthon*[1], the Chinthong three and the Amri two. The Rongkhong, the Chinthong and the Amri are the three original spatial socio-cultural groups representing the three Alongris. These divisions are the three well defined traditional socio-political divisions presided over and governed by *Lindoks* representing the different clan cluster. The Rongkhang, as noted above, has continued since time immemorial to enjoy the preferential treatment on socio-cultural occasions and has the place of precedence and prestige.

Administrators of the Alongri

It has been noted that the traditional Karbi administration is concerned with the institution of three *Alongris* — Rongkhang, Chinthong and Amri. As stated above a relatively full-length ethnographic accounts could be had in respect of the structure and function of the Ronghang Alongri; no data could be had for lack of knowledgeable persons with regard to the other two Alongris, i.e., Chinthong and Amri. The following is the brief pen-picture of the structure and function of the Ronghang Alongri.

Chart : I

The Rongkhang Alongri : the Structure

The chart concerning the structure of the Ronghang Alongri shows the different personnel meaning the whole institution in the hierarchical order. It is seen from the chart that there are two broad divisions, namely, civil and religious. The civil side is headed by the *Karbi Recho* who is also a *Lindok* belongs to the Ronghang sub-clan. He is assisted by three other *Lindoks*, namely, *Rongcheicho*, *Kiling* and *Rongpi*. These three *Lindoks* are equivalent in rank.

Next to them stand two officials called *Dili* and *Bey Bruteman*. They are equal in rank. The *Dili* is assisted by a congregation of officials who occupy certain position and rank. Similarly, the *Bey*

Bruteman is also assisted by another group of officials having hierarchical position and rank. Thus, it is seen that following the *Lindoks* the next in rank comes the *Dili,* who belongs to the Terang Dili sub-clan and who is the administrator-in-general of Rongkhang Alongri council. He manages the general day-to-day affairs of the council. He also looks after the defence and judiciary matters of the royal council. The *Dili* is followed in rank by the *Bor Pator* and the *Bor Miji.* They are equal in rank. The *Bor Pator* acts as the assistant to the administrator-in-general, and in the *Dili's* absence he can take over the defence matters temporarily. The *Bor Miji's* principal duty is to visit the *Longris* to supervise if the affairs under the *Habe* are running perfectly or not. He is entitled to take action or any other decision against any erring *Habe.* He has full right to dismiss or appoint a new Habe on behalf of the *Karbi Recho.*

The *Teron Rongpi* and the *Timung Rongpi* are two officials who follow the rank of the *Bor Pator* and the *Bor Miji.* The duty and function of the *Teron Rongpi* and the *Timung Rongpi* could hardly be intelligible during conversation with few knowledgeable people the ethnographer could meet. Moreover, the informants were reluctant to disclose the function and duties of the two functionaries despite vehement query. Officials in the lowest rung in the official hierarchy are the *Rongphu Borseno,* the *Rongchitim* and the *Rongling.* They act as the guards of the Nij Rongkhang.

The other set of hierarchy under the civil rank starts with the officials called the *Bey Bruteman* who occupies the topmost position. His functions and duties are identical in civil matters proper with that of the *Dili.* He acts as the legal adjudicator. The *Bey Bruteman* is followed in position and rank by the *Teron Miji* and the *Kiling Miji* who are equivalent officers. They act like rather assistants to the *Bruteman.* In absence of the *Bruteman* they function in his place.

Below the rank of the *Teron Miji* and the *Kiling Miji* come the *Rongphu Ferangke* and the *Rongling Ferangke.* They act as messengers of the royal court. They inform the villagers if any meeting is to be held in the royal court or if there is any important news to be conveyed to the villagers. These two officials are followed by the *Kro Nihang*, the *Khanalong*, the *Borsalai*, the *Phura Ingjai* and the *Lindok Riso* in the rank and position. They are also messengers of the royal court.

Apart from the functionaries of the civil division mentioned above, there is a set of religious functionaries in the royal court. The religious side of the royal court is headed by the *Karthar Bura*. Basically, he is the royal priest. He occupies the second in command in position in the royal council hierarchy, and therefore, takes the charge of the *Karbi Recho* in the latter's absence or death. His actual duty is to perform the annual worship which is arranged at Nij Rongkhang for the good, peace and prosperity of the kingdom.

Under the *Kathar Bura* there are two subordinates: the *Dengja Kethe* and the *Bey Miji*. The *Dengja Kethe* is the functionary who is involved in slaughtering the sacrificial animals in the Rongkher Puja Thanthepi which is held once in a year at Nij Rangkhang for the welfare and prosperity of the Kingdom. The *Dengja Kethe* is helped by his assistant *Dengjaso*. The other subordinate of the *Kather Bura*, the *Bey Miji*, stands in equal rank with *Dengja Kethe*. His duty is to drive away the evil spirits from any particular ritual where animals are sacrificed and holy verses are chanted. The *Bey Miji* has his own helpers; they are the *Kro Nilip* and the *Himtok Rongpi* who are equal in rank. However, the *Himtok Rongpi* has an additional duty over and above being an assistant of the *Bey Miji*. He supplies all materials especially *Him* (rice powder) required in the Rongker Puja. It is of absolute necessity on the part of the *Himtok Rongpi* to prepare *Him* during Rongker ritual.

The aforesaid delimination is an elaborate traditional system governing the day-to-day administration of the Karbi Rajya down to the level of the village. The system appears to the based on hierarchy both on the civil side in contradiction to the religious side. Apart from the Rajya level work, works at the subterritorial (*Longri*) and village (*Arong*) levels come under the jurisdiction of different officials already referred to in the foregoing paragraphs.

The Longri: The Sub-territorial Unit

As stated above the whole Karbi territory comprises twelve *Longris* which are sub-territorial units under the control of the *Karbi Recho*. The *Longri* level of Karbi traditional organisation is headed by an official called *Habe Kethe,* i.e., the foremost of *Habe* as there are more than two such office holders in each *Longri* except in Umchera Longri. Umchera Longri is also known as *Chouplit* meaning dark forest. Earlier, the habitation in Umchera Longri was thin and for this reason there was only one *Habe* in this *Longri.* The *Habe* of this *Longri* belongs to sub-clan called *Phangso*. It is also worth mentioning that there is no *Habe* in Lumbajong area. It is said that the Lumbajong area was under the Ahom domain for pretty long time, due to which the Karbi system of administration did not prevail there. The *Habes* are appointed by the *Lindok* in consultation with the council of *Pinpomar*. The *Habes* mostly come from two clans, namely, Inghty and Terang. The office of the *Habe* is invariably hereditary. A *Habe* is recognised and installed into office formally by the *Lindok* of the region. The occasion is solemnised by throwing a feast by the Habe-designate. The *Habe* continues to hold office till his death.

The *Habe* presides over all meetings held in the Longri council. It could be learnt that all Longri council meetings were held in the village dormitory called *Jirkedam*. The institution is also referred to as Terang Ahem and Terang Hangthar. But it has now become almost defunct. Nowadays, the meetings of the *Longri* are held in the house of the defunct dormitory chief called *Basopo* who is still functioning in his honorific capacity.

As several villages come under one *Longri,* there is more than one *Basapo* in a *Longri.* Above the *Basapo* there is an official called *Bruteman* meaning 'judge'. His main duty is to look after the legal proceedings in a *Longri* meeting. In hierarchy, the *Bruteman* is lower than that of the *Bey Bruteman* of the royal court. However, the functions of these two functionaries are more or less same as discussed above. In a *Longri* council, the *Bruteman* acts as a judge. In absence of the *Bruteman,* the *Basapo* of the Habe's village acts as the legal adviser.

Below the rank of the *Basapo* is the *Mutiar*. The word *Mutiar* might have been derived from the *Mukhtiar*, an Assamese word, very commonly used in the Assamese legal jurisprudence. The office of *Mutiar* is found only in Rongkhang area. The *Mutiar* serves as a messenger of the *Habe*. There might be more than one *Mutiar* under one *Habe*.

The other functionaries of the Longri council are: *Ferangke* and *Sarthe*. These two officials are below the rank of *Mutiar*. The *Ferangke* is higher than the *Sarthe*. His duty is to collect cash or kind from the villagers for the Rongkher Puja of the *Longri*. He also acts as the cashier of the Longri council.

The *Sarthe* is the lowest officer of a *Longri*. However, he has ample judiciary power concerning the common people under him.

All these functionaries mentioned above deal with the judiciary matters of the Longri council. The religious side of the *Longri* is looked after by the *Kurusor*, the priest. He presides over all the religious functions at the Longri level. In hierarchy, the office of the *Kurusor* is equal with the office of *Bruteman*.

All the *Longri* level functionaries are appointed by the *Habe Kethe* in consultation with the villagers of his domain and the matter is conveyed to the *Karbi Recho*. The *Habe Kethe* is the general administrator of the *Longri*. It is reported that the *Habe Kethe* of *Habepi Longri* is higher in rank than all *Habe Kethe* of all other *Longris*. He is regarded and honoured by all the *Longri* functionaries. He also gets a special honour and respect from the *Karbi Recho*. The *Habe Kethe* of Habepi Longri unlike the other *Habe Kethes*, is entitled to use the *Jambili Athon*.

The District Council appoints an official as a village functionary covering several villages. This official is called *Bor Gaonbura*. He is the official who carries an insignia in the form of a brass seal, i.e., tagged on his breast pocket. He receives a remuneration of rupees fifty per month. He is the man who collects *Chang-Khazana* or house tax from the villagers under his jurisdiction. He is also exempted from paying his *Chang-Khazana* for his service. The *Habe-Kethe* has no control or authority on the

Bor-Gaonbura. But a *Bor-Gaonbura* is invariably invited to join and participate in the deliberations in the *Longri* meeting presided over by the *Habe Kethe*.

Thus, we can say that the *Longri* level authority is equally hierarchical like the *Alongri* level authority. Each *Longri* is subdivided into manageable small territories presided over and governed by a sub-territorial leader called *Habe*. The *Habe Kethe* enjoys overriding powers and authority over the *Habe* who presides over smaller territory of his *Longri*. The authority of *Habe Kethe* reaches the masses through the *Sarthe* who occupies the basal portion of the Karbi political structure.

The Village Council

The *Sarthe* is head of the village council, locally known as *Mei*. Sartheship like Habeship is hereditary in character. The eldest son succeeds his father to Sartheship if otherwise he is acceptable to the people over whom he is to exercise authority. A physically handicapped person or suffering from leprosy is debarred from occupying such an exalted office. The *Sarthe* after selection has to be installed into the office by a *Habe*. Other functionaries of the *Longris* are also invited to attend thee installation ceremony which is also an occasion for a sumptuous feast by the villagers and invited guests. The *Lindok* or the *Pinpomar* in case of a *Habe* and a *Habe* in case of a *Sarthe* ceremonially puts on *Poho* (turban) to mark the occasion of holding the office. The *Habe* and the *Sarthe* must not henceforth put on *Lengti* (loin cloth used to cover the male organ). He thence puts on a *dhoti* (lower garment of the male). If someone inadvertently puts on a *Lengti* and if reported to the *Lindok* or *Pinpomar* he is liable to be fined. He may even lose his office if it is repeated. No case of transgression is available in both the village studies and delineated above. The informants say that the violator of this norm is usually fined by the *Pinpomar* in case of a *Habe*. A *Habe* can impose a similar fine on the *Sarthe* if the latter violates the norm. Usually the fine is rupees fifty in case of the *Habe* and rupees twentyfive in case of the *Sarthe*.

The functionaries who assist the *Sarthe* are: The *Bruteman*, who assists *Sarthe* in resolving disputes; the *Mutiar* or messenger of the village; the *Ferangke*, who collects money from the inhabitants for the Rongkher festival held in the village he also acts as a cashier of the village; the *Kurusor*, the priest of the village, whose presence is also required in making decisions and resolving disputes at the *Mei*. These functionaries selected by the inhabitants of the village are appointed by the *Habe* and are thus authorised to function by the *Habe* as well as the people of the village.

The villages are named after the currently functioning headman or *Sarthe*. As such, there is a keen desire on the part of an aspirant son of a *Sarthe* to go away from his parental village to start a new hamlet with a few families to assert his leadership. As the villages multiplied in due course there was a felt need for a superstructure to maintain the solidarity and unity among the villages so multiplied. Such a group of villages come to be organised under a sub-regional head called *Habe*, just as the village had its socio-political head in the person of the Sarthe.

The Three-Tier Political System

From the foregoing discussion, it is clear that the traditional political system of the Karbi is a three-tier one. The top tier is headed by the *Lindok*. The middle step is represented by the *Habe* till the same reaches the masses through the *Sarthe* who occupies the basal portion of the structure. The Ronghang Lindok or the *Karbi Recho* locally known as Raja is assisted by a council of elders who represent all the clans of the Karbi. For historical reasons, the Ronghang Lindok, as stated above enjoys an exalted position and honour among all the *Lindoks*. In the good olden days, a great Karbi king belonging to the Ronghang sub-clan not only gave the people peace and respect, he was the pivotal symbol of the social and political life of the Karbis. Lyall (1908) also referred to the Karbi chief as *Sot Recho* meaning a pure king. The middle tier of the traditional political system existing in the form of *Longri* is headed by the *Habe*, a nominee of the *Lindok*. The *Habe* governs the sub-territorial socio-political structure under the charge on behalf of the *Lindok* who appoints him; and he is solely responsible to the latter. The tier at the base is formed by innumerable villages each of which has its own local leader in the person of the *Sarthe*. Next to him stands the *Basapo*, his assistant who is the incharge of the bachelor's dormitory of the village. The village level organisation of the youths under the direct leadership of the village headman and his lieutenant, the *Basapo*, prepares the youths for future participation in a wider socio-political life. The youths of the village are so trained by the *Basapo* and the *Sarthe* as to make men of themselves so that they could rise in the social position up to highest rank. Traditionally, each Karbi village is to organise a bachelor's dormitory where the youths are trained to accept responsibilities of leadership after being conversant with the lore and mores of the Karbi society. It is an institution but for which the traditional organisation can run hardly smoothly.

Although presently the village dormitory is waning especially in the urban areas as already stated, its relevance and importance is still felt in the rural areas in connection with the performance of the community ritual *Chomankan*, marriage, mortuary rites and harvest festivals. Under such eventualities a temporary structure is built up to serve the immediate need. This shows that the spirit and function of the dormitory system still prevails and has remained more or less unimpaired.

In these three levels of regional, sub-regional and village level socio-political organisation, the total Karbi polity is reflected in the three-tier system presented above. Thus, the offices of the chief, the *Habe* and *Sarthe*, the people assert and glorify, and sanctified by the Karbi tradition and lores since time immemorial.

Administration of Justice

There is no codified law among the Karbis. However, the Karbis follow certain social norms which are prevailing in the society from time immemorial. Slight deviation of the prevailing norm is tolerated by the society. If someone commits serious offence, it is immediately brought to the notice of the *Sarthe* for adjudication. The *Sarthe* convenes a meeting of the village council locally known as *Mei* to which both the plaintiff and the defendant are summoned. The plaintiff expresses his grievances and the defendant responses to it in his own way. The adjudication is done in the preference of the villagers in general. All are allowed to join such a legal deliberation. In general, an infringement of traditional norm or dispute is resolved in one sitting but there are certain grievous issues, like incest (*Lichinem* or *Kurchenem*), adultery, rape, violation of marriage rules and pre-marital and extra-marital relations. Such cases take more than one session covering a prolonged period.

Only in serious cases the *Habe* also attends the sitting as a special invitee. Imposition of fine in cash is the normal punishment in such grievous offences. In case of incest the punishment is inflicted at three levels as will be evidenced from the following case:

> In the year 1971, an unmarried youth committed sexual intercourse with a girl of his own clan residing in his village Hamren, of course, with her consent. When the villagers came to know about the incident, it was reported to the *Sarthe*. He made an enquiry and on being satisfied prima facie with the case summoned the council. After hearing the case in detail the village council imposed a fine of rupees fifteen on the male offender. Then the *Sarthe* reported the matter to the *Habe* of his *Longri*. The *Habe* then summoned the offender to the Longri council. After due hearing the offender, the *Habe* sentenced him to a fine of rupees fifty and reported the case to the *Rechomei* through *Mutiar* for final disposal. The *Rechomei* summoned both the offenders and imposed a fine of rupees one hundred on the man and rupees fifty on the woman.

The amount of penalty money depends upon the degree of seriousness of the offence. The village council is empowered customarily to impose fine up to rupees one hundred only but the *Habe* and the *Lindoks* can impose much heavier penalty. In the above case it could be noted that the *Habe* and the *Pinpomar* inflicted heavier punishment. The sum realised as fine is distributed among the members of the council. The *Sarthe* gets one-third of the fine and the rest equally distributed among the members of the council. If the *Habe* is invited in the decision making, he gets half of the sum and the rest is equally distributed among the members of the council including the *Sarthe*. The amount is actually spent by these functionaries during the community feast, on the occasion of Sarthe's or Habe's assuming office or on festivals.

The secular disputes relating to abuse, assault and non-payment of debt or damage caused to the crops are brought to the village council for settlement. The disputes regarding the boundary of the *jhum* fields are also brought to the village council for settlement. But if conflicts arises between a Karbi and a non-Karbi, the matter is usually referred to the local court of law. Theft, murder, suicide and infanticide occur rarely in the Karbi society. Such cases are referred to the local court of laws where the *Bor Gaonbura* or the *Sarkari Gaonbura* acts as a government witness.

The violation of marriage negotiation is also treated as serious. The village council settles such cases and also sees that the *Ke-roi-dum*, the betrothal ring or the bracelet, is returned to the boy's family by the negotiated bride's parents.

The Karbis do not have any concept of the term divorce. They simply refer to the separation of the spouses as *Kasakok*. The villagers do not, however, encourage the separation of the husband and the wife. If it happens, the matter is thoroughly discussed in the village council. The *Sarthe* tries to resolve such cases amicably and prevents separation. He, however, encourages one to 'divorce' when his/her consort suffer from any incurable diseases like leprosy and insanity.

A man seeks separation on the ground of conjugal infidelity and neglect of maintenance of the family by the wife. Barrenness is not considered as a sufficient ground for separation. After separation, the wife loses the right over the husband's assets and the husband loses the right over the children. Social position of children is not affected except the right over the assets of their legal father is lost.

In addition to these administrative functions, the councils are also responsible for arranging various socio-religious ceremonies, such as *Rongkher* (annual village festival), *Chojun* (family welfare festival) and *Chomankan* (mortuary rite). Apart from the socio-religious ceremonies, untoward events like epidemics, natural calamity, etc., also come under the perview of the councils which allocate duties to able bodied members of the village. The *Rongkher* is a ceremony widely observed where the political functionaries of all the three councils of Karbi land are greatly involved. In the performance of lesser type of ceremonies, such as *Chojun* and *Chomankan* too, the village functionaries like *Sarthe, Basapo* and others are equally involved.

Collective Decision

It is worthwhile to mention here that the traditional political organisation of the Karbis virtually stands for collective decision. In the royal council a meeting is chaired by the *Lindok* and other *Pinpomar*. Full freedom is offered to any of these functionaries in such a meeting. The chief can take no decision of his own without referring to the council of advisers. After a full discussion of a matter that comes up for decision, all the participants place their views finally to arrive at an agreed solution which is nothing but a common consensus. The final outcome stands as the highest opinion held by the traditional leaders. There is no higher appellate authority over it. It, however, reserves the right to review its own decision in the light of fresh material gathered through its own efforts.

Appeals preferred by any of the *Habe* under its jurisdiction are heard by the body of *Pinpomar* presided over by the *Lindok*. Likewise, *Habes*, are the appellate authority over the decisions taken by the village level authority (*Sarthe*). The *Habe* is assisted by the council of the advisers, the *Bruteman*, the *Basapo*, the *Mutiar*, the *Feranka*, and the *Sarthe*. No individual decision can be imposed on the Longri level authority (*Habe*) which is equally collective as in the case of Alongri level authority, where the limited monarchy symbolizes the collective authority of the Karbi society.

Transmission of Message

In the difficult terrain of Karbi land, the people have devised their indigenous method of transmitting messages across the hills. The messages are carried by the specific messenger on foot. It is always a verbal one and the messenger carries along with him a traditional looped ring which called the *Lam Kido*. The urgency and seriousness of the message depends on the closely woven nature of the *Lam Kido*. The closer the loop, the more urgent is the message. It is restricted within the traditional functionaries of the three councils. In the year 1975, the Rechomei (royal council) warned Sri Sing Tisso, the *Habe Kethe* of Habepi Longri, through *Lam Kido* for his negligence of duty and misdemeanour. The incumbent ignored the *Recho's Lam Kido* for two times. Ultimately, he was put to more ominous Lam Kido called Habe Kapelam meaning suspension from the office of Habeship. For this reason, the suspended Habe had to pay a fine of rupees one hundred besides other associates offerings such as ten bottles of *Arak* and *Banta* (betel leaf and betel nut) to the *Recho*. The suspended *Habe* regained the office of Habeship after he made all the penalties to the *Recho*. He had to spend a sum of rupees six hundred approximately. He was reinstated to the office of *Habe* through a *Lam Kido* of the *Recho*.

Oath

Among the Karbis, justice is administered after taking into consideration the fact of the oath taken; it is known as *Seme*. In case, the accused denies the allegation, he is asked to take an oath before *Dengja-Kethe* or *Dengjaso*, the officials of the royal council.

In the olden days, the *Oocha* (magician man) played a significant role in the administration of justice. The *Oocha* was something like a magician judge who administered justice from supernatural point of view. He is believed to be endowed with supernatural powers that enables him to conjure up wild animals. Wild animals are believed to be under his beck and call and obey his command. In the Karbi society, the attack of wild animals is much dreaded. Any attack by the wild animal is considered as bad omen, and if a person is killed by an animal, misfortune befalls a family, and very often it means the social boycott of the family. Therefore, no person would try to utter untruth before an *Oocha* because the latter is possessed of the extraordinary supernatural power to let loose an animal on a lying person.

An oath has its own intrinsic value of its own. It is believed to act spontaneously. As false oath is certain to befall some serious calamity in the life of the oath-taker. Similarly, an oath on truth has its own merit and benefit. Nowadays, the Oochas are diminishing in number but the popular faith still persists, and this perhaps explains why the Karbis approach the traditional authorities for redress of their grievances. The people find solace in the dispensation of justice by the traditional authorities.

Note

1. *Jambili Anthon* : It is a symbolical finely and smoothly dressed wooden rod, about five feet high; fitted on a cubical wooden platform, with five out-flaring branches, each with artistic design of engraving and modelling representing five clans. Under the Jambili Anthon, the Karbis recite the holy verses such as Masira Kohir.

REFERENCES

FORTES, M.; E.E. EVANS-PRITCHARD, 1940, *African Political Systems.* London: Oxford University Press.

LYALL, C., 1908, *The Mikirs.* London: Oxford University Press.

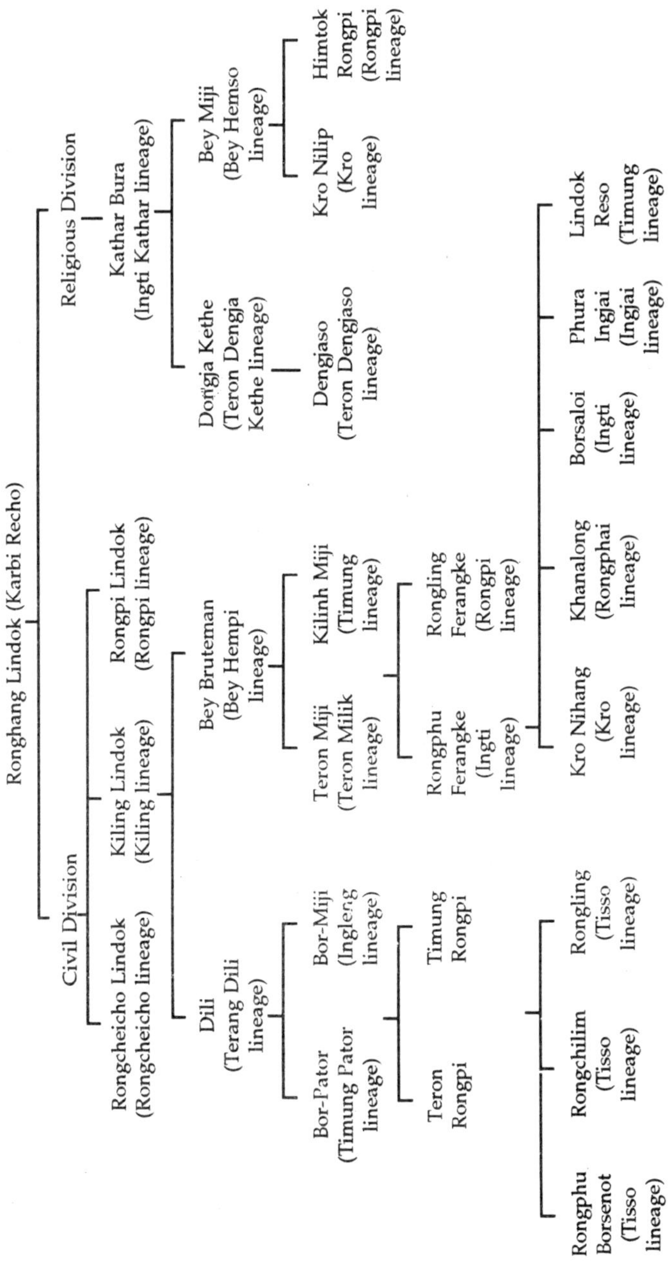

Chart 16.1 : The Rongkhang Alongri : The Structure.

17

The Tarao : A Dwindling Tribe of Manipur

Mutum Bokul Singh

Manipur lies in the extreme north-eastern region of India. A large number of tribes are sparsely populated in five hill districts. Each of them has their own dialects, customs, beliefs and practices, etc., which are some of the determinant factors to distinguish one tribe to other culturally. Among the non-Scheduled Tribes, mention can be made of the Tarao, the Kharam, the Paomei, etc. Of them, the tribe Tarao is a least known as well as the smallest tribal community. From 1983 they all are confined in the rugged hill tracts of Chandel district and distributed in four villages. They claim that they have originated from Kabow Valley (now in Myanmar). Their neighbouring tribes are Moyon, Monsang, Purum, Lamkang, Maring, etc. As the tribe is small in numerical strength, in last two-three decades many of the earlier scholars often speak to them as a dwindling tribe of the State.

The Tarao is one of the oldest tribes of Manipur because they arrived in Tengnoupal area (Chandel district) before 14th century A.D. Moreover, according to the Old Chronicles of Manipur, the Loiyumba Shilyen, the Royal Edict of King Loiyumba (1072-1122 A.D.) refers to the duties to be performed and tributes to be paid by the Taraos of south-east Manipur (Kabui, 1976 : 3).

The racial elements of the ethnic groups of Manipur are said to be constituted of the Indo-Mongoloids who speak the

Tibeto-Burman languages and some Caucasoid elements. More subtly, the Naga dialects of Manipur can be grouped into two sub-families: the Naga group and the Naga-Bodo group. But the Kuki dialects belong to Kuki-Chin linguistic sub-family to which the Meitei also belongs. Again the Kuki-Chin speakers are divided into two groups — those Kuki tribes who came earlier to Manipur are called 'Old Kukis' and those who came during 18th century onwards are said to be of the 'New Kukis'.

Owing to the present situation, the shifting identity is a peculiar phenomenon among the tribes of Manipur. As a result, the several tribes of 'Old Kuki' groups, evidenced by earlier writings, now claim themselves as Naga. They are Anal, Moyon, Monsang, Lamkang, Koireng, Kharam, Tarao, etc. While describing the ethnological affinity of Tarao tribe, most of the eminent scholars such as Shakespear (1912), Bose (1934), Needham (1958) and Levi-Strauss (1969) placed the Taraos under 'Old Kuki' groups. But today, they have a strong claim for Naga identity.

Demographic Profile

The total population of Tarao was 532 persons as on December 1988 (Male = 53.01% and Female = 46.99%). The sex ratio was 112.8. The tribe can be classified into three broad age-group categories — children (40.86%), working age group (54.51%), and old age group (4.64%) respectively. The clan-wise populations in order of percentages are Khulpu (38.72%), Katrimsa (31.58%), and Chanasa (29.70%).

The population growth of this tribe has been discouraging since the days yore. During the last decade there has been a raise in population. Historically, the mortality rate was reportedly high enough. More strikingly, it was repeatedly slashed by epidemics and other kind of unknown diseases. Even during the last two decades, the highest incidence of death toll was occurred in 1974. It was around 10.16 per cent of the total population of this tribe. The infant mortality rate in 1984 was 333.33 per 1000 live births while in 1985 it was somewhat reduced to 55.55 per 1000 live births. Neo-natal mortality is very rare among the natives. In the year 1981 there were three cases of neo-natal death but all were males. From 1961 to 1983 there have been only four cases of foetal deaths. Its highest record was 500 per 1000 livebirths in 1972. Other records on still-birth in 1980 comes 200 per 1000 livebirths whereas the rate was increased 1000 per 1000 livebirths in 1982. These are some of the statistical striking features on mortality rates in Tarao society.

The biological and social variables and their relative roles in determining the fertility and mortality pattern in the Tarao population were examined carefully. It is important to put a note that there are eight couples who have no child issue throughout their lives. Another finding is that the couples marrying between the two lineages — *Mathangmanai* (*Khulpu* clan) and *Shaloishanei* (*Katrimsa* clan) — are reportedly of short life span.

Migration is an important component of population change. The Taraos are one of the most mobile people of Manipur. They keep on moving from one place to another that has been continued till 1983. The main reason for migration is, as reported, when they faced a number of death tolls and sufferings from unknown diseases they felt that the village was not suited for settlement. So that they go on searching another suitable place for settlement. Similarly, religion is also another factor that lead the people to migrate. Some of them wanted to convert into Christianity, while others wanted to continue their tradition. Thus, sometimes a conflict between the two groups does take place which ultimately leads to migration. In this way, a section of people used to leave the village and settled somewhere else. As reported by informants, wars caused the Tarao population in an alarming number of deaths. For instance, during Khongchai War (1917) in Manipur and other World Wars, the population of Taraos was surprisingly reduced. They further report me that after war there was mass sufferings from diseases and that led to a remarkable death toll. However, other ethnic groups in the State do not find such situations. Over and above, it is also reported that prior to the practice of midwifery came into the Tarao society the child was brought out from mother's womb by a crude surgical operation in their home. It was usually conducted by her father-in-law with a local knife called *takshi* where the life of the child was mostly saved but it led to maternal death. Besides, poor ventilation, damp and lack of sunshine in domicile area, poor bathing, worse toilet amenities and insanitary system, lack of modern education, treatment of illness by local beliefs, etc., are other possible factors for population declination in past. But today there has been lots of improvement in the health and hygienic conditions of the people by modern education, Christianisation, westernisation, and modern health care and treatments.

Social and Cultural Life

Family

In the dynamic sense, the basic unit of the social structure in every society is the family. The specific pattern of family life in any given social structure is the product of the *mores* and varies with time, place and peoples. Therefore, the family has been seen as a universal social institution, as an inevitable part of human society. Looking to the tracing of descent system, the Tarao is a patrilineal and unilineal society. With regard to residence pattern, it is patrilocal. From the point of view of authority it is patriarchy. Basing on the membership type of the family the Tarao has a type of conjugal family (parents and their children). In addition, there is consanguine family, made up of either parents and the units blood relatives. As far as back to very past, consanguine family was outnumbered.

Traditionally speaking, the joint family organisation was strongly influenced by customs. As the Tarao society has patrilineal descent system a male child seemed to have a greater importance than girls. By reason of the fact that only the male members have the right to inherit their fathers property. For ease of reference to joint family organisation, a belief behind this is that once the Meitei Maharaja had a plan to grow some fruits like orange, lemon, guava, pomegranate, etc., in a village called Komalthabi (Chandel district). At that time the Meitei King engaged the Tarao tribe to look after the plantation as caretakers. Very unfortunately, there was no satisfactory products in the said year. For that reason, the Meitei King was very angry with them and scolded them — "You the Tarao people should not exceed more than 20 (twenty) families; if it exceeds let you/them succumb to death as a punishment given by the God". To this, they were disappointed and the same had happened in the following year when the number of families increased in the village. By such circumstances, the people of Tarao, then, amended a custom on the practice of joint family system. Henceforth, the people have been influenced by custom to restrict the number of families at village level as well as they were told themselves that they had better to maintain the number as far as practiceable. When it is beyond the control of limit some are supposed to leave the village with a mutual consent of the chief. In a formal and mannered style, they established a new village somewhere else. In this way, the people, from time to time, split up the families in order to maintain its number, particularly during those olden days. But it is no longer applicable today. As and when the Christianity came to this society they have started nuclear family organisation because they felt that they were free from traditional customs by conversation to Christianity. Again and again, modernisation, westernisation and Christianisation must have led the people to split up the joint family organisation.

A father has certain rights and duties because he holds major responsibilities in both outside and inside the family. He is in great demand in lineage or clan organisation. Next to him is his eldest son. In tradition, both inheritance and succession passed down from father to eldest son only. But today, a new phenomenon of change is of equal sharing of the property among brothers. However, succession of chieftainship, and headmanship of each clan or lineage remain unchanged till today, i.e., primogeniture. An eldest son and an eldest man of each lineage belonging to various clans have several functional rights to perform duties sanctioned by the society. These are seen in marriage, death ceremony, religion, economic activities, calendaric festivals, etc.

Clan Organisation

A clan is the most important part of social organisation in tribal society. It can be said that clan is the extensive form of lineages constituting blood relation through ancestral stock. Every Tarao individual belongs to a family known as *tolloikung*.

Each belongs to a larger group called *salai* (lineage). Again each *salai* is composed of a number of families. More usually, a number of *salais* combines to form a *shakei* (clan), the largest social group of the Taraos. There are three clans having three ancestral stocks who may be mythologically related to a common ancestor. The three clans and their sub-divisions are as below:

1. Khulpu:
   - (a) Khulpuin
   - (b) Tlangsa
   - (c) Khullan
   - (d) Mathangmanai
   - (e) Rabdousa

2. Katrimsa:
   - (a) Tulekshanei
   - (b) Tuilamthangna
   - (c) Shaloishanei
   - (d) Lunglan (extinct)

3. Chanasa:
   - (a) Tleitlap
   - (b) Thamoin
   - (c) Leikhan
   - (d) Peitrim (extinct)

The operational nature of social networks may be based on social values, beliefs, norms, traditions and customs. Keeping in mind the theoritical concepts, some measurable observations are made on the inter-clan and intra-clan relationships that have taken place at different occasions in Tarao society. Such relationships are clearly seen in the establishment of new villages, particularly while searching its settlement site; in the annual worshipping of *Shangkhuleima*, a supreme Goddess of the community; in constructing a new house; in traditional form of marriage by preference on others; in most of the agricultural activities associated a number of rituals and festivals; in other economic activities such as hunting, fishing, etc.; while sharing of flesh of hunted animals; etc. To carry out such customary activities they form a team representing an eldest male survivor from each clan.

This is known as *phungreiya-changreiya* who have played a central role in every sphere of their life cycle. In fact, the team is made by four men from the clans: Khulpu, Katrimsa, Chanasa and Khullan (a lineage of Khulpu clan) respectively. In Tarao society, they are very important specialists whose memberships or status succeed to their eldest sons by customs. They perform many observances conducted for well being of the community as a whole. In absence of anyone, the work is always held up. On this evidence, it shows that their roles and physical presence have a high social values in this society.

The following food items are tabooed from eating by the persons who belonged to Khulpu shakei. The restricted food items are *Keitangsha* (an animal once hurt by tiger) *shangmang* (an animal found dead in the forest), *koikir* (a kind of wild grass), *marum* (eagle), tiger, *sharkhei* (wild cat), *nungok* (a pig like animal), and *shaphabee* (armadilos). It is reported that the tiger is not eaten by the Taraos since they were attacked by the tiger when their mythological ancestors came out of subterranean world to the present earth. *Thingsayo* (a bulb bearing parasitic plant), *kundun* (a creeper) and all kinds of mushrooms are some of the food taboo for the people of Katrimsa clan and Tlangsa lineage of Khulpu clan. A belief associated with *kundun* is that once the Taraos were being chased by enemies. At that time they hid in the bush of *kundun* creepers. That is why they do not take it because they show their gratitude towards the creeper for being saved their lives from enemies. Henceforth, the people of Katrimsa and Tlangsa have been observing as a taboo. Similarly, Chanasa shakei has also a taboo that any vegetables which tied with thatch grass (*paddi*) are not eaten. Because some of the Chanasa people were once saved by this thatch in an accident. Moreover, the people of Katrimsa clan treat elephants as human beings because once a Tarao girl named Trimjur of Katrimsa clan, who was a well-known of her laziness, ran into nearby forest by neglecting her duty from husking of paddy. But she was surprisingly disappeared in the forest and ultimately people came to know that she was supposed to transform into an elephant. For that they do not kill or eat the flesh of elephants. A similar belief is also found among the people of Tlangsa where bear is not taken since it is believed to transform from a Tlangsa girl.

Marriage

For back-pointing, it is customary for a Tarao boy to seek his spouse outside his own clan. A better understanding of what is referred is that they practise clan-exogamy by tribe-endogamy. As I have noted of their clan organisation in the preceding part, there are three intermarrying clans. In the earlier interpretations made by Shakespear (1912) and Levi-Strauss (1969), the marriage cycle of Tarao was always moved in clockwise direction only. Soon after them, it is reported to move in reverse direction. In fact, it is due to the relaxation of mate selection. The strict reason to traditional mate selection is of preferential marriage. But the time has brought to them to undergo marriage by elopement. After that selection can be made in both directions. By the reason of the fact of MoBrDa marriage by preference, an ideal form of alliance, it must have to move in one direction only. At that time, the eyes and mind of boy's parents always paid attention on searching a suitable *amnei* (MoBrDa) within the circle but under the rules of alliance culture. But looking to the recent tendency, a man is having much freedom in selecting his wife as compared with past.

Changwang, a formal marriage is a contract made between the parents of both sides. For a series of its negotiations, a male mediator (*thimintong*) bears a great role in their culture. An ideal betrothal girl is locally known as *amnei* (MoBrDa). In those days, the consent of the boy or girl was seldom taken into account. Moreover, in a formal way, a traditional marriage mostly came through *yurkhu* (child marriage). *Yurkhu* is a ritual ceremony for the reservation of a betrothal female child. It is usually done within a month after birth. Relating this fact, once this has been done he/she does not permit to marry anyone else. Because they are bound by their customs to marry each other but when they attain marriageable ages. It shows that they cannot deny the matter. Here are three phases/steps for a formal marriage without which it does not get social sanction. They are (i) *mouhai*, (ii) *shiluk-ngathal*, and (iii) *amante* or *meilosheh* respectively. At each interval between the above three steps a mediator carries on the urgent go-between the two sides for the fixation of day/date of each phase.

Mouhai is the first formal visit for negotiation by boy's party to girl's family. Such a visit is usually under the supervision of a mediator. At the time of this visit, boy's party carry something with them like a pig/cow, rice-beer, etc., to offer to girl's parents and relatives. As and when the negotiation has come to the point of fulfilment of each side they all enjoy the drinks and meat arranged by boy's party. Here a son-in-law (*makcha*) of the boy's family plays a remarkable role and has a special status because most of the activities involved in marriage are carried out by him and under his active supervision.

Shiluk-ngathal takes place after two or three months of *mouhai*. On this second visit, the boy's parents offer a box (made of split bamboo) containing full of dry fish, rice-beer, pig, etc., to girl's parents in order to get the permission of sexual intercourse of the would be couples. In one sense it is the day of marriage. For this, a grand feast is to be arranged by boy's family. Here there will be a simple ritual ceremony by which the would-be couples get social sanction of their marriage. In this feast, the bride (*therei*) and groom (*changrei*) have a special seating arrangement and should have dinned together in presence of all. As noted that such a grand feast along with a ritual will give a social recognition of the status of husband and wife. After that they all including bridegroom come back home, leaving the bride at her house. By custom, the bride may not come on this day. Usually, the parents and relatives of the boy will bring the bride to her husband's house on another day. It may be on the following day or after days or within a month. During these days, the boy may go for a regular visit to his wife's house, particularly at night, which he continues till the bride has come to his house. When the bride arrives to her husband's house she is to be solemnised with certain ritual acts which signify her to entry into her husband's lineage.

The payment of bride-place is known as *amante*. The bride-place of a Tarao girl consists of a gong, one or more cattle, a pig, etc. These are given to the girl's parents in presence of the village chief with his administrative assistants and other two witnesses who are selected by the chief from other clans. In case the boy's parents could not pay the bride price, their son has to undergo three years long service to the bride's family by living as husband and wife. This service, in lieu of bride price, is known as *meilosheh*. Unlike the other Indian tribes, such service in Tarao society is with consummation. For this service, the bridegroom has taken away to the bride's family by his parents and relatives, friends, etc., on a day. Here the groom puts on new clothes and carries with him the implements for fishing, hunting, war, etc. In this way, he renders his sincere service to his father-in-law's family for a period of three years continuously. After the stipulated period is over the man with his wife and their children comes back to his own parental house. He then establishes a new house in due course.

Other forms of marriage are (i) *yurkhu* (child marriage), (ii) *kikloumou* (MoBrDa marriage by preference), (iii) *tlan* (marriage by elopement), (iv) *tulmeipaolou* (widower marriage), (v) *tulmeinaolou* (widow marriage), and (vi) marriages solemnized in Church. As and when a female betrothal child (MoBrDa) is born or available the boy's parents would go for obtaining a promise from the girl's parents and to reserve her for their son by a ritual. After such reservation is made she then is not permitted to marry anyone else than the betrothed boy. But the actual marriage would take place when they have attained marriageable ages. Such act in Tarao society is known as *yurkhu*. By customs, a Tarao girl is obliged to marry her father's sister's son. This marriage by preference is called *kikloumou*. In those days, MoBrDa marriage was supposed to be the ideal union among this tribe. This alliance system is found in most of the tribes of Manipur. Among the Taraos, marriage by elopement is known as *tlan*. In this case, *mouhai* or *shiluk-ngathal* is not required. It comes direct to either the payment of bride price or service. Widow or widower are also permitted to remarry but after the lapse of one or more years of the death or divorce. Most of such marriage occurred between widow and widower. Sororal union are found but no levirate union. Traditional type of marriages have been disappearing fast and is being replaced by Church marriage today.

Kinship

Kinship is the most important aspect in the study of the social structure of a society. Kinship terminology of Tarao tribe is closely related with the Iroqois type. In Tarao society, there is an emphasis on the integration through the feeling of blood brotherhood (*lukhangeenshung*). Affinal kinship (marital relationship) is narrow-range because of their alliance system that strictly is based on MoBrDa marriage. But the patrilineal consanguineous kinship (same blood) is comparatively in broad-range. Although even more weightage is given to father's line the entire kinship network is divided into two sets of relatives, i.e., one set through father (*pa-eenshung*) and other through mother (*nu-eenshung*). For general viewpoints, the kinship bond between genealogically distant kinsmen is weaker than that of the genealogically closed one. But in actual scene, the relationship to a father's line is stronger than others since it is patrilineal society. In addition to this organisation, four types of relationships can be made here. They are *lukhang-eenshung* (close relatives), *shakei-eenshung* (far relative), *pa-eenshung* (paternal relative) and *nu-eenshung* (maternal relative). The recognition of consanguineal kin organisation in Tarao society reveals two levels like clan and lineage.

Within each king group, behaviour, verbal and non-verbal, etc., constitute kinship usages. With reference to Tarao customs, some of the kinship dimensions are being observed and seen in the obligations to share goods, service, sexual discrimination against near relatives, food habit between relatives or kins, dinning behaviour or attitude of a daughter-in-law, cooking of rice on special occasions by a daughter-in-law, the manner of distribution of the flesh of the hunted animal, different parts of anatomical flesh to be shared by particularised persons, kinship role in hunting/fishing, transmission of property, succession of hereditary status, reciprocal gifts in child birth, marriage, death, etc.

Among the Taraos, some of the behavioural observations of avoidence are found between a daughter-in-law and a father-in-law; a son-in-law and his parents-in-law; and limited social relations between brothers and sisters. Another custom is that brothers and sisters may not occupy the same sleeping room. However, to dine together over the same dining basket is a common practice. Family customs are the medium through which this has imparted. Restrictions regarding the exchange of clothes are found between a man with his sisters' husbands and wife's brothers; a mother-in-law and a daughter-in-law; a son-in-law and father-in-law; etc. For instance, a man who uses the loin cloth of his daughter's husband is treated badly. A father never shares the rice-beer with his sons and son-in-laws. But among the females it is of lesser restriction. And there is no evidence on the sharing of drinks between brother and sister jointly. A woman during her monthly period cannot serve anything that is associated with religion. By customs, a married brother cannot easily enter the rooms occupied by his married brothers. On the other hand, in an easy manner, a daughter-in-law should not get into the room of her father-in-law and to her husband's elder brother's room. Likewise, a son-in-law is not expected to enter the room of his parents-in-law.

The Tarao kinship terminology is more or less closely related with the Iroquois system (Fig. 1a, 1b, 2). There are more than thirty terms found in the addressing system of the Tarao tribe. *Pa* stands for father and Nu for mother; *Pappi* for FaEBr and MoESiHu whereas *Nupi* for FaEBrWi and MoESi; *Patte* for FaYBr and MoYSiHu while *Nute* to FaYBrWi and MoYSi. *Marang* covers HuFa, FaESiHu, FaYSiHu, HuFabr, etc. There respective wives are *Nee*. The term *Pu* is used for FaFa, FaFaBr, MoFa, MoFaBr, BrWiFa, BrWiFaBr, HuMoFa, etc. The term *Pi* is for their respective wives. Mother's elder or younger brother is addressed as *Pute* while *Pite* for MoEBrWi and MoYBrWi. In case of marrying one's MoBrDa by preference he can address as *Pu* and *Pi* instead of *Pute* and *Pite*. The term *Ute* is used in both elder brother and sister whereas *Kanao* for both younger brother and sister. But there are different terms for multiple brothers and sisters of the same parents.

Economy

The diversity of natural environment has resulted in the diversity of economies practised by societies. The Taraos are found in the foothills and also in high densed forests. Given the simple technology, the impact of the natural environment is considerable. The mode of production of material goods for subsistence in this tribe is of mixed type. They practise shifting cultivation. It is hoe-culture type of cultivation. With past reference, one can say the Taraos are good hunters and gatherers. Even today they practise it to some extent. Group hunting has been disappearing fast but individual hunting is still done. Today some are practising wet-cultivation on plains. Kinship plays a vital role in carrying out the entire agricultural cycle associating a number of festivals at each phase. A strong bond of inter-clan or intra-clan relationship is clearly seen in economic activities. For instance, certain clan or lineage or both have specific duty to initiate the activities which are duly followed by others. The land belonged to a particular clan is locally known as *niktom-rem* while land owned collectively by the people of a lineage is known as *eenshunna-ram*. Individual ownership of land is also recognised. Such land may be mortgaged or sold out according to the wills of the owners. There is also common land/property of the village.

Both man and woman have equal load of works particularly in economic activities. But most of the domestic affairs are in the hands of women. The preparation of local rice-beer is usually done by women. Most of the traditional clothes were woven from locally available fibre tree, from which they first prepare yarn and then wove clothes for their family use. Besides that, women are working in basketry at a remarkable extent. By doing so they maintain their kitchen. Moreover, basketry is a household industry in Tarao society. Women of all the groups are hard workers in bamboo works. They themselves collect the raw materials from forests and readymade items are sold in nearby market (pallel) or at Imphal Bazar.

It will not be out of place to mention that there is an interesting custom for storing of foodgrains in granary. Its storing should be initiated by an eldest daughter of each family. And at the end also she has to carry the remnants to declare the storing closed. Prior to the conversion to Christianity, as per custom, at village level, every Tarao family was obliged to subscribe one chicken, 5 (five) litres of rice-beer and a pig or a cow to the village chief. This was made on instalment basis. The family who fails to do so must receive a severe punishment from the Chief's side. Such annual contribution made to the Chief is locally known as *aarel-yurel-oksan*. When visitors/outsiders visit his village he then seeks such subscription to extend hospitality to the visitors. However, he never forces a particular family to pay it instant. The collection of such items is utilised in authority sitting or meeting for the well-being of the village as whole or other council meetings. Besides, a Tarao family is required to subscribe a few bags of paddy which are accumulated to the Church's granary. This is to make payment to the Church Pastor and Church chowkidar in the form of monthly salaries.

Village Administration

It is common fact that a community has some common interests and common ways of doing things bound by their own customs and traditions which are ultimately controlled by village administration. Particularly among the Taraos of Manipur, a public opinion is also a very powerful influence in the life of its individual members. A Tarao village is administered by 19 officials headed by a *Kurung* (Chief). *Kurungship* has still been hereditary from the days yore. There is a specific clan called Khulpu in which *Kurungship* has been handed down from father to eldest son by generations. It still shows that no other person from other clans can hold *Kurungship*. The total picture of administrative officials are given below:

1. Kurung
2. Senapati
3. Khullak
4. Lunglak
5. Yupal
6. Khanglak
7. Naharak
8. Loithil
9. Wangkherirak
10. Roumilak
11. Mata-rampu
12. Tongpra
13. Lalchingpa
14. Chingsanglak
15. Mantri

16. Ningolak
17. Sellungba
18. Keirungba, and
19. Lallupchingba.

The first six officials, i.e., Kurung, Senapati, Khullak, Lunglak, Yupal and Khanglak are treated as more important administrators, Loithil is another administrator whose duty is to go-between the Meitei King and the Taraos. Giving of seasonal crops and clothes as presentations to the Meitei King was done by him. Each administrator has specific duty or function that have been seen in festivals and in council meeting or hearings while occupying their respective seats. Each village has an alarm bell. Nobody is allowed to use it without any responsible cause. When it is heard every available man in the village will come forward with at least a weapon with them.

Religion

Religion is the relations between human beings with supernatural forces and suprasensoty beliefs which seem to bind together men and supernatural powers. Beliefs and rituals have been found to be the main component parts of religion everywhere. During the pre-Christianity period, every family was a follower of *shangkhuleima*, a Tarao girl who belonged to Khulpu shakei. The goddess is also known as rapu. Actually the terms *shangkhuleima* was given by the Meitei King. A shrine of *rapu* is located just above the Burma road near Tengnoupal. The people of Tarao worshipped this goddess once in a year. The Meitei King also worship her by every two years. Because she was married with the God of water of Meitei (called *Wangbrel*) — so that there had been close relationship between the two communities. It might probably be after the Tarao came under the Metei suzerainty. In due course, the Taraos were engaged by the King for looking after the temple. This temple is locally known as *raputhang* in Tarao dialect. On the other hand, it was the supreme god of this tribe. When a better relationship had come with the Meitei King they were exempted from the forced labour to be rendered to the King. Annual worshipping of *rapu* by the Taraos tribe continued till 1966. It was performed in the month of either

Phalwa (October) or *Matulbu* (November). It last for five days. Most of the religious activities were done by *phungreiya-changreiya*, a team comprising four individuals, who are socially sanctioned for the purpose, from Khulpu clan, Khullan lineage (of Khulpu clan), Katrimsa and Chanasa clans respectively. Each of them has obliged to do specific duty to be performed. Anyone absent in the team held up the works. It indicates these four men have a great social value in their culture. Other religious activities are carried out by two village priests known as *amlan* and amchan. They always go together to perform rituals jointly. Sacrifice of either animal or bird and followed by a religious feast or a grand feast are associated in most of the festivals, at every phase of agricultural activities. Besides the religious activities *phungreiya-changreiya* performs many thing in the society.

Animism, animatism, dream, divination, fertility cult, magic, taboo, totemism, witchcraft, shamanism, etc., constitute the core religion of the people. The Tarao people believe in a number of deities and spirits. They are *arao* (family deity), *kashalai* (deity resting at the top of the first pillar), *markheengkungmarim* (domicile deity), *bulon* (family heart deity), *enkharkouthou* (deity resides at front door), *samalchakhai* (evil spirit), *amarui* (evil spirit), *ramrapu* (forest deity), *mayamthou, monungsa, makhathim,* etc. The *arao* deity is associated with the birth ceremony (*neothathlou*). Here a cock for male child or a hen for female is to be sacrificed. *Markheengkungmarim* is with *yurkhu* (child marriage), araochal (a ceremony for the adoption of a child), and others. The deity of family hearth is called *bulon*. The head of the family used to drop a little rice upon it before he starts eating. When an individual is suffering from any disease/illness the family has to perform this ritual at the threshold of the house. The Tarao believes that there is a deity resting at the top of the first pillar of a house. It protects the family from evil spirits. Generally the corpse's head is directed towards its pillar. At that time deity is removed and placed somewhere in the courtyard till the dead body has been taken to burial ground. *Enkharkung* is another magico-religious act conducted by village priest at the threshold of the front door. It was to be used to perform when a child is suffering from illness. In the agricultural cycle also there are a series of rituals which are performed from time to time. Another interesting finding is that every lineage has a sacred spear which was kept in the house of the eldest surviving male member of that lineage. This is used either in war, head hunting, and in killing of sacrificed animals. The spear is tabooed from touch by female members in the family or from persons belonging to other lineage or clan.

REFERENCES

DAS, R.K., 1985, *Tribal Social Structure: A Study of the Maring Society of Manipur*. New Delhi: Inter India Publication.

KABUI, G., 1976, The Tarao: A Forgotten Tribe of Manipur, *Resistance*.

LEVI-STRAUSS, C., 1969, *The Elementary Structure of Kinship*. Oxford: Oxford University Press.

SHAKESPEAR, J., 1912, *The Lushai-Kuki Clans*. London: MacMillan and Co.

SINGH, M.B., 1989, *The Tarao of Manipur (Social and Demographic Change)*. Unpublished Ph.D. Thesis. Manipur University, Manipur.

SINGH, M.B., 1990, 'Tribal Culture of Manipur'. In *Tribal Profile of Manipur*. Edited by G. Kabui. Imphal: Centre for Tribal Studies, Manipur University.

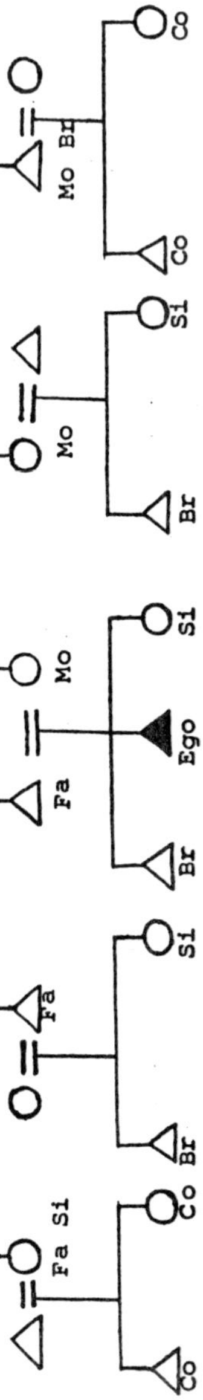

Fig. 17.1(a): Iroquois Kinship System

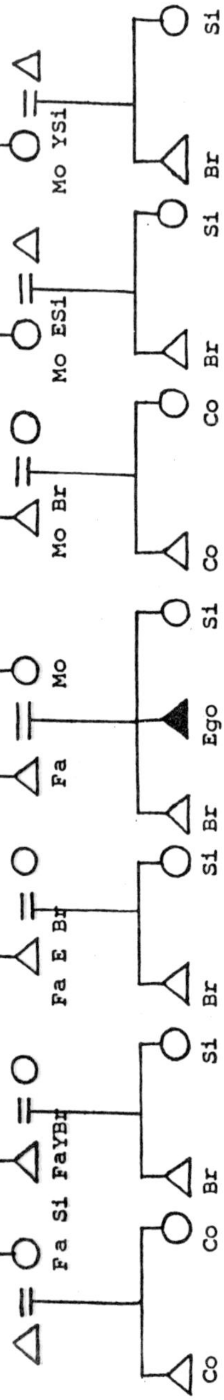

Fig. 17.1(b): Tarao Kinship System

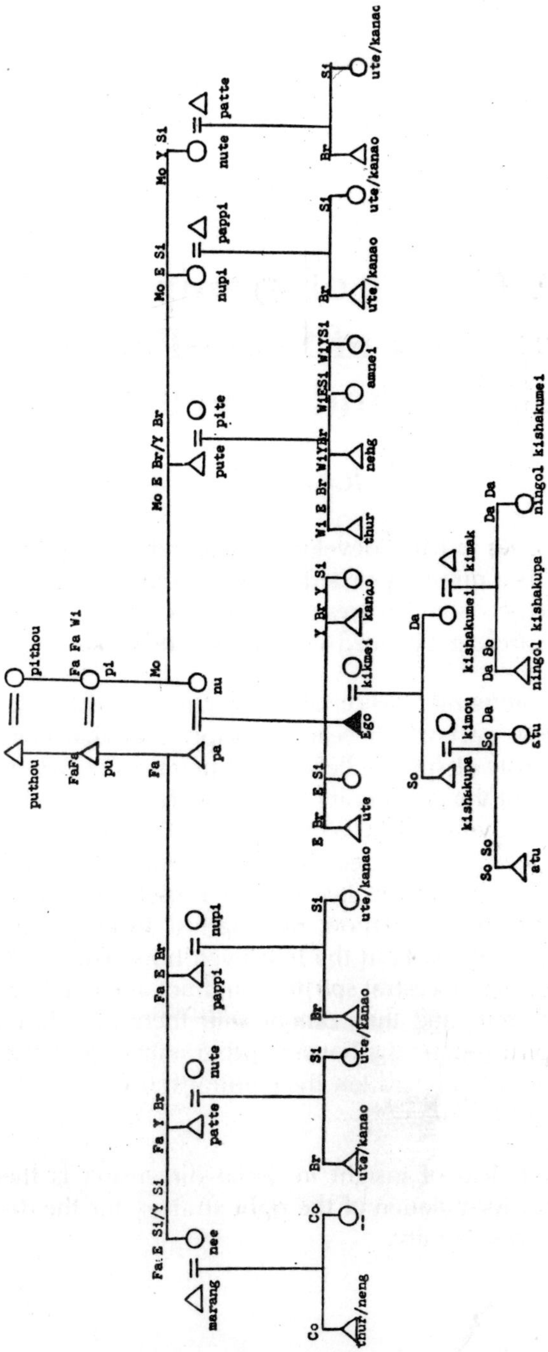

Fig. 7.2. Tarao Kinship System.

18

The Chotes of Manipur : An Appraisal of Socio-Political Tradition and Development

R.K. Kar

The main issues in tribal development in India today are philosophical. It is a question of better appreciation of the nature of socio-politico-economic forces operating there or likely to operate as these areas get opened up (Sharma, 1978).

Each community has certain distinctive characteristic roots in the remote past which bear the impress of that culture as regards the role of specific beliefs and practices in determining the response of the community to specific items of development programme. Roy Burman (1968) reports "...though commodious houses had been constructed by the Government for the tribal Rabhas, they continued to live in their traditional type of huts without light and ventilation; they agreed to keep only their cattle and poultry birds in the improved huts. The Rabhas explained that their ancestral spirits would not agree to live in the new type of huts and they cannot shift there abandoning the ancestral spirits. Here, the housing programme, executed without taking into consideration the cultural tradition of the community, proved a failure".

A good deal of insight in social dimension is therefore necessary for formulation of the right strategy for the development of any community.

The political goals of development imply an evolution towards demographic process and forms of Government. The approach to different tribal groups would, however, depend upon the existing socio-political organisation. The political life of the tribals of India reflects a paradoxical situation in which democracy and monarchy co-exist. Dhebar Commission has also noted that the pattern ranges from highly authoritarian to highly democratic. Each tribal group therefore, would have to be worked out on an individual basis (Mathur, 1968).

Political structure of a similar community is the product of their traditional political life which at the same time combines political affairs. Thus the political characters of a society may broadly be looked at through their social organisation.

Every head of a community at different levels like clan, village and territory is generally honoured, obeyed and accepted as head of the group. The tribal leader governs the community only because he is backed by the majority or the whole of the group. The tribal village works actively as a political unit. Sometimes secular and sacerdotal spheres of activity (e.g., Santal, Bhil, Munda) are kept under the jurisdiction of two different heads.

Most of the tribes have village council or assembly of elders known as Panchayat at the village level (e.g., Adi, Bhil, Gond, Ho, Munda, Oraons and Santal). These bodies look after the general welfare and integrity of the society. The verdict of the tribal Panchayat or headman of the village is law to the tribal people. The sanction behind it is the great faith in the elders and village leadership.

While introducing certain innovations in the political systems, certain specific characteristics of the traditional institutions need careful understanding and appreciations. To illustrate this Chattopadhaya (1968) reports of the differential results obtained in the introduction of the official Panchayat system in one rural area in West Bengal and a tribal area in Bihar. After the introduction of official Panchayats the power of the *Majlis* went down, but *punc* retained its influence. In the West Bengal village there live eight castes of Hindus (Brahmin, Sadgope, Napit, Teli, Bagdi,

Ahir and Munchi), a dozen families of Santhals and about half a dozen families of Muslims. Among the Hindus, the Brahmins are the most wealthy in the village and next in order comes the Sadgops. Between them they have always controlled the *Majlis*. Consequently when *Majlis* lost its semi-official status, very soon the lower castes declared their intention of disobeying *Majlis* and uptil now they are continuing to do so.

But, in case of Hos, their *panc* had always been a body composed of *Mundas* and elders, and the former men were traditionally chosen by the Hos themselves, quite irrespective of their wealth and social status. They could have no objection to the presence of the elders in the *panc* since every one knew that they could also choose to sit in the *panc* when they grew old enough. Hence there was no question of group exploitation here under the protective wing of a political authority. Official Panchayats are important bodies which carry on the development work at the lowest level. So, it should be closest to the people. The members of the Panchayat would be those persons who are most influential in the villages. And here lies the snag. 'Influential' persons in the village are not always representatives of all groups.

It is thus imperative that socio-political system of a community determines its broad responses to the development programme, or where it is consciously taken into consideration, it plays the crucial role in determining the broad strategy of the programme.

In this background the paper attempts a brief appraisal of the traditional socio-political organisation of the Chotes of Manipur as well as the introduction of a relatively more secular body among the people, replacing the traditional one. Data for the paper were collected in 1984 mainly from Bishenpur district of Manipur.

The Land

Manipur is a small State in India that has an area of 22,356 sq. km., and a population of 14,33,691 (1981 figure). It occupies India's eastern borderland, and extends between latitudes 23°5' and 25°41' North and longitudes 93°2' and 94°47' East.

The land consists of both hills and valley. The Meiteis who are the dominant population of the State live mostly in the valley, and the hill area is the abode of the *Nagas* (hill people who are not Meiteis).

Manipur's boundaries fall into two categories: (i) interstate, and (ii) international. On the north, west and south-west lie the sister States of Nagaland, Assam and Mizoram. On the eastern border lies the Myanmar, giving that part of the country an international character. Out of her 859 km of the boundary, 505 km is interstate and 354 km international. The State has in all eight districts (administrative units), namely, (i) Central District, (ii) South District, (iii) East District, (iv) North District, (v) West District, (vi) Tengnoupal, (vii) Bishanpur, and (viii) Thoubal.

The Chotes and their Socio-Political Structure

The Chotes of Manipur are a small endogamóus group who are commonly referred to as Kuki-Chin. They show a clear historical connection with the Purum, the best described of the Kuki tribes (e.g., Dun, 1986; Das, 1945). But, now the Government of Manipur is said to have recognized both Puram and the Chote tribes as belonging to the Chote tribal group of Manipur. They are of Mongoloid stock and speak Tibeto-Burman language.

According to 1971 census the total Chote population is 1905, the highest concentration being in the Tengnoupal district (more than 60 per cent). Das (1945) observed that the people are divided into five clans, viz., *Marim, Makam Kheyang, Thao* and *Paros*. Among these he finds a number of sub-clans. But, during the present investigation, the Chotes were found to have seven clans.

According to a legendary belief, the tribe originally lived in a cave known as *Huipithoranga*. The cave was covered by a flat rock. As per the command of God, a wild buffalo, with the horn broke open the cave. The Chote men and women then came out on the ground for the first time. It is further believed that after some days of their coming over the ground, all the people, but two were eaten up by *Kamkier angpa* (tiger). Kachohte (a young boy) and Thanidam (a young girl) were, however, carefully protected by their God *Phakhangba* from the wild beast and enemies.

In course of time seven sons were born to this couple. Their names were: (i) Yahlung, (ii) Hiyang, (iii) Marim, (iv) Makan, (v) Thao, (vi) Rungkung, and (vii) Parpa. It is said that these seven brothers are the ancestors of the seven clans that exist among the people today. The names of the clans are also derived from the names of these seven brothers. The clans are strictly endogamous. Traditionally one can marry only in one or more selected clans. Thus a *Hiyang* boy can marry only a *Parpa, Marim, Rungkung* or a *Thao* girl, but not a *Yuhlung* girl.

The sub-clan is an intermediate social grouping between clan and family. It consists of a number of either nuclear or limited joint families or both. In the present study 49 per cent of the families are nuclear and 15 per cent joint. The rest are broken families. Each sub-clan has a *Pipa* who is regarded as the head of the group, and this is an important socio-religious post. The eldest son of the *Pipa* succeeds his father. If a person has no son, his youngest brother assumes the office. The smallest social unit in the Chote society is the nuclear family. The family is patrilineal. Thus, we find a social structure like Tribe-Clan-Sub-clan-Family.

The village community among the people exists as a distinct socio-political unit. The individual, as an inhabitant of a village has certain duties and obligations towards society. A person has a social obligation to take part in the proceedings of the Village Council regarding any dispute and any other matter involving the community as a whole. A villager has also to pay for communal worship performed for the welfare of the entire village. No work is done on *genna* (population) days. Each individual helps to clear the village road when called upon to do so. Whenever it is necessary, each villager is required to take up arms in defence of his village against raids by neighbouring villages. These and similar other duties, one has to discharge traditionally as a member of the village community.

A Chote village is organized in a three-tier structure. The three formal groups (*bungkung*) are formed primarily on the basis of ageset system. They are: (i) *Urinta,* (ii) *Tangarinta,* and (iii) *Luithei* or *Nungakluithei.*

The *Urinta-bungkung* is the highest body, and its members are the elderly members of the various clans. *Tangarinta* is the second highest body, the members of which are next to those of *Urinta* in age-structure. It looks after the customary religious activities, fair and festivals, and annual festivals of the village shrines, etc. The third council, Luitheir is the voluntary group which may also be regarded as dormitory group.

Urinta: It comprises seven office-bearers, namely, (i) *Khullakpa,* (ii) *Luplakpa,* (iii) *Juh Paipa,* (iv) *Keirungpa,* (v) *Keirungnapong* (vi) *Hachari,* and (vii) *Hachari Naopong.* Traditionally, all the seven clans are represented in the body of office-bearers. These tribal officers have their respective duties and roles to perform. Among the Chotes, the protector of the village is *Khullakpa* (*khul*-village, *Lakpa*-overseer or protector). House of the *Khullakpa* is known as *Hubankung.* He presides over the *Thoubei* (village meeting). During the past decades, the *Khullakpas* represented the respective villages in the *durbar*[1].

Luplakpa is the additional village head, and presides over the village meetings in the absence of the *Khullakpa* (or *Hulakpa*). *Juh Paipa, Keirungpa* and *Keirungnaopong* are held responsible for collecting fines and making arrangements on various occasions. *Juh Paipa* arranges *Zu* (rice bear) in community congregations. He remains also incharge of controlling the audience in the village council meetings. *Keirungpa* and *Keirungnapong* are responsible for selecting particular animal to be offered at a community rite, and collecting subscriptions from the villages. *Hachari* is said to be the attendant of the village head. In the absence of *Keirungpa, Hachari Naopong* sometimes serves as public crier.

The posts are not exactly hereditory. But, when an office-bearer dies or resigns prematurely, his posts goes to the next lower office-bearer, and the last office, i.e., *Hachari Naopong* is

1. Manipur has witnessed a lot of political upheavals in the past. Before 1891 (British annexation) absolute monarchy was the prevalent system of administration. The king was assisted by a durbar (court) that acted as an advisory council in the day-to-day administration of the State.

filled by the son of the deceased office-bearer. If all the offices fall vacant, the villagers meet together and select the *Khullakpa* first and then other then other posts are filled through election on subsequent days.

Tangrinta: It is the next powerful body in a Chote village. The members belong to the next age-group representing different clans. The following are the office-bearers of the *Tangrinta* in order of status:

(i) *Pakhangiak*
(ii) *Jupai*
(iii) *Lomjuiahai* (or *Lomjui*)
(iv) *Lomjuiyaima*
(v) *Lomjuinaha* (or Lomjuinapong)
(vi) *Juhjong,* and
(vii) *Juh-jong naopong*

The body is subordinate to *Urinta* and the members are elected by the villagers. The first two office-bearers of *Tangrinta* take important role in *Thaubei,* and sit by the side of *Khullakpa* and *Luplakpa*.

Luitheir bungkung: This is the third and the lowest council. This is in fact the bachelors' dormitory. Its membership includes four age-grades each having a distinct and specific role of its own as a constituent part of *Luitheir bungkung*. It is the volunteer force of the village. The four age-grades are: (i) *Tangsa,* (ii) *Hancha,* (iii) *Hithan,* and (iv) *Leibak.*

Tangsa, again has three sub-groups, namely, *Tanglaichang, Tuisakchang,* and *Tanghungechang. Tanglaichang* is the seniormost of the three sub-groups, and a senior member from it heads the *Luithai bungkung.* He is called *Pakhanglakpa* which, in rank is equivalent to *Tangrinta* head. Both these heads conduct the *Urinta* meeting in the absence of *Khullakpa* and *Luplakpa*. The other member of the *Tangsa* act as the main volunteer force in organizing community dance and ceremonial rites.

Hancha also consists of three sub-groups, namely, *Tanglai hancha, Tuisakchang hancha,* and *Tanghungchang hancha*. Duties of the members of the *Hancha* include teaching of songs to the junior members of *Hithang* and *Laibak*.

The last two groups, *Hithang* and *Laibak* include boys and girls who are the beginners in the process of socialization. The members of the *Leithei bungkung* also act as a defence force for the village.

The Village Authority

The traditional Village Council among the Chotes had been functioning very effectively, and was instrumental in maintaining the village life at a very useful level of interaction. In the mid-1950's this has been substituted by another body, namely, Village Authority. The Village Authority Act was passed by the Government of Manipur in 1956. It consists of a minimum of six members including the Chief. The members are elected at random from among the villagers irrespective of clan affiliation and age. A minimum age, however, is prescribed to contest for the membership.

A village needs to have at least 25 households to have this body of its own. Otherwise Village Authority body cut across villages. Its main pre-occupation is to co-ordinate and execute development activities in the village.

The original idea of introducing the scheme was to rationalize the developmental activities in different tribal areas to achieve a parity in this sphere, and thereby to accelerate the process of bringing the people in the mainstream of the country.

Concluding Observation

There are significant differences among various groups of people with regard to their antecedants, complexity of social organizations, customs and institutions. Thus the processes of development should not be a matter of devising a general scheme for all the communities. Before formulating any scheme for a group; its overt and covert problems, and its traditional socio-political structure need to be understood and appreciated in proper and total perspective.

With regard to the Chotes of Manipur, if we carefully examine the state of affair in their village level organization, we find that the village life has gradually become relatively less integrated since the introduction of the Village Authority.

In the Village Authority there is more secular scope for contesting the election for membership. Consequently internal cliche and dissensions are now increasing in most of the villages. In many villages it is seen that some people still continue their loyalty to the traditional *Urinta* which still functions as a parallel village organization.

In many cases the election for Village Authority membership is fought on the basis of party affiliation. Various 'fair' and 'unfair' means are very often adopted to win or get the party nominees won the election. In a number of cases, it so happens that the members from the present generation overpower those from the older generation. Thus, the rift in these cases is a vertical one (between the generations).

The Village Authority does not necessarily have representatives from all the clans, which the traditional council had. It is therefore suggested that the Village Authority body be formed by taking representatives from all the clans.

In the Village Council the members were the elderly persons of the village. Respect for age and experience, however, 'primitive' it appear to many, has deep root in the society. An abrupt change in the age-structure of the leadership is bound to have its obvious repercussions in the community. In order to have a smooth transition, it is therefore felt that the Village Authority be composed of proportionate representatives from all age-groups.

Traditionally, each village has a council. A tribal village is something more than a revenue unit. Very often it has a socio-religious dimension too. In the Village Authority Act a minimum size of the village is a prerequisite condition to have an independent Village Authority body. Otherwise it cuts across villages. It is therefore suggested that irrespective of the size, each Chote village should have its own Village Authority.

It is also thought that a harmony between the two systems can be better achieved if the Village Authority makes it a point to see that the other two traditional bodies, namely, *Tangarinta* and the *Luithai* in the Chote society, can function independently and effectively. Finally, it is genuinely felt that a harmonious synthesis between the two systems could have been achieved, and the resultant conflicts could have been minimised if the inner details of the traditional village organization were properly understood and appreciated beforehand.

REFERENCES

CHATTOPADHAYA, G., 1968, Application of anthropology to administration: Case studies in rural and tribal areas. In *Applied Anthropology in India*. Edited by L.P. Vidyarthi, pp 349-355, Allahabad: Kitab Mahal.

DAS, T.C., 1945, *The Purums*. Calcutta: University of Calcutta.

DUN, CAPTAIN, 1886, Gazettier of Manipur (Cited in Devi Bina Kumari, 1976). *Studies on Socio-Cultural Life of the Chana Village*, Manipur. Unpublished M.A. dissertation in Sociology, Dibrugarh University.

MATHUR, J.S., 1968, Tribal development administration in India. In *Applied Anthropology in India*. Edited by L.P. Vidyarthi, pp 137-149, Allahabad: Kitab Mahal.

ROY BURMAN, B.K., 1968, Anthropological concepts of problems of planning and research for social development. In *Applied Anthropology in India*. Edited by L.P. Vidyarthi, pp 42-61, Allahabad: Kitab Mahal.

SHARMA, B.D., 1978, *Tribal Development: The Concept and the Frame*. New Delhi: Prachi Prakashan.

Index